Bulletin No. 233   Series F, Geography, 41

DEPARTMENT OF THE INTERIOR
UNITED STATES GEOLOGICAL SURVEY
CHARLES D. WALCOTT, Director

A

GAZETTEER OF WEST VIRGINIA

BY

HENRY GANNETT

WASHINGTON
GOVERNMENT PRINTING OFFICE
1904

Notice

In many older books, foxing (or discoloration) occurs and, in some instances, print lightens with wear and age. Reprinted books, such as this, often duplicate these flaws, notwithstanding efforts to reduce or eliminate them. The pages of this reprint have been digitally enhanced and, where possible, the flaws eliminated in order to provide clarity of content and a pleasant reading experience.

Originally published
Washington D. C.
1904

Reprinted by:

Janaway Publishing, Inc.
732 Kelsey Ct.
Santa Maria, California 93454
(805) 925-1038
www.janawaygenealogy.com

2006, 2014

ISBN: 978-1-59641-012-1

Made in the United States of America

LETTER OF TRANSMITTAL.

DEPARTMENT OF THE INTERIOR,
UNITED STATES GEOLOGICAL SURVEY,
Washington, D. C., March 9, 1904.

SIR: I have the honor to transmit herewith, for publication as a bulletin, a gazetteer of West Virginia.

Very respectfully,

HENRY GANNETT,
Geographer.

Hon. CHARLES D. WALCOTT,
Director United States Geological Survey.

A GAZETTEER OF WEST VIRGINIA.

By Henry Gannett.

GENERAL DESCRIPTION OF THE STATE.

The State of West Virginia was cut off from Virginia during the civil war and was admitted to the Union on June 19, 1863. As originally constituted it consisted of 48 counties; subsequently, in 1866, it was enlarged by the addition of two counties, Berkeley and Jefferson, which were also detached from Virginia.

The boundaries of the State are in the highest degree irregular. Starting at Potomac River at Harpers Ferry, the line follows the south bank of the Potomac to the Fairfax Stone, which was set to mark the headwaters of the North Branch of Potomac River; from this stone the line runs due north to Mason and Dixon's line, i. e., the southern boundary of Pennsylvania; thence it follows this line west to the southwest corner of that State, in approximate latitude 39° 43$\frac{1}{4}$' and longitude 80° 31', and from that corner north along the western boundary of Pennsylvania until the line intersects Ohio River; from this point the boundary runs southwest down the Ohio, on the northwestern bank, to the mouth of Big Sandy River. The Big Sandy and Tug Fork nearly to its head then form the boundary. Thence the line follows a very irregular course, turning east and northeast, but with frequent breaks in direction as it coincides with the irregular boundaries of the counties which were set off to form the State.

The topographic features of West Virginia are simple. Nearly all the area of the State consists of a greatly dissected plateau which slopes from a crest line near the eastern boundary in a northwesterly direction to Big Sandy and Ohio rivers. Ohio River at the mouth of the Big Sandy, which is the lowest part of the State with the exception of the territory surrounding Harpers Ferry, has an altitude of about 500 feet, and the plateau level along the Ohio is 200 or 300 feet higher. From this level, which may be taken as the base of the plateau, the land rises to the northeast, and along the Allegheny Front has an average altitude of perhaps 4,000 feet. The streams of this plateau have cut deep gorges, and in most parts of it are so numerous that the plateau is reduced to an alternation of sharp ridges and deep, narrow canyons.

The principal rivers are the Ohio, which borders the State on the west and which is navigable throughout the portion bordering the boundary; the Big Sandy, which is navigable for small craft up to the junction of Tug and Levisa forks; the Guyandot; the Kanawha, which is navigable nearly to the falls above Charleston; the Little Kanawha; and the Monongahela. All of these are tributaries of the Ohio, and head in the plateau, with the exception of Kanawha River, the main branch of which, known as New River, heads in northwestern North Carolina and cuts a gorge throughout the entire breadth of the plateau in its course to the Ohio.

The mean altitude of the State above sea level is estimated at 1,500 feet. The areas within certain zones of altitude are as follows:

Areas in West Virginia at different altitudes.

	Square miles.
500–1,000	7,900
1,000–1,500	6,000
1,500–2,000	4,200
2,000–3,000	5,280
3,000–4,000	1,200
4,000–5,000	200

The gross area of the State—that is, including all bodies of water as well as land—is 24,780 square miles. The land area, after deducting the river surface, is 24,645 square miles.

The first census of population and industries of the State was taken in 1870. The following table shows the population at that and at each subsequent census, with the rate of increase:

Census of West Virginia at each census since 1870.

Year.	Population.	Rate of increase.
		Per cent.
1870	442,014	
1880	618,457	39.9
1890	762,794	23.3
1900	958,800	25.7

In 1900 the population was essentially of a rural character, as there were only four cities which had more than 8,000 inhabitants each, namely, Wheeling, Huntington, Parkersburg, and Charleston. The combined population of these four cities was only 73,603, or 8 per cent of the total population of the State, while in the United States at large one-third of all the people live in cities of this class.

The average number of persons to a family was 5.1, a number exceeded by Texas only, in which there were 5.2 persons to a family.

Males were largely in excess of females, the proportion being 521 males to 479 females. This condition is unusual in the eastern part of the country, there being no other State east of the Mississippi in which the proportion of males is as large as in West Virginia.

Another unusual feature is represented by the race distribution. Out of every 1,000 persons 955 were white and but 45 colored, while in the District of Columbia and Maryland the proportion of negroes is vastly greater. The proportion of foreign born was also very small; out of 1,000 persons 977 were born in the United States and only 23 in foreign countries. Of all the States of the Union, West Virginia has the largest proportion of native white inhabitants; out of every thousand inhabitants no fewer than 922 were whites born in the United States. There are States having a smaller proportion of foreign blood, but those States, like Mississippi, have a large proportion of negroes.

Persons more than 10 years of age who were unable to read and write comprised 11.4 per cent of all the inhabitants of the State, 10.3 per cent being white inhabitants, and 32.3 per cent being negroes.

Of the whole number of inhabitants of the State over 10 years of age, 46.4 per cent were engaged in gainful occupations. Of this number, nearly one-half, or 46.6 per cent, were engaged in agricultural pursuits, 3.6 per cent in professions, 17.3 per cent in domestic and other personal service, 11.7 per cent in trade and transportation, and 20.8 per cent in manufactures and mining.

Agriculture is the principal industry of the State. In 1900 there were 92,874 farms. Of these, nearly four-fifths, or 78.2 per cent, were owned by their occupiers, the remainder being rented either for a money rental or for a share of the proceeds, the latter plan being the one most in vogue. The total area in farms amounted to 10,654,513 acres. Of this, a little more than half, 5,498,981 acres, was under cultivation; this is 51.6 per cent of the entire farm area and 34.9 per cent, or more than a third, of the whole area of the State. The average size of the farms was 114.7 acres, considerably less than the average of the United States. The total value of the farms, including land, buildings, implements, and live stock—in short, the entire farm capital—was $203,907,349, an average per farm of $2,196.

The following table shows the distribution of the value among the different items:

Value of farm lands, buildings, and accessories in West Virginia.

Land	$134,269,110
Buildings	34,026,560
Implements	5,040,420
Live stock	30,571,259

The farm products had a value of $44,768,979, an average value per farm of $482. This was 22 per cent of the whole amount of farming capital. The following table shows the divisions of live stock and farm products:

Statistics of live stock and farm products in West Virginia.

Cattle	639,782	Wheat	bushels..	4,326,150
Horses	185,188	Oats	do....	1,833,840
Mules	11,354	Potatoes	do....	2,245,821
Sheep	968,843	Hay	tons..	644,535
Swine	442,844	Tobacco	pounds..	3,087,140
Corn ....bushels..	16,610,730	Dairy produce		$5,088,153

Although primarily a farming State, West Virginia has a considerable number of manufactures and they are rapidly increasing in importance. These manufactures are mainly in the narrow strip in the north lying between Pennsylvania and Ohio River, in and about Wheeling.

The total number of manufacturing establishments in the State was 4,418. They had a capital of $55,904,238, employed 33,272 hands, and paid $12,969,237 in wages. Raw materials cost $43,006,880, and the products had a gross value of $74,838,330. The following table gives the principal articles of manufacture, with the value of the products:

Statistics of principal manufactures in West Virginia.

Steam railway cars	$2,943,557
Clay products	1,541,239
Coke	3,529,241
Flour	5,541,353
Foundry products	1,401,852
Glass	1,871,795
Iron and steel	16,514,212
Lumber	10,612,837
Leather	3,210,753

In mineral products West Virginia takes high rank, especially in coal, petroleum, and natural gas. The coal produced in 1901 amounted to 24,068,402 short tons, and was exceeded only by Pennsylvania and Illinois. In making coke from its coal it was exceeded by Pennsylvania only, the amount produced being 2,283,700 short tons. Its petroleum production was 14,177,126 barrels, which was exceeded only by Pennsylvania and Ohio. Its natural gas had a value of $3,954,472. Coal, petroleum, and natural gas are found in various places throughout the State. Indeed, most of the plateau seems to be underlain with coal, and within this area petroleum and natural gas may exist.

Of iron ore Virginia and West Virginia together produced 925,394 long tons, and West Virginia smelted 166,597 long tons.

Originally West Virginia was entirely covered by dense forests. In the higher country these were largely coniferous. In Pocahontas

County, above the crest of the Allegheny Plateau, are found extensive tracts covered with white pine similar to that of New England and the Lake States. Farther down the slopes the hard woods become relatively more abundant, and the coniferous species disappear near Ohio River. In the lower portions of the State, near Ohio River, these forests have been largely cut away to make way for cultivation of the soil and to supply needed lumber, but in the eastern part there are vast tracts still untouched by lumbermen. It is estimated that timber still covers not less than 18,400 square miles, or 73 per cent of the area of the State, and that the State still contains not far from 35,000,000,000 feet B. M. In 1900 the Census reported that a little over half a billion feet were cut for lumber purposes, besides that used for firewood, fence posts, etc.

GAZETTEER.

Aaron; branch, a very small right-hand tributary to Kanawha River in Kanawha County.

Aaron; creek, a small right-hand tributary to Guyandot River, a branch of Ohio River, in Lincoln County.

Aaron; creek, a left-hand branch of Deckers Creek in Monongalia County.

Aaron; fork, a small right-hand branch of Little Sandy Creek, a tributary to Elk River, in Kanawha County.

Aarons; post village in Kanawha County.

Abb Camp; branch, a small right-hand tributary to Clear Fork, a branch of Tug Fork of Big Sandy River, in McDowell County.

Abbot; creek, a right-hand branch of Fifteenmile Fork of Cabin Creek, a tributary to Kanawha River, in Kanawha County.

Abbott; branch, a small left-hand tributary to Big Ugly Creek, a branch of Guyandot River, in Lincoln County.

Abbott; post village in Upshur County.

Aberdeen; post village in Lewis County.

Abram; creek, a right-hand tributary to North Fork of Potomac River in Mineral and Grant counties.

Absalom; run, a small left-hand tributary to Right Fork of Steer Creek in Gilmer County.

Academy; post village in Pocahontas County.

Acme; post village in Kanawah County on the Chesapeake and Ohio Railway.

Acord; branch, a small left-hand tributary to Laurel Branch, a tributary to Clear Fork of Guyandot River, in Wyoming County.

Ada; post village in Mercer County on the Norfolk and Western Railway and on East River. Altitude, 2,225 feet.

Adairs; run, a small left-hand tributary to New River in Mercer County.

Adaline; post village in Marshall County.

Adam; post village in Calhoun County.

Adamston; post village in Harrison County.

Adkin; post village in Wyoming County.

Adkin; branch, a very small right-hand tributary to Tug Fork of Big Sandy River in McDowell County.

Adkins; branch, a small right-hand tributary to Beech Fork of Twelvepole Creek, a branch of Ohio River, in Wayne County.

Adkins; branch, a small right-hand tributary to Dunloup Creek, a branch of New River, in Fayette County.

Adkins; fork, a small left-hand branch of Rich Creek, a tributary to East Fork of Twelvepole Creek, in Wayne County.

Adkins; fork, a very small left-hand tributary to Clear Fork of Guyandot River in Wyoming County.

Adkins; fork, a very small left-hand tributary to Spruce Fork of Little Coal River in Logan County.

GAZETTEER OF WEST VIRGINIA. 11

Adlai; post village in Pleasants County.
Adley; branch, a small right-hand tributary to Dry Fork, a branch of Tug Fork of Big Sandy River, in McDowell County.
Adolph; post village in Randolph County.
Adonijah; fork, a left-hand branch of Big Sycamore Creek, a tributary to Elk River, in Clay County.
Adonis; post village in Tyler County.
Advent; post village in Jackson County.
Afton; post village in Preston County.
Akron; post village in Tyler County.
Alam; village in Greenbrier County on Meadow River.
Alaska; post village in Mineral County.
Alaska; station in Fayette County on the Chesapeake and Ohio Railway and on New River.
Albatross; post village in Putnam County.
Albert; post village in Tucker County on the Virginia and Southwestern Railway.
Albion; Post village in Nicholas County.
Albright; post village in Preston County.
Alderson; branch, a very small right-hand tributary to Winding Gulf, a branch of Guyandot River, in Raleigh County.
Alderson; county seat of Monroe County on the Chesapeake and Ohio Railway. Altitude, 1,548 feet. Population, 518.
Aldrich; branch, a small right-hand tributary to Cranberry River in Webster County.
Aldrich; fork, an indirect left-hand tributary to Dry Fork, a branch of Tug Fork of Big Sandy River, in McDowell County.
Aleck; run, a small left-hand tributary to Right Fork of Buckhannon River in Upshur County.
Alexander; post village in Upshur County.
Alfred; post village in Gilmer County on the Baltimore and Ohio Railroad.
Algeria; post village in Pleasants County.
Algoma; village in McDowell County, on the Norfolk and Western Railroad.
Alice; post village in Gilmer County.
Alkires Mills; post village in Lewis County.
Allegheny Front; the escarpment of the Allegheny Plateau in Pendleton, Grant, and Mineral counties. Elevation, 2,000 to 4,500 feet.
Allegheny Plateau; westernmost member of the Appalachian system, extending as a greatly dissected plateau through southern New York, Pennsylvania, and Maryland, occupying the greater part of West Virginia, and, under the name of Cumberland Plateau, extending across eastern Kentucky and middle Tennessee into northern Alabama.
Allen; creek, a small right-hand tributary to Guyandot River in Raleigh and Wyoming counties.
Allen; creek, a small left-hand branch of Birch River, a tributary to Elk River, in Webster and Nicholas counties.
Allen Knob; summit in Greenbrier County. Altitude, 3,704 feet.
Allensville; post village in Berkeley County.
Alliance; post village in Harrison County.
Alma; post village in Tyler County.
Alpena; post village in Randolph County.
Alpha; post village in Doddridge County.
Alta; post village in Greenbrier County.
Altizer; post village in Calhoun County.

Alton; post village in Upshur County on the Baltimore and Ohio Railroad. Altitude, 1,813 feet.
Alum; creek, a small right-hand tributary to Tug Fork of Big Sandy River in Mingo County.
Alum; creek, a small right-hand tributary to Coal River, a branch of Kanawha River, in Kanawha County.
Alumbridge; post village in Lewis County.
Alvaro; post village in Kanawha County.
Alvon; post village in Greenbrier County.
Alvy; post village in Tyler County.
Amblersburg; post village in Preston County on the Baltimore and Ohio Railroad.
Amboy; post village in Preston County.
Ambrosia; post village in Mason County on the Ohio Central Lines Railroad.
Amma; post village in Roane County.
Amos; fork, a small right-hand branch of Old Lick Creek, a tributary to Holly River, in Webster County.
Amos; post village in Marion County.
Amos; run, a small right-hand branch of Laurel Creek, a tributary to Elk River. in Webster County.
Amos; run, a small creek in Webster County.
Anchor; post village in Boone County.
Andy; post village in Wetzel County.
Angel; fork, a small left-hand tributary to Coal River in Kanawha and Putnam counties.
Angel; post village in Kanawha County.
Angerona; post village in Jackson County on the Baltimore and Ohio Railroad.
Anglin; creek, a small right-hand branch of Meadow River, tributary to Gauley River, in Nicholas County.
Anita;, village in Marion County.
Ann; run, a right-hand branch of Simpson Creek in Harrison County.
Annamoriah; post village in Calhoun County.
Ansted; town in Fayette County on a branch of the Chesapeake and Ohio Railway. Altitude, 1,225 feet. Population, 1,090.
Anthem; post village in Wetzel County.
Anthony; creek, a small left-hand tributary to Birch River, a branch of Elk River, in Nicholas County.
Anthony; creek, a left-hand tributary to Greenbrier River in Greenbrier County.
Anthony; post village in Greenbrier County on the Chesapeake and Ohio Railway.
Antioch; post village in Mineral County.
Apgah; post village in Kanawha County.
Applegrove; post village in Mason County on the Baltimore and Ohio Railroad.
Aracoma; town in Logan County. Population, 444.
Arbovale; post village in Pocahontas County.
Arbuckle; creek, a small left-hand tributary to New River in Fayette County.
Arbuckle; post village in Mason County on the Ohio Central Lines.
Arbutus; post village in Kanawha County.
Arca; post village in Wirt County.
Arches; post village in Wetzel County.
Arden; post village in Barbour County on the Baltimore and Ohio Railroad.
Arkansas; branch, a very small right-hand branch of Right Fork of Twelvepole Creek, a tributary to Ohio River, in Wayne County.
Arlee; post village in Mason County.
Arlington; post village in Upshur County on the Norfolk and Western Railway.

GAZETTEER OF WEST VIRGINIA.   13

Armour; creek, a small right-hand tributary to Kanawha River in Kanawha and Putnam counties.
Armstrong; creek, a left-hand tributary to Kanawha River in Fayette County.
Arnettsville; post village in Monongalia County.
Arnold; post village in Lewis County on the Baltimore and Ohio Railroad.
Arnoldsburg; post village in Calhoun County.
Arroyo; post village in Hancock County on the Pittsburg, Cincinnati, Chicago and St. Louis Railway.
Arthur; post village in Grant County.
Arvilla; post village in Pleasants County.
Asbury; post village in Greenbrier County.
Ash; branch, a small right-hand tributary to Paint Creek, a branch of Kanawha River, in Kanawha and Fayette counties.
Ash; fork, a small right-hand branch of Twentymile Creek, a tributary to Gauley River, in Nicholas and Clay counties.
Ash; post village in Mason County.
Ashbridge; branch, a small right-hand tributary to Salt Lick Fork of Little Kanawha River in Braxton County.
Ash Camp; run, a right-hand branch of Long Drain in Wetzel County.
Ashland; post village in McDowell County.
Ashley; post village in Doddridge County on the Norfolk and Western Railway.
Ashton; post village in Mason County on the Baltimore and Ohio Railroad.
Aspinwall; post village in Lewis County.
Assurance; post village in Monroe County.
Astor; post village in Taylor County.
Athens; post village in Mercer County.
Atkinsville; post village in Raleigh County.
Atlas; post village in Upshur County.
Atwood; post village in Tyler County.
Auburn; post village in Ritchie County.
Audra; post village in Barbour County.
Augusta; post village in Hampshire County.
Aurora; post village in Preston County on the Baltimore and Ohio Railroad.
Austen; post village in Preston County on the Baltimore and Ohio Railroad.
Auvil; post village in Tucker County.
Avon; post village in Doddridge County.
Avondale; post village in McDowell County on the Baltimore and Ohio Railroad.
Ayers; post village in Calhoun County.
Back; creek, a right-hand branch of the Potomac River in Berkeley County.
Back; creek, a small right-hand branch of Indian Creek, a tributary to New River, in Monroe County.
Back; creek, a small left-hand tributary to Second Creek, a branch of Greenbrier River, in Monroe County.
Back Allegheny; mountain at head of Shavers Fork of Cheat River in Randolph, Pocahontas, and Greenbrier counties.
Backbone Knob; summit in Logan County.
Back Fork; mountain in Webster and Randolph counties.
Back Fork of Elk; right-hand branch of Elk River in Webster and Randolph counties.
Backus; post village in Fayette County.
Baden; post village in Mason County.
Badway; branch, a small left-hand tributary to Spice Creek, a branch of Tug Fork of Big Sandy River, in McDowell County.

Bailey; branch, a very small left-hand tributary to Indian Creek, a branch of Guyandot River, in Wyoming County.

Bailey; branch, a very small right-hand tributary to Winding Gulf, a branch of Guyandot River, in Raleigh County.

Bailey; branch, a very small right-hand tributary to Pocotaligo River, a branch of Kanawha River, in Putnam County.

Baileysville; post village in Wyoming County.

Baker; fork, a small left-hand branch of Elk Twomile Creek, a tributary to Elk River, in Kanawha County.

Baker; fork, a small left-hand tributary to Elk River in Braxton County.

Baker; post village in Hardy County on the Norfolk and Western Railway.

Bakers; run, a left-hand tributary to Lost River in Hardy County.

Bakerton; post village in Jefferson County on the Baltimore and Ohio Railroad.

Balderson; post village in Wood County.

Bald Knob; summit in Boone County.

Bald Knob; summit in Harris County. Elevation, 1,552 feet.

Bald Knob; summit in Lewis County.

Bald Knob; summit in the eastern part of Pocahontas County on the Virginia State line. Altitude, 4,242 feet.

Baldknob; post village in Boone County.

Baldwin; branch, a small left-hand tributary to Pinnacle Creek, a branch of Guyandot River, in Wyoming County.

Baldwin; post village in Gilmer County.

Ball; creek, a right-hand branch of Tanner Fork of Little Kanawha River in Gilmer County.

Ball; creek, a small left-hand branch of Charley Creek, a tributary to Mud River, in Cabell County.

Ballard; fork, a small left-hand tributary to Horse Creek, a branch of Little Coal River, in Boone County.

Ballard; fork, a small right-hand tributary to Mud River, a branch of Guyandot River, in Boone County.

Ballard; post village in Monroe County.

Ballengee; post village in Summers County.

Balls; post village in Marshall County.

Balser; mountain, a summit in Pocahontas County.

Baltimore; run, a small left-hand tributary to Back Fork of Elk River in Webster County.

Bancroft; post village in Putnam County.

Bank; post village in Pendleton County.

Bank Camp; branch, a small right-hand tributary to Left Fork of Mud River, a branch of Guyandot River, in Lincoln County.

Bannen; post village in Marshall County.

Bannock Shoal; run, a small right-hand tributary to Williams River in Webster and Pocahontas counties.

Bans; branch, a very small left-hand tributary to Clear Fork, a branch of Guyandot River, in Wyoming County.

Barbecue; fork, a left-hand branch of Grass Run in Gilmer County.

Barbecue; run, a small right-hand branch of Maul Creek in Braxton County.

Barbour; county, situated in the northern part of the State, in the Alleghany Plateau, here not greatly dissected; it is drained by tributaries to the Monongahela. Area, 393 square miles. Population, 14,198—white, 13,390; negro, 808; foreign born, 230. County seat, Philippi. The mean magnetic declination in 1900 was 3°. The mean annual rainfall is 50 inches, and the mean annual temperature 45° to 50°. The county is traversed by the Baltimore and Ohio Railroad.

Barboursville; town in Cabell County on the Chesapeake and Ohio Railway. Altitude, 578 feet. Population, 429.
Bardane; post village in Jefferson County.
Bargers Springs; post village in Summers County.
Barker; creek, a left-hand tributary to Guyandot River in Wyoming County.
Barker Ridge; mountains in Wyoming County.
Barn; post village in Mercer County.
Barn; run, a small left-hand tributary to Right Fork of Steer Creek in Gilmer County.
Barnes Mills; post village in Hampshire County.
Barnett; run, a right-hand branch of Wheeling Creek in Marshall County.
Barns Creek; right-hand branch of Mud River in Lincoln County.
Barnum; post village in Mineral County on the West Virginia Central and Pittsburg Railway.
Barrackville; post village in Marion County on the Baltimore and Ohio Railroad. Altitude, 901 feet.
Barren; branch, a small right-hand tributary to Dunloup Creek, a branch of New River, in Fayette County.
Barren; creek, a small right-hand tributary to Elk River, a branch of Kanawha River, in Kanawha County.
Barren She; creek, a small right-hand tributary to Dry Fork, a branch of Tug Fork of Big Sandy River, in McDowell County.
Barren She; mountain, a summit in Nicholas County. Elevation, 3,000 feet.
Barren She; run, a small right-hand tributary to North Fork of Cherry River in Nicholas County.
Barren She; run, a small left-hand branch of Buffalo Creek, a tributary to Elk River, in Clay County.
Bartholomew; fork, a left-hand branch of Buffalo Creek in Marion County.
Bartlett; creek, a small right-hand tributary to Dry Fork, a branch of Tug Fork of Big Sandy River in McDowell County.
Bartley; post village in Wyoming County.
Barton Knob; summit of Cheat Mountain in Randolph County.
Bartram; post village in Wayne County.
Basin; post village in Wyoming County.
Basnett; village in Marion County.
Bat; run, a left-hand tributary of Fish Creek in Wetzel County.
Batoff; creek, a small left-hand branch of Piney Creek, a tributary to New River, in Raleigh County.
Battern; fork, a small left-hand branch of East Fork of Twelvepole Creek, a tributary to Ohio River, in Wayne County.
Battle; run, a right-hand branch of Little Wheeling Creek in Ohio County.
Bauffman Knob; summit between Elk and Gauley rivers in Webster County.
Bayard; town in Grant County on North Fork of Potomac River and on the West Virginia Central and Pittsburg Railway. Population, 540. Altitude, 3,150 feet.
Bayards Knob; summit in Randolph County. Altitude, 4,150 feet.
Bays; fork, a small left-hand branch of Middle Fork of Davis Creek, tributary to Kanawha River, in Kanawha County.
Bays; post village in Fayette County.
Beach; fork, a right-hand branch of Twelvepole Creek in Wayne County.
Beach Lick; run, a small right-hand tributary to South Fork of Cherry River in Greenbrier County.
Bealls Mills; post village in Lewis County.
Bean Camp; creek, a small right-hand branch of Marrowbone Creek, a tributary to Tug Fork of Chattarawha River, in Logan County.

Bear; branch, a small right-hand tributary to Mud River, a branch of Guyandot River, in Lincoln County.
Bear; branch, a very small right-hand tributary to Laurel Branch, a tributary to Clear Fork of Guyandot River, in Wyoming County.
Bear; branch, a very small right-hand branch of Blue Creek, a tributary to Elk River, in Kanawha County.
Bear; branch, a small left-hand tributary to Horse Creek, a branch of Little Coal River, in Lincoln County.
Bear; creek, a small right-hand tributary to Guyandot River, a branch of Ohio River, in Lincoln County.
Bear; creek, a left-hand tributary to North Fork of Cherry River in Greenbrier County.
Bear; mountain, a summit near the eastern border of Pocahontas County.
Bear; run, a small right-hand tributary to Little Birch River in Braxton County.
Bear; run, a small left-hand tributary to Elk River in Braxton County.
Bear; run, a small left-hand tributary to Little Kanawha River in Gilmer County.
Bear; run, a small right-hand tributary to Oil Creek in Lewis County.
Bear; run, a right-hand tributary to South Fork of Fishing Creek in Wetzel County.
Bear Camp; run, a small left-hand branch of Left Fork of Buckhannon River in Randolph and Upshur counties.
Beard; post village in Pocahontas County on the Chesapeake and Ohio Railway.
Bearden Knob; summit of Brown Mountain in Tucker County.
Beards; fork, a right-hand branch of Loop Creek, a tributary to Kanawha River in Fayette County.
Bear Garden; fork, a small right-hand tributary to Salt Lick Fork of Little Kanawha River in Braxton County.
Bear Garden Knobs; summits in Greenbrier County, one of which reaches an altitude of 3,262 feet.
Bearhole; fork, a small right-hand tributary to Guyandot River in Wyoming County.
Bear Knob; summit in Randolph County.
Bear Pen; branch, a small right-hand branch of Rock Camp Fork of Twentymile Creek, a tributary to Gauley River in Nicholas and Clay counties.
Bear Run; fork, a small right-hand branch of Lilly Fork of Buffalo Creek, a tributary to Elk River, in Clay and Nicholas counties.
Bear Spring; branch, a small left-hand tributary to Huff Creek, a branch of Guyandot River, in Wyoming County.
Bearsville; post village in Tyler County.
Beartown; branch, a small left-hand tributary to Dry Fork, a branch of Tug Fork of Big Sandy River, in McDowell County.
Beartown; fork, a small right-hand tributary to Pinnacle Creek, a branch of Guyandot River, in Wyoming County.
Beartown Ridge; mountains in Wyoming County.
Bearwallow; branch, a very small right-hand tributary to North Fork of Elkhorn Creek in McDowell County.
Bear Wallow; branch, a small right-hand tributary to Dingus Run, a branch of Guyandot River, in Logan County.
Bear Wallow; hill in McDowell County. Altitude, 3,170 feet.
Bear Wallow; run, a small right-hand tributary to Back Fork of Elk River in Webster and Randolph counties.
Bear Wallow Knob; summit in Fayette County. Altitude, 2,460 feet.
Bear Wallow Knob; summit in Greenbrier County. Elevation, 4,030 feet.
Bear Wallow Ridge; mountains in Wyoming County.
Beatrice; post village in Ritchie County.
Beatysville; post village in Jackson County.

GAZETTEER OF WEST VIRGINIA.

Beauty; post village in Fayette County.
Beaver; branch, a very small left-hand tributary to Guyandot River in Wyoming County.
Beaver; creek, a small left-hand tributary to Greenbrier River in Pocahontas County.
Beaver; creek, a small right-hand tributary to Meadow River in Greenbrier County.
Beaver; creek, a right-hand branch of Black Water River in Tucker County.
Beaver; creek, a right-hand tributary to Piney Creek, a branch of New River, in Raleigh County.
Beaver; creek, a small right-hand tributary to Valley River in Randolph and Barbour counties.
Beaver; creek, a small left-hand tributary to Valley River in Randolph County.
Beaver; post village in Nicholas County on the Chesapeake and Ohio Railway.
Beaver; run, a small right-hand tributary to Holly River in Webster County.
Beaver; run, a small right-hand tributary to Patterson Creek, a branch of North Branch of Potomac River, in Mineral County.
Beaver; run, a small right-hand tributary to Gauley River in Webster County.
Beaver Dam Ridge; short spur of Black Mountain in Pocahontas County.
Beaver Lick; mountain, long narrow ridge, lying east of Greenbrier River in Greenbrier and Pocahontas counties. Elevation, 2,500 to 3,500 feet.
Beaver Pond; branch, a small left-hand tributary to Pond Fork of Little Coal River in Boone County.
Bebee; post village in Wetzel County.
Beccas; creek, a small right-hand tributary to Valley River in Randolph County.
Beckley; county seat of Raleigh County. Population, 342. Altitude, 2,300 feet.
Beckwith; post village in Fayette County on Laurel Creek.
Becky; run, a small left-hand tributary to South Fork of Cherry River in Greenbrier County.
Bedington; post village in Berkeley County on the Cumberland Valley Railroad.
Bee; branch, a very small left-hand tributary to Indian Creek, a branch of Guyandot River, in Wyoming County.
Bee; branch, a very small right-hand tributary to Clear Fork, a branch of Guyandot River, in Wyoming County.
Bee; branch, a very small right-hand tributary to Tug Fork of Big Sandy River in McDowell County.
Bee; branch, a small right-hand tributary to Sand Lick Creek, a branch of Marsh Fork of Coal River, in Raleigh County.
Bee; run, a small left-hand tributary to Cranberry River in Webster and Nicholas counties.
Bee; run, a very small right-hand tributary to Elk River in Braxton County.
Bee; run, a left-hand branch of Cheat River in Preston County.
Bee; post village in Putnam County.
Beech; branch, a very small left-hand tributary to Guyandot River, a branch of Ohio River, in Logan County.
Beech; branch, a very small right-hand tributary to Big Huff Creek, a branch of Guyandot River, in Logan and Wyoming counties.
Beech; creek, a small right-hand branch of Tug Fork of Chattarawha River, a tributary to Ohio River, in Logan County.
Beech; creek, a small left-hand branch of Spruce Fork of Little Coal River in Logan County.
Beech; fork, a small left-hand tributary to Birch River, a branch of Elk River, in Nicholas and Webster counties.
Beech; fork, a right-hand branch of Shaver Fork in Braxton County.

Beech; fork, a large right-hand tributary to Twelvepole Creek, a branch of Ohio River, in Wayne County.

Beech; fork, a small right-hand branch of Lilly Fork of Buffalo Creek, a tributary to Elk River, in Clay and Nicholas counties.

Beech; mountain, a short spur from Rich Mountain in Randolph and Nicholas counties.

Beech; post village in Calhoun County.

Beech; run, a small left-hand branch of Big Laurel Creek, a tributary to Cherry River, in Greenbrier County.

Beech; run, a right-hand head fork of Left Fork of Buchannon River in Randolph County.

Beechcreek; post village in Mingo County on the Norfolk and Western Railway. Altitude, 1,019 feet.

Beech Flat Knob; summit in Randolph County.

Beechgrove; post village in Ritchie County on the Baltimore and Ohio Railroad.

Beechhill; post village in Mason County,

Beech Knob; summit in Greenbrier County. Altitude, 4,161 feet.

Beech Lick; run, a right-hand branch of Pyles Fork of Buffalo Creek in Marion County.

Beechwood; post village in Monongalia County on the Baltimore and Ohio Railroad.

Beechy; branch, a small left-hand tributary to East Fork of Twelvepole Creek, a branch of Ohio River, in Wayne County.

Beechy; fork, a small left-hand branch of Fuqua Creek, a tributary to Coal River, in Lincoln County.

Bee Knob; summit in Braxton County.

Bee Knob; summit in Greenbrier County.

Bee Knob; summit in Randolph County.

Bee Knob; summit in Webster County. Altitude, 3,280 feet.

Beelers Station; post village in Marshall County.

Bee Lick Knob; summit in Fayette County. Altitude, 3,118 feet.

Bee Tree; branch, a small left-hand tributary to Devils Fork, a branch of Guyandot River, in Raleigh County.

Bee Tree; run, a small left-hand tributary to Back Fork of Elk River in Randolph County.

Bee Tree Ridge; short spur from Frank Mountain in Pocahontas County.

Behler; post village in Monongalia County.

Belcher; branch, a very small right-hand tributary to Tug River in McDowell County.

Belcher; branch, a very small left-hand tributary to Tug Fork of Big Sandy River in McDowell County.

Belcher; branch, a small left-hand tributary to Pinnacle Creek, a branch of Guyandot River, in Wyoming County.

Belfont; post village in Braxton County.

Belgrove; post village in Jackson County.

Belington; town in Barbour County on the Baltimore and Ohio, the Belington and Beaver Creek, the Roaring Creek and Belington, and the West Virginia Central and Pittsburg railroads. Population, 430.

Bell; creek, a right-hand branch of Twenty Mile Creek, a tributary to Gauley River, in Nicholas, Fayette, and Kanawha counties.

Belle; post village in Kanawha County.

Belleville; post village in Wood County on the Baltimore and Ohio Railroad.

Bellton; post village in Marshall County on the Baltimore and Ohio Railroad.

Belmont; post village in Pleasants County on the Baltimore and Ohio Railroad.

Belva; post village in Nicholas County on the Chesapeake and Ohio Railway.
Ben; creek, a small right-hand branch of Tug Fork of Big Sandy River in Mingo County.
Ben; run, a small left-hand tributary to Indian Fork in Lewis County.
Ben; run, a small left-hand tributary to Elk River, a large branch of Kanawha River, in Clay County.
Ben; run, a small right-hand tributary to Elk River in Braxton County.
Bend; branch, a very small right-hand tributary to Spruce Fork of Little Coal River in Logan County.
Bend; branch, a small left-hand branch of Dunloup Creek, a tributary to New River, in Fayette County.
Bender; run, a small left-hand tributary to left fork of Steer Creek in Braxton County.
Bendolph; village in Marion County.
Ben Lomond; post village in Mason County on the Baltimore and Ohio Railroad.
Bennett; fork, a small indirect right-hand tributary to Pond Fork of Little Coal River, a branch of Coal River, in Boone County.
Bennett; post village in Gilmer County.
Benson; post village in Harrison County.
Bent; creek, a very small left-hand branch of Marrowbone Creek, a tributary to Tug Fork of Chattarawha River, in Logan County.
Bent Mountain; ridge in Mercer County.
Bentons Ferry; post village in Marion County on the Baltimore and Ohio Railroad. Altitude, 883 feet.
Benwood; city in Marshall County, on the Baltimore and Ohio and the Pittsburg, Cincinnati, Chicago and St. Louis railroads. Altitude, 645 feet. Population, 4,511.
Berea; post village in Ritchie County.
Bergoo; fork, a left-hand tributary to Elk River in Webster and Randolph counties.
Bergoo; post village in Webster County.
Berkeley; county situated in the northeastern part of the State, limited on the north by the Potomac; the surface consists in the main of a rolling valley traversed by Little North and Sleepy Creek mountains. Area, 257 square miles. Population, 19,469—white, 17,704; negro, 1,765; foreign born, 237. County seat, Martinsburg. The mean magnetic declination in 1900 was 4° 25'. The mean annual rainfall is 40 to 50 inches, and the mean annual temperature 50° to 55°. The county is traversed by the Baltimore and Ohio and the Cumberland Valley railroads.
Berkeley; run, a left-hand branch of Tygart Valley River in Taylor County.
Berkeley Springs; county seat of Morgan County on the Baltimore and Ohio Railroad. Population, 781.
Berlin; post village in Lewis County.
Bernards Town; post village in Webster County.
Bernie; post village in Lincoln County.
Berry; branch, a very small right-hand tributary to Mud River, a branch of Guyandot River, in Lincoln County.
Berry; branch, a small left-hand tributary to Winding Gulf, a branch of Guyandot River in Raleigh County.
Berry; run, a left-hand tributary of Berkeley Run in Taylor County.
Berryburg; post village in Barbour County on the Baltimore and Ohio Railroad.
Bert; post village in Tyler County.
Bethany; village in Brooke County. Population, 245.
Bethel; post village in Mercer County.
Betsy; run, a right-hand branch of North Fork of Fishing Creek in Wetzel County.
Beury; post village in Fayette County on the Chesapeake and Ohio Railway.

Beverage Knob; summit in Upshur County.

Beverly; town in Randolph County on the West Virginia Central and Pittsburg Railway. Altitude, 2,250 feet. Population, 464.

Bias; branch, a very small right-hand tributary to Spruce Fork of Little Coal River in Boone County.

Bible Knob; summit in Pendleton County.

Bicketts Knob; summit in Monroe County. Altitude, 3,327 feet.

Bickle Knob; summit in Randolph County. Altitude, 4,020 feet.

Big; branch, a small right-hand tributary to Cranberry River in Webster County.

Big; branch, a very small right-hand branch of West Fork of Twelvepole Creek, a tributary to Ohio River, in Wayne County.

Big; branch, a very small right-hand tributary to Dry Fork, a branch of Tug Fork of Big Sandy River, in McDowell County.

Big; branch, a small right-hand tributary to Wide Mouth Creek, a branch of Bluestone River, in Mercer County.

Big; branch, a very small right-hand tributary to Elkhorn Creek, a branch of Tug Fork of Big Sandy River, in McDowell County.

Big; branch, a very small right-hand tributary to Guyandot River in Mingo County.

Big; branch, a small left-hand tributary to Spruce Fork of Little Coal River in Boone County.

Big; branch, a very small left-hand tributary to Middle Fork of Mud River, a branch of Guyandot River in Lincoln County.

Big; branch, a small left-hand tributary to Lilly Fork of Buffalo Creek, a branch of Elk River, in Clay County.

Big; branch, a small left-hand tributary to Second Creek, a branch of Greenbrier River, in Monroe County.

Big; branch, a small left-hand tributary to Clear Fork, a branch of Tug Fork of Big Sandy River, in McDowell County.

Big; branch, a very small left-hand tributary to Guyandot River in Wyoming County.

Big; creek, a small left-hand branch of Big Hart Creek, a tributary to Guyandot River, in Lincoln County.

Big; creek, a very small left-hand branch of Twelvepole Creek, a tributary to Ohio River, in Wayne County.

Big; creek, a left-hand branch of Trace Fork of Mud River in Lincoln and Putnam counties.

Big; creek, a left-hand tributary to Mud River, a branch of Guyandot River, in Lincoln County.

Big; creek, a very small right-hand tributary to Greenbrier River in Summers County.

Big; creek, a small right-hand branch of Guyandot River, a tributary to Ohio River, in Logan County.

Big; creek, an indirect right-hand tributary to Dry Fork, a branch of Tug Fork of Big Sandy River, in McDowell County.

Big; creek, a small right-hand tributary to Gauley River, a branch of Kanawha River, in Fayette County.

Big; fork, a left-hand branch of Strange Creek in Braxton County.

Big; fork, a very small left-hand tributary to Gilbert Creek, a branch of Guyandot River, in Mingo County.

Big; mountain, a short ridge between Laurel Creek and Little Laurel Creek in Nicholas County.

Big; mountain, a ridge west of South Branch of Potomac River in Pendleton County. Elevation, 2,000 to 2,500 feet.

Big; run, a left-hand tributary to North Fork of Potomac River in Pendleton County.

GAZETTEER OF WEST VIRGINIA.

Big; run, a small left-hand tributary to Elk River in Webster and Randolph counties.
Big; run, a small indirect left-hand tributary to West Fork of Monongahela River in Lewis County.
Big; run, a small left-hand tributary to Buckhannon River in Upshur County.
Big; run, a left-hand tributary to Thorn Run, a branch of South Branch of Potomac River, in Pendleton County.
Big; run, a small left-hand tributary to Red Creek in Randolph County.
Big; run, a small left-hand tributary to Gauley River, entering it between Miller Ridge and Hamrick Ridge, in Webster County.
Big; run, a small left-hand tributary to Elk River in Webster County.
Big; run, a small left-hand tributary to Dry Fork of Cheat River in Tucker County.
Big; run, a small left-hand tributary to Spruce Run, a small branch of Cheat River, in Preston County.
Big; run, a small right-hand tributary to Shavers Fork of Cheat River in southeastern part of Randolph County.
Big; run, a small right-hand tributary to East Fork of Greenbrier River in Pocahontas County.
Big; run, a small right-hand branch of Laurel Fork, a tributary to Back Fork of Holly River, in Webster County.
Big; run, a right-hand tributary to North Fork of Fishing Creek in Wetzel County.
Big; run, a small right-hand tributary to Elk River in Webster County.
Big; run, a left-hand branch of Little Kanawha River in Gilmer County.
Big; run, a small right-hand tributary to Valley River in Randolph County.
Big; run, a left-hand branch of Pyles Creek in Marion County.
Big; run, a left-hand branch of Leading Creek in Gilmer County.
Big; run, a small right-hand tributary to South Branch of Potomac River in Hampshire County.
Big; run, a small right-hand tributary to Elk River in Braxton County.
Bigbattle; post village in Doddridge County.
Big Beechy; creek, a very small left-hand tributary to Elk River in Clay County.
Big Beechy; run, a small left-hand tributary to Williams River in Webster County.
Bigbend; post village in Calhoun County on the Chesapeake and Ohio Railway.
Big Briery Knob; summit in Nicholas County. Altitude, 3,738 feet.
Big Buffalo; creek, a small left-hand tributary to Elk River in Braxton County.
Big Buffalo; creek, a left-hand tributary to Cheat River in Preston County.
Big Clear; creek, a right-hand branch of Meadow River in Greenbrier County.
Big Clear; mountain, a curved range in Greenbrier County. Elevation, 3,000 to 4,000 feet.
Big Clear Creek; village in Greenbrier County.
Big Coal; river, a large, left-hand branch of Kanawha River.
Big Cove; run, a small right-hand tributary to Valley River in Barbour County.
Big Cub; branch, a very small left-hand tributary to Tug Fork of Big Sandy River in McDowell County.
Big Cub; creek, a small right-hand tributary to Guyandot River in Wyoming County.
Big Ditch; run, a small right-hand tributary to Gauley River in Webster County.
Big Draft; small right-hand tributary to Anthonys Creek, a branch of Greenbrier River, in Greenbrier County.
Big Elk; run, a small left-hand tributary to Coal River, a branch of Kanawha River, in Raleigh County.
Big Hart; creek, a small left-hand branch of Guyandot River, a tributary to Ohio River, in Lincoln County.
Big Hollow; short right-hand tributary to Kanawha River in Kanawha County.

Big Huff; creek, a right-hand branch of Guyandotte River in Logan and Wyoming counties.

Big Isaac; post village in Doddridge County.

Big Jarrell; fork, a left-hand branch of Hopkins Fork, a tributary to Coal River, in Boone County.

Big Jenny; branch, a small right-hand tributary to Tug Fork of Big Sandy River in McDowell County.

Big Jonathan; run, a small left-hand tributary to Cheat River in Tucker County.

Big Knob; summit in Clay County.

Big Knob; summit in Greenbrier County.

Big Knob; summit in Kanawha County. Altitude, 1,487 feet.

Big Laurel; branch, a small right-hand tributary to Beaver Creek, a branch of Piney Creek, in Raleigh County.

Big Laurel; creek, a small left-hand tributary to Gauley River in Webster County.

Big Laurel; creek, a left-hand tributary to Cherry River, a branch of Gauley River, in Nicholas and Greenbrier counties.

Big Laurel; creek, a small right-hand branch of Kiah Fork of Twelvepole Creek in Wayne County.

Big Laurel; creek, a right-hand tributary to Elk River, a branch of Kanawha River, in Clay County.

Big Laurel; run, a left-hand tributary to Valley River in Randolph County.

Big Laurel; run, a small left-hand branch of Blue Creek, a tributary to Elk River, in Kanawha County.

Biglick; branch, a very small left-hand tributary to Gilbert Creek, a branch of Guyandot River, in Mingo County.

Big Lynn; creek, a small left-hand branch of East Fork of Twelvepole Creek, a tributary to Ohio River, in Wayne County.

Big Moses; post village in Tyler County.

Big Otter; post village in Clay County.

Big Paw Paw; creek, left-hand branch of Monongahela River, in Mineral County.

Big Ridge; mountains in Raleigh County.

Big Ridge; broken mountainous range in Greenbrier County. Elevation, 2,500 to 3,000 feet.

Big Ridge; mountains in Wyoming County.

Big Ridge; short spur in Pocahontas County. Elevation, 2,500 to 3,000 feet.

Big Ridge; short spur in Hardy County. Elevation, 2,000 feet.

Big Right; fork, a small left-hand branch of Loop Creek, a tributary to Kanawha River, in Fayette County.

Big Rock; summit in Fayette County. Altitude, 2,538 feet.

Big Rock; summit in Peters Mountain in Monroe County.

Big Rocky; run, a small right-hand tributary to South Fork of Cherry River in Greenbrier County.

Big Run; gap in hills in Webster County.

Big Sandy; creek, a right-hand tributary to Elk River, a large branch of Kanawha River, in Kanawha County.

Big Sandy; post village in McDowell County.

Big Sandy; river, a large left-hand branch of Ohio River. It turns in the crest of the Alleghany Plateau and flows nearly northwest to its mouth at Catlettsburg, forming through most of its course the boundary line between West Virginia and Kentucky. Drainage area, 4,050 square miles. It is navigable the entire length. Sometimes called the Chatterawha.

Big Sang Kill; very small left-hand branch of Right Fork of Twelvepole Creek, a tributary to Ohio River, in Logan County.

Big Sewell; knob of Big Sewell Mountain in Fayette County.

GAZETTEER OF WEST VIRGINIA.

Big Sewell; mountain, a short, curved ridge in Fayette County. Elevation, 3,000 to 3,500 feet.
Big Spring; fork, a right-hand head fork of Elk River in Pocahontas County.
Bigsprings; post village in Calhoun County.
Big Spruce Knob; summit in Pocahontas County. Altitude, 4,652 feet.
Big Staunch; branch, a small right-hand tributary to Dry Fork, a branch of Tug Fork of Big Sandy River, in McDowell County.
Big Sulphur; creek, a small right-hand branch of Big Ugly Creek, a tributary to Guyandot River, in Lincoln County.
Big Sycamore; creek, a left-hand tributary to Elk River in Clay County.
Big Top; summit in the central part of Pocahontas County.
Big Twomile; creek, a small left-hand tributary to Mud River, a branch of Guyandot River, in Cabell County.
Big Ugly; creek, a right-hand tributary to Guyandot River, a branch of Ohio River, in Lincoln and Boone counties.
Big Whitestick; creek, a small left-hand tributary to Piney Creek, a branch of New River, in Raleigh County.
Big Wolf Knob; summit on boundary line between Lincoln and Logan counties.
Bill; branch, a very small right-hand tributary to Guyandot River in Wyoming and Logan counties.
Bill; creek, a small left-hand tributary to Kanawha River in Putnam County.
Bill; fork, a small right-hand tributary to O'Brien Fork in Braxton County.
Billie; branch, a very small left-hand branch of Blue Creek, a tributary to Elk River, in Kanawha County.
Bills; creek, a small left-hand tributary to Sugar Creek, an indirect tributary to Valley River, in Barbour County.
Billy; branch, a very small right-hand tributary to West Fork of Twelvepole Creek, a branch of Ohio River, in Wayne County.
Billy; branch, a very small right-hand tributary to Middle Fork of Mud River in Lincoln County.
Binola; post village in Wood County.
Birch; fork, a right-hand tributary to Marsh Fork, a left-hand head fork of Coal River, in Raleigh County.
Birch; river, a left-hand branch of Elk River in Braxton and Nicholas counties.
Birch Pen; run, a small right-hand tributary to Laurel Fork of Holly River in Webster County.
Birch River; post village in Nicholas County.
Birch Root; run, a small left-hand branch of Big Buffalo Creek in Preston County.
Bird; post village in Tyler County.
Bird; run, a small left-hand tributary to Knapp Creek, a branch of Greenbrier River, in Pocahontas County.
Bird Knob; summit in Clay County. Altitude, 1,880 feet.
Bishop; branch, a very small left-hand tributary to Paint Creek, a branch of Kanawha River, in Fayette County.
Bishop Knob; summit in Webster County.
Bismarck; post village in Grant County, situated along the Allegany Front. Altitude, 2,863 feet.
Black; fork, a small left-hand branch of Cabin Creek, a tributary to Guyandot River, in Wyoming County.
Black; mountain, a summit in Pocahontas County.
Black; run, a right-hand head fork of Laurel Fork of Cheat River in Randolph County.
Black; run, a small right-hand tributary to North Fork of Greenbrier River in Pocahontas County.

Blackbird Knob; summit in Tucker County.
Blackburn; branch, a small right-hand tributary to Sand Lick Creek, a branch of Marsh Fork of Coal River, in Raleigh County.
Black Lick; creek, a small right-hand tributary to Bluestone River in Mercer County.
Black Lick; creek, a small right-hand tributary to Little Skin Creek in Lewis County.
Black Oak; mountain in Mercer County.
Blacksville; town in Monongalia on the Chesapeake and Ohio Railway. Population, 180.
Black Water; river, a right-hand branch of Dry Fork of Cheat River in Tucker County.
Blaine; island in Kanawha River, near Charleston in Kanawha County.
Blaine; post village in Mineral County on the West Virginia Central and Pittsburg Railway. Altitude, 1,689 feet.
Blake; branch, a left-hand branch of Smithers Creek, a tributary to Kanawha River, in Fayette County.
Blake; creek, a small right-hand tributary to Kanawha River in Putnam and Kanawha counties.
Blake; fork, a left-hand branch of Lynn Camp Run in Wetzel County.
Blaker Mills; post village in Greenbrier County.
Bland; run, a right-hand branch of Church Fork of Fish Creek in Wetzel County.
Blandville; post village in Doddridge County.
Blayney; run, a left-hand tributary of Castleman Run in Ohio County.
Blaze; branch, a small right-hand tributary to Dunloup Creek, a branch of New River, in Raleigh and Fayette counties.
Blaze; fork, a small left-hand tributary to the right-hand head fork of Grassy Creek in Webster County.
Blenn; run, a left-hand branch of Little Fishing Creek in Wetzel County.
Blennerhassett; post village in Wood County on the Baltimore and Ohio Railroad.
Bletcher; branch, a left-hand branch of Mud River in Cabell County.
Blizzard; run, a small right-hand tributary to South Fork of Cherry River in Greenbrier County.
Bloomery; post village in Hampshire County. Altitude, 700 feet.
Bloomington; post village in Roane County.
Blown Timber; fork, a right-hand tributary to Crooked Fork in Braxton County.
Blue; creek, a left-hand tributary to Elk River in Kanawha and Clay counties.
Blue; post village in Tyler County.
Bluecreek; post village in Kanawha County on the Charleston, Clendennin and Sutton Railroad.
Bluefield; city in Mercer County on the Norfolk and Western Railway. Altitude, 2,557 feet. Population, 4,644.
Blue Knob; branch, a small left-hand tributary to South Fork of Cherry River in Greenbrier County.
Blue Knob; creek, a small right-hand tributary to Elk River, a large branch of Kanawha River, in Clay County.
Blue Knob; summit in Greenbrier County.
Blue Knob; summit in Lincoln County.
Blue Knob; summit in Pocahontas County. Altitude, 4,368 feet.
Blue Knob; summit in Randolph County.
Blue Ridge; mountains, the easternmost ridge of the Appalachian System, with the exception of a few short outliers. It extends from Maryland, southwestward to the southern boundary of the State. From Harpers Ferry, where it is cut through by the Potomac in a water gap, and where it has an altitude of from

1,000 to 1,200 feet, it runs southwestward, increasing rapidly in altitude until at Stony Man, near Luray, and the Peaks of Otter, near Lynchburg, it has an altitude of 4,000 feet. James and Roanoke rivers, which head in the valley behind the ridge, have cut deep gaps in it. In the southern part of the State it changes from a ridge to a plateau with an escarpment facing southeast, and in this form enters North Carolina.

Blue Spring; post village in Randolph County.

Bluestone; river, a left-hand branch of New River.

Blue Sulphur Springs; post village in Greenbrier County on the Chesapeake and Ohio Railway. Altitude, 598 feet.

Bluff; fork, a small left-hand branch of Devils Fork, a tributary to Guyandot River, in Raleigh County.

Bluff; post village in Mercer County.

Blundon; post village in Kanawha County.

Board; branch, a very small right-hand tributary to Indian Creek, a branch of Guyandot River, in Wyoming County.

Board; post village in Mason County.

Board Tree; branch, a very small left-hand tributary to Blue Creek, a branch of Elk River, in Kanawha County.

Board Tree; branch, a small right-hand tributary to Twentymile Creek, a branch of Gauley River, in Nicholas County.

Board Tree; gap in Nicholas County, caused by Board Tree Branch in Nicholas County.

Board Tree; post village in Marshall County on the Baltimore and Ohio Railroad.

Boar Knob; summit in Braxton County. Elevation, 1,466 feet.

Boaz; post village in Wood County.

Bob; run, a small left-hand tributary to Elk River in Webster County.

Bobby; creek, a small right-hand branch of Big Ugly Creek, a tributary to Guyandot River, in Lincoln County.

Bob Peak; summit in the central part of Upshur County.

Bob Ross; branch, a very small left-hand tributary to Beech Fork of Twelvepole Creek, a branch of Ohio River, in Wayne County.

Bobs Ridge; short spur between Greenbrier and Alleghany mountains in Greenbrier County. Elevation, 2,000 to 2,500 feet.

Boggs; fork, a small left-hand tributary to Lower Sleith Fork in Braxton County.

Boggs; post village in Webster County on the Baltimore and Ohio Railroad.

Boggs; run, a left-hand tributary to Spring Creek, a branch of Greenbrier River, in Greenbrier County.

Boggs; run, a left-hand branch of Ohio River in Marshall County.

Boggs Knob; summit in Greenbrier County.

Boggs Knob; summit in Fayette County. Altitude, 3,600 feet.

Bois; post village in Webster County.

Bolair; post village in Webster County.

Bolivar; town in Jefferson County. Population, 781.

Bond; creek, a small left-hand tributary to Ohio River in Ritchie County.

Bone Town; gap at mouth of Robinson Creek at its junction with Buffalo Creek, in Clay County.

Booher; post village in Tyler County.

Boomer; branch, a very small right-hand tributary to Kanawha River, in Fayette County.

Boomer; post village in Fayette County on the Ohio Central Lines.

Boone; county, situated in the southern part of the State, on the Allegheny Plateau. It is here deeply dissected. It is drained by Coal and Little Coal rivers. Area, 512 square miles. Population, 8,194—white, 8,059; negro, 135; foreign born, 7.

County seat, Madison. The mean magnetic declination in 1900 was 1°. The mean annual rainfall is 50 to 60 inches, and the mean annual temperature 50° to 55°.

Boone; post village in Fayette County.

Booths; creek, a right-hand branch of West Fork River in Marion County.

Boothsville; post village in Marion County.

Booton; branch, a small right-hand tributary to Beech Fork of Twelvepole Creek, a branch of Ohio River, in Wayne County.

Booton; creek, a very small left-hand tributary to Guyandot River, a branch of Ohio River, in Cabell County.

Boreman; post village in Wood County.

Borland; post village in Pleasants County.

Botkins Ridge; spur in Pendleton County.

Bottom; creek, a small right-hand tributary to Elkhorn Creek, a branch of Tug Fork of Big Sandy River in McDowell County.

Bowen; creek, a right-hand branch of Beech Fork of Twelvepole Creek in Wayne County.

Bowen; post village in Wayne County.

Bowers; creek, a small right-hand branch of Beech Fork of Twelvepole Creek, a branch of Ohio River, in Wayne County.

Bowlby; post village in Monongalia County.

Box; post village in Pendleton County.

Boyd; branch, a very small left-hand tributary to Clear Fork of Coal River in Raleigh County.

Boyd; branch, a very small right-hand tributary to Paint Creek, a branch of Kanawha River, in Fayette County.

Boyer; fork, a small right-hand branch of Piney Creek, a tributary to New River, in Raleigh County.

Boyer; post village in Pocahontas County.

Boyer; run, a small right-hand tributary to Cedar Creek in Braxton County.

Brackin; creek, a small left-hand branch of Meadow River, a tributary to Gauley River, in Fayette County.

Bradford; branch, a very small left-hand tributary to Kanawha River in Kanawha County.

Bradford; post village in Randolph County.

Bradshaw; creek, a left-hand tributary to Dry Fork, a branch of Tug Fork of Big Sandy River in McDowell County.

Bradshaw; creek, a small right-hand branch of Indian Creek, a tributary to New River, in Summers County.

Bradshaw; post village in McDowell County, situated on Bradshaw Creek.

Bradshaw Hill; a knob of Gauley Mountain in Randolph County.

Brady; fork, a left-hand branch of Grass Lick and tributary to Left Fork of Steer Creek in Braxton County.

Brady; post village in Pocahontas County.

Bragg; branch, a small right-hand tributary to Tommy Creek, a head fork of Guyandot River, in Raleigh County.

Bragg; fork, a small right-hand branch of Horse Creek, a tributary to Little Coal River, in Boone County.

Bragg Knob; summit in Clay County. Elevation, 1,674 feet.

Braines; creek, a right-hand branch of Raccoon Creek, a tributary to Valley River, in Preston County.

Brake; run, a small right-hand tributary to South Fork of Potomac River in Hardy County.

Bramwell; town in Mercer County on the Norfolk and Western Railway and on Bluestone River. Altitude, 2,247 feet. Population, 825.
Branch; mountain, a short ridge in Hardy County. Elevation, 1,500 to 2,500 feet.
Branch; post village in Pendleton County.
Brandonville; town in Preston County. Population, 68.
Brandywine; post village in Pendleton County.
Brant; creek, a very small right-hand tributary to Peters Creek, a branch of Gauley River, in Nicholas County.
Braxton; county, situated in the central part of the State on the Allegheny Plateau. It is here deeply dissected. It is traversed and drained by Little Kanawha and Elk rivers. Area, 541 square miles. Population, 18,904—white, 18,717; negro, 187; foreign born, 53. County seat, Sutton. The mean magnetic declination in 1900 was 2°. The mean annual rainfall is 40 to 50 inches, and the mean annual temperature 50° to 55°. The county is traversed by the Baltimore and Ohio Railroad.
Breading; post village in Mingo County.
Breckenridge; creek, a small left-hand tributary to Marsh Fork of Coal River in Raleigh County.
Breeden; creek, a very small left-hand branch of Right Fork of Twelvepole Creek, a tributary to Ohio River, in Logan County.
Bridge; branch, a very small right-hand branch of Laurel Fork, a tributary to Clear Fork of Guyandot River, in Wyoming County.
Bridgeport; town in Harrison County on the Baltimore and Ohio Railroad. Altitude, 979 feet. Population, 464.
Brier; creek, a left-hand tributary to Indian Creek, a branch of Guyandot River, in Wyoming County.
Brier; creek, a right-hand tributary to Coal River, a branch of Kanawha River, in Kanawha County.
Brier; post village in Wyoming County.
Brier Patch; mountain, a peak in the Allegheny Mountains in Randolph County. Altitude, 4,480 feet.
Briery; run, a small right-hand tributary to South Fork of Cherry River in Greenbrier County.
Briery Knob; summit in Nicholas County. Altitude, 1,850 feet.
Briery Knob; summit in Pocahontas County. Elevation, 4,534 feet.
Brierylick; run, a right-hand tributary of Right Fork of Steer Creek in Gilmer County.
Briery Ridge; short spur in Webster County, north of Gauley River.
Brighton; post village in Mason County.
Brillian; post village in Putnam County.
Brink; post village in Marion County.
Briscoe; post village in Wood County.
Bristol; post village in Harrison County on the Baltimore and Ohio Railroad.
Brittain; post village in Taylor County.
Broad; branch, a small left-hand tributary to Big Ugly Creek, a branch of Guyandot River, in Lincoln County.
Broad; run, a small right-hand tributary to Elk River, a branch of Kanawha River, in Kanawha County.
Broad; run, a small right-hand branch of Wolf Creek, a tributary to Greenbrier River, in Monroe County.
Brock; run, a small right-hand branch of Holly River, a tributary to Elk River, in Braxton County.
Brook; branch, a very small left-hand tributary to Guyandot River in Wyoming County.

Brook; creek, a left-hand tributary to Laurel Creek in Webster County.

Brook; run, a small right-hand tributary to Middle Fork of Tygarts Valley River in Randolph County.

Brooke; county, situated in the northern part of the State, in the Panhandle, bordering on Ohio River. Area, 97 square miles. Population, 7,219—white, 7,079; negro, 139, foreign born, 335. County seat, Wellsburg. The mean magnetic declination in 1900 was 3°. The mean annual rainfall is 40 inches, and the mean annual temperature 50° to 55°. The county is traversed by the Pittsburg, Cincinnati, Chicago and St. Louis Railway.

Brooklin; town in Raleigh County on the Chesapeake and Ohio Railway. Population, 632.

Brooks; branch, a very small right-hand tributary to New River in Summers County.

Brooks; post village in Summers County on the Chesapeake and Ohio Railway.

Brooks; run, a very small left-hand branch of Big Laurel Creek, a tributary to Cherry River, in Greenbrier County.

Brookside; post village in Preston County.

Broom; branch, a small left-hand branch of Alum Creek, a tributary to Coal River, in Kanawha County.

Broomfield; post village in Marion County.

Brosius; post village in Morgan County.

Brown; creek, a small right-hand tributary to Tug Fork of Big Sandy River in McDowell County.

Brown; creek, a small right-hand tributary to Big Clear Creek, a branch of Meadow River, in Greenbrier County.

Brown; mountain, a broken mountainous country in Tucker County. Elevation, 3,500 feet.

Brown; post village in Harrison County on the Baltimore and Ohio Railroad.

Brown; run, a left-hand tributary to North Fork of Dunkard Creek in Monongalia County.

Brown; run, a right-hand branch of Fish Creek in Wetzel County.

Browning; fork, a left-hand tributary to Gilbert Creek, a branch of Guyandot River, in Mingo County.

Browns; branch, a very small right-hand branch of Indian Creek, a tributary to New River, in Monroe County.

Browns; branch, a small right-hand tributary to West Fork, a branch of Pond Fork of Little Coal River, in Boone County.

Browns; creek, a small right-hand branch of Knapp Creek, a tributary to Greenbrier River, in Pocahontas County.

Browns; creek, a left-hand tributary to Coal River, a branch of Kanawha River, in Kanawha County.

Browns; knob in Taylor County.

Browns; mountain, a ridge in Pocahontas County between Browns and Knapp creeks. Elevation, 2,500 to 3,000 feet.

Browns; run, a left-hand tributary to the Ohio River in Marshall County.

Browns; run, a right-hand tributary to Little Wheeling Creek in Ohio County.

Bruce; village in Nicholas County.

Bruceton Mills; town in Preston County. Population, 80.

Bruffs; fork, a head fork of Big Sandy Creek in Preston and Barbour counties.

Brush; creek, a small left-hand branch of Coal River, a tributary to Kanawha River, in Boone County.

Brush; creek, a small left-hand tributary to Mud River, a branch of Guyandot River, in Cabell County.

Brush; creek, a right-hand tributary to Bluestone River in Mercer County. It rises in Stony Ridge.
Brush; creek, a small right-hand tributary to New River in Monroe County.
Brush; fork, a small left-hand tributary to Buckhannon River in Upshur County.
Brush; fork, a small left-hand tributary to Cedar Creek in Gilmer and Braxton counties.
Brush; run, a very small right-hand branch of Cedar Creek in Braxton County.
Brush; run, a right-hand branch of Indian Fork in Lewis County.
Brush; run, a right-hand branch of Lost Run in Taylor County.
Brush; run, a left-hand branch of Pyles Fork of Buffalo Creek in Marion County.
Brush; run, a right-hand branch of Buffalo Creek in Marion County.
Brush; run, a left-hand branch of Fishing Creek in Wetzel County.
Brush Camp Low Place; gap at the head of Leatherwood Fork, a left-hand branch of Elk River, in Randolph County.
Brush Fence; run, a small right-hand tributary to Gauley River in Webster County.
Brushfork; post village in Mercer County.
Brushy; branch, a very small right-hand tributary to Paint Creek, a branch of Kanawha River, in Kanawha County.
Brushy; branch, a very small left-hand tributary to Gilbert Creek, a branch of Guyandot River, in Mingo County.
Brushy; creek, a small left-hand branch of East Fork of Twelvepole Creek, a tributary to Ohio River, in Wayne County.
Brushy; creek, a small right-hand tributary to Seneca, a branch of North Fork of Potomac River, in Pendleton County.
Brushy; fork, a small left-hand branch of Huff Creek, a tributary to Guyandot River, in Wyoming County.
Brushy; fork, a small left-hand branch of Peters Cave Fork of Horse Creek, a tributary to Little Coal River, in Lincoln County.
Brushy; fork, a left-hand tributary to Strange Creek in Nicholas County.
Brushy; fork, a small right-hand branch of Muddlety Creek, a tributary to Gauley River, in Nicholas County.
Brushy; fork, a small right-hand tributary to Teter Creek, a branch of Valley River, in Barbour County. It rises in Laurel Hills.
Brushy; fork, a small right-hand tributary to Bluestone River in Mercer County.
Brushy; fork, a small right-hand tributary to Elk River in Braxton County.
Brushy; fork, a right-hand branch of Dunkard Creek in Monongalia County.
Brushy; fork, a small right-hand tributary to Spruce Fork of Little Coal River in Logan County.
Brushy; mountain, a short ridge in Greenbrier and Pocahontas counties. Elevation, 3,000 feet.
Brushy; run, a left-hand branch of Lunice Creek, tributary to South Branch of Potomac River, in Grant County.
Brushy; run, a name applied to the upper course of North Mill Creek, a right-hand tributary to South Branch of Potomac River, in Pendleton and Grant counties.
Brushy Flat; spur from Big Knob in Greenbrier County.
Brushfork; post village in Mercer County.
Brushy Knob; summit in Lincoln County.
Brushy Knobs; summit in Preston County.
Brushy Meadow; creek, an indirect right-hand tributary to Gauley River in Nicholas and Greenbrier counties.
Brushy Ridge; short, narrow range in Greenbrier County. Elevation, 2,500 feet.
Brushyrun; post village in Pendleton County.

Bryan; post village in Mason County.

Buck; creek, a small right-hand tributary to Greenbrier River in Pocahontas County.

Buck; fork, a small left-hand branch of Big Hart Creek, a tributary to Guyandot River, in Logan County.

Buck; fork, a right-hand head fork of Sand Creek, a tributary to Guyandot River, in Lincoln County.

Buck; fork, a small right-hand tributary to Dry Fork, a branch of Tug Fork of Big Sandy River, in McDowell County.

Buck; mountain, a short ridge in Hardy County.

Buck; post village in Summers County.

Buck; run, a very small right-hand tributary to Elk River in Braxton County.

Buck; run, a right-hand tributary to Right Fork of Simpson Run in Taylor County.

Buck; run, a right-hand tributary to South Fork of Fishing Creek in Wetzel County.

Buckeye; branch, a very small left-hand tributary to Gauley River in Webster County.

Buckeye; creek, a small left-hand tributary to Elk River in Braxton County.

Buckeye; fork, a head fork of Little Skin Creek in Lewis County.

Buckeye; post village in Pocahontas County on the Chesapeake and Ohio Railway.

Buck Garden; branch, a small right-hand tributary to Peter Creek, a branch of Gauley River, in Nicholas County.

Buckhannon; county seat of Upshur County on the Baltimore and Ohio Railroad. Altitude, 1,500 feet. Population, 1,589.

Buckhannon; mountain, a broken, mountainous ridge in the western part of Lewis County.

Buckhannon; river, a large left-hand branch of Tygarts Valley River in Upshur, Barbour, and Randolph counties.

Buckhorn; fork, a left-hand branch of Little Sycamore Creek, a tributary to Elk River in Clay County.

Buckhorn; post village in Preston County.

Buck Knob; summit in Greenbrier County.

Buck Knob; summit in Pocahontas County. Altitude, 4,356 feet.

Buckles; branch, a small right-hand tributary to Twenty Mile Creek, a branch of Gauley River, in Fayette County.

Buckley; mountain, a short ridge east of Greenbrier River in Pocahontas County. Elevation, 3,000 feet.

Buck Lick; small right-hand tributary to Gauley River, a large branch of Kanawha River, in Nicholas County.

Buck Lick; run, a left-hand tributary to Spruce Run, a small branch of Cheat River, in Preston County.

Buena; post village in Tucker County.

Buffalo; creek, a very small left-hand branch of Guyandot River, a tributary to Ohio River, in Logan County.

Buffalo; creek, a small left-hand branch of Little Huff Creek, a tributary to Guyandot River, in Wyoming County.

Buffalo; creek, a small left-hand tributary to Mud River, a branch of Guyandot River, in Lincoln County.

Buffalo; creek, a right-hand branch of Guyandot River in Logan County.

Buffalo; creek, a very small right-hand tributary to New River in Fayette and Summers counties.

Buffalo; creek, a very small right-hand branch of Tug Fork of Big Sandy River, a tributary to Ohio River in Logan County.

Buffalo; creek, a small right-hand tributary to North Branch of Potomac River in Grant County.

Buffalo; creek, a left-hand tributary to Elk River, a large branch of Kanawha River, in Clay County.

Buffalo; creek, a right-hand branch of Little Kanawha River in Braxton County.
Buffalo; creek, a small left-hand branch of Ohio River, rising in Pennsylvania and flowing west through Brooke County into Ohio River.
Buffalo; fork, a left-hand tributary to East Fork of Greenbrier River in Pocahontas County.
Buffalo; fork, a right-hand branch of Smithers Creek, a tributary to Kanawha River, in Kanawha County.
Buffalo; fork, a small right-hand branch of Hughes Creek, a tributary to Kanawha River, in Kanawha County.
Buffalo; fork, a small right-hand tributary to Clear Fork of Coal River in Raleigh County.
Buffalo; run, a left-hand branch of Right Fork of Middle Fork of Little Kanawha River in Webster County.
Buffalo; run, a small left-hand branch of Deer Creek, a tributary to North Fork of Greenbrier River, in Pocahontas County.
Buffalo; run, a small right-hand tributary to Cheat River in Preston County.
Buffalo; run, a left-hand branch of South Fork of Fishing Creek in Wetzel County.
Buffalo; village in Putnam County on the Ohio Central Lines. Population, 364.
Buffalo Bull Knob; summit in Webster County.
Buffalo Hills; short ridge west of South Branch of Potomac River in Pendleton County. Elevation, 2,000 to 2,500 feet.
Buffalolick; post village in Roane County.
Buffalo Lick; very small left-hand tributary to Elk River in Kanawha County.
Buffalo Ridge; summit in Marthas Ridge in Pocahontas County.
Buffington; run, a right-hand branch of Cheat River in Preston County.
Buffs; branch, a left-hand branch of Hurricane Creek, a tributary to Kanawha River, in Putnam County.
Bula; post village in Monongalia County.
Bull; creek, a small left-hand tributary to Pond Fork of Little Coal River in Boone County.
Bull; creek, a small left-hand tributary to Tug Fork of Big Sandy River in McDowell County.
Bull; creek, a small left-hand tributary to Ohio River in Wood County.
Bull; creek, a small right-hand tributary to Coal River, a branch of Kanawha River, in Boone County.
Bull; creek, a very small right-hand branch of Tug Fork of Big Sandy River, a tributary to Ohio River, in Wayne County.
Bull; run, a left-hand branch of Cheat River in Preston County.
Bull; run, a left-hand branch of Wheeling Creek in Marshall County.
Bull; run; a left-hand branch of French Creek in Upshur County.
Bull; run, a small left-hand tributary to Cheat River in Tucker County.
Bull; run, a right-hand tributary to Cedar Creek in Gilmer County.
Bull Fork; run, a left-hand branch of Little Kanawha River in Braxton County.
Bull Lick; branch, a small right-hand branch of Kelly Creek, a tributary to Kanawha River, in Kanawha County.
Bullrun; post village in Preston County.
Bullskin; branch, a small right-hand branch of Little Sandy Creek, a tributary to Elk River, in Kanawha County.
Bulltown; post village in Braxton County.
Bumble Bee; run, a small left-hand tributary to South Fork of Cherry River in Greenbrier County.
Bungers; post village in Greenbrier County.
Bunkerhill; post village in Berkeley County on the Cumberland Valley Railroad.

Bunners; post village in Marion County.
Burch; post village in Mingo County.
Burchfield; post village in Wetzel County.
Burdett; post village in Putnam County.
Burditt; creek, a small right-hand tributary to Gauley River in Greenbrier County.
Burk; creek, a very small right-hand tributary to Elkhorn Creek in McDowell County.
Burker; run, a right-hand branch of North Fork of Fishing Creek in Wetzel County.
Burkes; creek, a very small left-hand tributary to Elk River in Kanawha County.
Burlington; post village in Mineral County. Altitude, 800 feet.
Burner; mountain, a short ridge at the head of Greenbrier River in Pocahontas County.
Burner; run, a left-hand branch of Fish Creek in Wetzel County.
Burning Rock; triangulation station in Wyoming County.
Burning Spring; branch, a very small right-hand tributary to Kanawha River in Kanawha County.
Burning Springs; post village in Wirt County.
Burns; run, a small left-hand tributary to Salt Lick Fork of Little Kanawha River in Braxton County.
Burnside; branch, a very small tributary of Coal River, in Boone County.
Burnsville; post village in Braxton County on the Baltimore and Ohio Railroad. Altitude, 758 feet.
Burnt; fork, a small right-hand branch of Slab Fork, a tributary to Guyandot River, in Raleigh County.
Burnt Bottom; branch, a very small right-hand tributary to Pinnacle Creek, a branch of Guyandot River, in Wyoming County.
Burnt Cabin; branch, a small right-hand tributary to Laurel Fork, a branch of Spruce Fork of Little Coal River, in Boone County.
Burnt Cabin; run, a right-hand branch of Tygart Valley River in Marion County.
Burnt Camp; branch, a very small right-hand tributary to Pond Fork of Little Coal River in Boone County.
Burnthouse; post village in Ritchie County.
Burnt Ridge; mountains in Raleigh County.
Burnt Ridge; short ridge between the heads of Greenbrier and North Fork of Pocahontas River in Pocahontas County.
Burton; post village in Wetzel County on the Baltimore and Ohio Railroad. Altitude, 1,060 feet.
Bush; run, a small right-hand tributary to French Creek in Upshur County.
Buster Knob; summit in Fayette County.
Butcher; branch a small left-hand tributary to New River in Fayette County.
Butcher; fork, a left-hand branch of Sand Fork in Gilmer and Lewis counties.
Butcher; run, a small left-hand tributary to Cedar Creek in Gilmer and Braxton counties.
Butcher; run, a small left-hand tributary to Right Fork of Steer Creek in Gilmer County.
Butler; post village in Mason County.
Buzzard; branch, a small right-hand tributary to Paint Creek, a branch of Kanawha River, in Kanawha County.
Buzzard; branch, a small right-hand tributary to North Fork of Elkhorn Creek in McDowell County.
Buzzard; creek, a left-hand branch of Trace Creek in Putnam County.
Buzzard; run, a left-hand branch of Cheat River in Monongalia County.
Byrne; post village in Braxton County.

GAZETTEER OF WEST VIRGINIA. 33

Byrnside; post village in Putnam County.
Cabell; county, situated in the western part of the State bordering on Ohio River, which, with the Guyandot, drains it. Its surface is broken, being upon the lower slopes of the plateau. Area, 261 square miles. Population, 29,252—white, 27,713; negro, 1,537; foreign born, 378; county seat, Huntington. The mean magnetic declination in 1900 was 1°. The mean annual rainfall is 40 to 50 inches, and the mean annual temperature 50° to 55°. The county is traversed by the Chesapeake and Ohio and the Ohio River railroads.
Cabell; creek, a right-hand tributary to Mud River, a branch of Guyandot River, in Cabell County.
Cabell; creek, a very small right-hand tributary to Guyandot River, a branch of Ohio River, in Cabell County.
Cabin; branch, a very small right-hand tributary to Laurel Branch, a branch of Clear Fork of Guyandot River, in Wyoming County.
Cabin; creek, a small right-hand tributary to Guyandot River in Wyoming County.
Cabin; creek, a left-hand branch of Kanawha River in Kanawha and Fayette counties.
Cabin; fork, a small indirect right-hand tributary to Pond Fork of Little Coal River, a branch of Coal River, in Boone County.
Cabin; run, a small left-hand branch of Patterson Creek, a tributary to North Branch of Potomac River, in Mineral County.
Cabin; run, a small left-hand branch of Right Fork of Holly River in Braxton County.
Cacapehon; post village in Hampshire County.
Cacapon; mountains, a short ridge in Hampshire and Morgan counties. Elevation, 2,500 feet.
Cacapon; river, a large right-hand branch of Potomac River, rising in Hardy County, and flowing in a generally northeastern direction through Hardy, Hampshire, and Morgan counties. In its upper course it is known as Lost River.
Cairo; town in Ritchie County on the Baltimore and Ohio and on the Cairo and Kanawha Valley railroads. Altitude, 658 feet. Population, 653.
Calcutta; post village in Pleasants County.
Calders Peak; one of the summits of Swoopes Knobs in Monroe County.
Caldwell; post village and railway station in Greenbrier County, located on Howards Creek; also on Chesapeake and Ohio Railway. Altitude, 1,766 feet.
Caldwell; run, a left-hand branch of Saltlick Creek in Braxton County.
Calf; run, a left-hand branch of Indian Fork of Ellis Creek in Lewis County.
Calhoun; county, situated in the western part of the State on the Alleghany Plateau. Area, 276 square miles; population, 10,266—white, 10,183; negro, 83; foreign born, 26. County seat, Grantsville. The mean magnetic declination in 1900 was 1° 10′. The mean annual rainfall is 40 to 50 inches, and the mean annual temperature 50° to 55°.
Calhoun; post village in Barbour County.
Calis; post village in Marshall County.
Calvin; post village in Nicholas County.
Camden; post village in Lewis County on the Ohio River Railroad.
Camden on Gauley; post village in Webster County on the Baltimore and Ohio Railroad.
Cameron; town in Marshall County on the Baltimore and Ohio Railroad. Altitude, 547 feet. Population, 964.
Camp; branch, a very small left-hand tributary to Loop Creek, a branch of Kanawha River, in Fayette County.

Bull. 233—04——3

Camp; branch, a very small right-hand tributary to Dingus Run, a branch of Guyandot River, in Logan County.
Camp; branch, a small right-hand tributary to Tug River in McDowell County.
Camp; branch, a very small right-hand tributary to Dunloup Creek, a branch of New River, in Fayette County.
Camp; branch, a right-hand tributary of Beech Fork of Twelve Pole Creek in Cabell County.
Camp; creek, a very small left-hand tributary to Elk River in Clay County.
Camp; creek, a left-hand tributary to Bluestone River, a branch of New River, in Mercer County.
Camp; creek, a right-hand tributary to Little Coal River, a branch of Coal River, in Boone County.
Camp; creek, a small right-hand tributary to East Fork of Twelvepole Creek, a branch of Ohio River, in Wayne County.
Camp; creek, a very small right-hand tributary to Elk River, a large branch of Kanawha River, in Clay County.
Camp; creek, a right-hand tributary to Laurel Creek in Braxton and Webster counties.
Camp; creek, a very small right-hand branch of Tug Fork of Big Sandy River, a tributary to Ohio River, in Wayne County.
Camp; run, a left-hand branch of North Fork of Dunkard Creek in Monongalia County.
Camp; run, a right-hand tributary of Buffalo Creek in Marion County.
Camp; run, a left-hand tributary of Fishing Creek in Wetzel County.
Camp; post village in Doddridge County.
Campbell; creek, a right-hand tributary to Kanawha River in Kanawha County.
Campbell; fork, a small left-hand branch of Bell Creek, a tributary to Gauley River, in Kanawha County.
Campbell; run, a left-hand branch of Pyles Fork of Buffalo Creek in Marion County.
Campbell; post village in Calhoun County.
Campcreek; post village in Mercer County on Camp Creek.
Campus; post village in Wyoming County.
Canaan; mountain, a broken, mountainous country in Tucker and Grant counties. Elevation, 3,500 to 4,000 feet.
Canaan; post village in Upshur County.
Cane; branch, a very small right-hand tributary to Kanawha River in Fayette County.
Cane; branch, a very small right-hand tributary to Coal River, a branch of Kanawha River, in Kanawha County.
Cane; fork, a small left-hand branch of Davis Creek, a tributary to Kanawha River, in Kanawha County.
Cane; fork, a small right-hand branch of Cabin Creek, a tributary to Kanawha River, in Kanawha County.
Canebrake; branch, a very small left-hand tributary to Guyandot River, a branch of Ohio River, in Mingo County.
Canfield; post village in Braxton County.
Cannel Coal Hollow; short left-hand tributary to Elk River in Clay County.
Cannelton; post village in Kanawha County on the Ohio Central Lines. Altitude, 639 feet.
Cannoy; branch, a very small right-hand branch of Tug Fork of Big Sandy River, a tributary to Ohio River, in Logan County.
Canoe; run, a left-hand tributary to Monongahela River in Lewis County.
Canoe; run, a very small right-hand tributary to Elk River in Braxton County.
Cansada; post village in Clay County.

GAZETTEER OF WEST VIRGINIA.

Canterbury; post village in Mingo County, on the Norfolk and Western Railway.
Cantikee; branch, a very small right-hand tributary to Guyandot River in Mingo County.
Canton; village in Marion County.
Cantwell; post village in Ritchie County.
Capehart; post village in Mason County.
Caperton; post village in Fayette County on New River and on the Chesapeake and Ohio Railway. Altitude, 990 feet.
Capon Bridge; post village in Hampshire County, located on Cacapon River.
Capon Iron Works; post village in Hardy County.
Capon Springs; post village in Hampshire County.
Captina; post village in Marshall County on the Baltimore and Ohio Railroad.
Carberry; run, a right-hand tributary of Buffalo Creek in Marion County.
Carbondale; post village in Fayette County.
Carder; run, a right-hand branch of Lost Run in Taylor County.
Carder; run, a left-hand branch of Husted Creek in Taylor County.
Caress; post village in Braxton County.
Carkin; post village in Kanawha County.
Carmel; post village in Preston County.
Carnes Knob; summit in Clay County.
Caro; fork, a small left-hand tributary to Joe Creek, a branch of Coal River, in Boone County.
Carpenter; creek, a small right-hand branch of Second Creek, a tributary to Greenbrier River, in Monroe and Greenbrier counties.
Carpenter; fork, a small left-hand tributary to Little Birch River in Braxton County.
Carpenter; run, a left-hand branch of Little Fishing Creek in Wetzel County.
Carrel; post village in Wayne County.
Carron Knob; summit in Nicholas County. Altitude, 2,382 feet.
Carrson; fork, a right-hand tributary of North Fork of Fishing Creek in Wetzel County.
Carter; branch, a small right-hand tributary to Loop Creek, a branch of Kanawha River, in Fayette County.
Carter; run, a right-hand branch of Wheeling Creek in Ohio County.
Carthage; post village in Jackson County.
Cartwright; branch, a small left-hand tributary to Buffalo Creek, a branch of Guyandot River, in Logan County.
Cascade; run, a right-hand branch of Buffalo Creek in Brooke County.
Cascara; post village in Doddridge County.
Casey; creek, a small left-hand tributary to Pond Fork of Little Coal River in Boone County.
Cashmere; post village in Monroe County.
Cass; post village in Pocahontas County on the Chesapeake and Ohio Railway.
Cassiday; fork a small left-hand branch of Left Fork of Middle Fork of Tygarts Valley River in Randolph County.
Cassity; post village in Randolph County.
Cassville; post village in Monongalia County.
Castle; branch, a very small right-hand tributary to Big Huff Creek, a branch of Guyandot River, in Wyoming County.
Castle; mountain, a ridge situated between South and North branches of Potomac River in Pendleton County. Elevation, 3,000 feet.
Castle; post village in Wyoming County.
Castleman; run, a left-hand branch of Buffalo Creek in Ohio and Brooke counties.
Catawba; post village in Marion County on the Baltimore and Ohio Railroad.

Cave; mountain on West and South branches of Potomac River in Pendleton and Grant counties. Elevation, 1,500 to 3,000 feet.

Cave; run, a small left-hand tributary to Little Kanawha River in Upshur County.

Cave; post village in Pendleton County.

Cavill; creek, a right-hand branch of Guyandot River in Cabell County.

Cecil; post village in Taylor County on the Baltimore and Ohio Railroad.

Cedar; branch, a very small left-hand tributary to Paint Creek, a branch of Kanawha River, in Fayette County.

Cedar; branch, a very small left-hand branch of Dunloup Creek, a tributary to New River, in Fayette County.

Cedar; branch, a very small right-hand tributary to Pinnacle Creek, a branch of Guyandot River, in Wyoming County.

Cedar; branch, a very small right-hand tributary to Beech Fork of Twelvepole Creek, a branch of Ohio River, in Wayne County.

Cedar; branch, a very small right-hand tributary to New River in Summers County.

Cedar; creek, a very small right-hand tributary to Clear Fork of Guyandot River in Wyoming County.

Cedar; creek, a small left-hand branch of Slab Fork, a tributary to Guyandot River in Wyoming County.

Cedar; creek, a large left-hand branch of Little Kanawha River in Gilmer and Braxton counties.

Cedar; run, a small right-hand tributary to Wolf Creek, a branch of Greenbrier River, in Monroe County.

Cedarburg; post village in Wyoming County.

Cedarcliff; post village in Mineral County.

Cedargrove; post village in Kanawha County.

Cedar Knob; summit in Pendleton County.

Cedarville; post village in Gilmer County, located on Cedar Creek.

Centennial; post village in Monroe County.

Center; post village in Monongalia County.

Centerpoint; post village in Doddridge County.

Centerville; town in Wayne County. Population, 156.

Central City; town in Cabell County on the Baltimore and Ohio and the Chesapeake and Ohio railroads. Population, 1,580.

Centralia; post village in Braxton County on the Baltimore and Ohio Railroad.

Central Station; post village in Doddridge County.

Century; post village in Barbour County on the Baltimore and Ohio Railroad.

Ceredo; village in Wayne County on the Baltimore and Ohio, the Chesapeake and Ohio, and the Norfolk and Western railroads. Altitude, 545 feet. Population, 1,279.

Chandler; branch, a small left-hand branch of Twomile Creek, a tributary to Kanawha River, in Kanawha County.

Channel; run, a small right-hand tributary to Valley River in Randolph County.

Chap; post village in Boone County.

Chapel; post village in Braxton County.

Chapmanville; post village in Logan County.

Chappel; branch, a very small left-hand tributary to Kanawha River in Kanawha County.

Charles Knob; summit in Grant County.

Charleston; capital of the State and county seat of Kanawha County on the Charleston, Clendennin and Sutton, the Chesapeake and Ohio, and the Ohio Central railroads. Altitude, 600 feet. Population, 1,099.

Charlestown; county seat of Jefferson County on the Baltimore and Ohio and Norfolk and Western railroads. Altitude, 514 feet. Population, 2,392.

Charley; branch, a very small left-hand tributary to Mud River, a branch of Guyandot River, in Lincoln County.
Charley; creek, a small right-hand tributary to Mud River, a branch of Guyandot River, in Cabell and Putnam counties.
Charley Ridge; summit in Pocahontas County.
Charlotte; branch, a very small left-hand branch of Right Fork of Twelvepole Creek, a tributary to Ohio River, in Wayne County.
Charlotte; post village in Monongalia County.
Cheat; mountain, a short ridge in the northern part of Pocahontas County. Elevation, 4,000 feet.
Cheat; river, a large eastern branch of the Monongahela. It drains the eastern part of the State through a number of branches and flows generally northward to its mouth near the north boundary of the State.
Cheatbridge; post village in Randolph County.
Cheat View; summit in Monongalia County. Elevation, 2,212 feet.
Chelyan; post village in Kanawha County on the Chesapeake and Ohio Railway.
Chenowith; creek, a small right-hand tributary to Valley River in Randolph County. It rises in Chenowith Knob of Cheat Mountain.
Chenowith Knob; summit in Randolph County. Altitude, 3,870 feet.
Cherry; fork, a small right-hand tributary to Little Kanawha River in Upshur and Lewis counties.
Cherry; post village in Wirt County.
Cherry; river, a large left-hand branch of Gauley River which rises in two forks, North and South, in Greenbrier County, and flows northwestward into Nicholas County to its junction with the Gauley.
Cherry; run, a right-hand tributary of Potomac River on the boundary between Morgan and Berkeley counties.
Cherry Glades; marsh at the head of Cherry River in Greenbrier and Pocahontas counties.
Cherry Pond; mountain in Boone and Raleigh counties.
Cherryrun; post village in Morgan County on the Baltimore and Ohio and the Western Maryland railroads.
Chesterville; post village in Wood County.
Chestnut; post village in Mason County.
Chestnut; run, a left-hand branch of Leading Creek in Gilmer County.
Chestnut Bottom; run, a right-hand tributary of Ellis Creek in Gilmer County.
Chestnut Knob; branch, a very small right-hand branch of Buffalo Creek, a tributary to Elk River, in Clay County.
Chestnut Lick; small left-hand branch of Left Fork of Steer Creek in Gilmer County.
Chestnut Ridge; short spur in Greenbrier County. Elevation, 2,500 to 3,000 feet.
Chestnut Ridge; short spur in Pocahontas County.
Chestnut Ridge; short spur in Monongalia and Preston counties. Elevation, 2,275 feet.
Chew; run, a small right-hand branch of Big Laurel Creek, a tributary to Cherry River, in Greenbrier County.
Chicken; run, a right-hand tributary of Right Fork of Simpson Creek in Taylor County.
Chiefton; post village in Marion County.
Childress; branch, a left-hand tributary of Buch Fork of Twelve Pole Creek in Wayne County.
Childs; post village in Wetzel County.
Chilton; post village in Kanawha County on the Kanawha and Coal River Railway.
Chimney Ridge; mountains in Monroe County.

Chimney Rock; run, a small left-hand tributary to Elk River in Randolph County.

Chrisley, fork, a small right-hand tributary to Laurel Creek, a branch of Coal River, in Boone County.

Christian; fork, a small right-hand tributary to Brush Creek, a branch of Bluestone River, in Mercer County.

Christian; post village in Logan County.

Christopher; run, a right-hand branch of Cheat River in Monongalia County.

Chub; fork, a small right-hand branch of Naul Creek in Braxton County.

Church; fork, a right-hand branch of Fish Creek in Wetzel County.

Church Knob; summit in Upshur County.

Churchville; post village in Lewis County.

Cicerone; post village in Roane County.

Circleville; post village in Pendleton County.

Cirtsville; post village in Raleigh County. Altitude, 1,640 feet.

Cisko; post village in Ritchie County.

Clapboard; run, a small left-hand tributary to Valley River in Randolph County.

Claremont; post village in Fayette County on the Chesapeake and Ohio Railway and on New River.

Clarence; post village in Roane County.

Claria; post village in Calhoun County.

Clark; branch, a very small right-hand tributary to Elkhorn Creek in McDowell County.

Clark; gap in Great Flat Top Mountain in Mercer County.

Clarksburg; county seat of Harrison County on the Baltimore and Ohio Railroad. Population, 4,050. Altitude, 1,031 feet.

Claude; post village in Taylor County.

Clawson; post village in Pocahontas County.

Clay; branch, a head fork of Big Cub Creek, a tributary to Guyandot River, in Wyoming County.

Clay; county, situated in the central part of the State, in the Alleghany Plateau; it is here deeply dissected. It is drained mainly by Elk River. Area, 348 square miles. Population, 8,248—white, 8,230; negro, 18; foreign born, 48. County seat, Clay. The mean magnetic declination in 1900 was 1° 30′. The mean annual rainfall is 40 to 50 inches, and the mean annual temperature 50° to 55°. The county is traversed by the Charleston. Clendennin and Sutton Railroad.

Clay; county seat of Clay County.

Clayton; post village in Summers County.

Clear; fork, a left-hand tributary to Tug Fork of Big Sandy River in McDowell County.

Clear; fork, a right-hand branch of Guyandot River in Wyoming County.

Clear; fork, a stream in Raleigh County uniting with Marsh Fork to form Coal River.

Clearcreek; post village in Raleigh County. Altitude, 1,520 feet.

Clear Fork; gap in Guyandot Mountain in Raleigh and Wyoming counties.

Clear Drain; a right-hand branch of Fish Creek in Wetzel County.

Clements; post village in Barbour County on the Baltimore and Ohio Railroad.

Clen; fork, a right-hand branch of Laurel Branch of Clear Fork of Guyandot River in Wyoming County.

Clen; gap in spur of Guyandot Mountains, caused by Laurel Fork, in Wyoming County.

Clendenin; post village in Kanawha County on the Charleston, Clendennin and Sutton Railroad. Altitude, 624 feet.

Cleveland; post village in Webster County.

Cleveland Knob; summit in Nicholas County.

Cliff; run, a right-hand branch of Fish Creek in Wetzel County.
Cliff Knob; summit in Webster County. Altitude, 3,012 feet.
Clifftop; post village in Fayette County.
Clifton; village in Mason County on the Baltimore and Ohio Railroad. Population, 427.
Clifton Mills; post village in Preston County.
Clifty; post village in Fayette County.
Climer; creek, a very small left-hand tributary to Trace Fork of Mud River, a branch of Guyandot River, in Putnam County.
Clint; post village in Monroe County.
Clinton; post village in Ohio County.
Clinton Furnace; post village in Monongalia County.
Clintonville; post village in Greenbrier County.
Clio; post village in Roane County.
Cloat; run, a small left-hand tributary to Salt Lick Fork of Little Kanawha River in Braxton County.
Clover; creek, a small right-hand tributary to Greenbrier River in Pocahontas County.
Clover; run, a left-hand tributary to Cheat River, in Tucker County.
Clover Creek; mountain, a short ridge in Pocahontas County. Elevation, 3,000 to 4,000 feet.
Cloverdale; post village in Monroe County.
Cloverlick; branch, a small left-hand tributary to Laurel Branch, a tributary to Clear Fork of Guyandot River, in Wyoming County.
Clover Lick; fork, a left-hand branch of Oil Creek, in Lewis County.
Cloverlick; post village in Pocahontas County on the Chesapeake and Ohio Railway.
Clower; post village in Hardy County.
Cluster; post village in Pleasants County.
Clyde; post village in Wetzel County.
Coal; branch, a very small right-hand tributary to Davis Creek, a branch of Kanawha River, in Kanawha County.
Coal; fork, a left-hand branch of Cabin Creek, a tributary to Kanawha River, in Kanawha County.
Coal; fork, a small left-hand branch of Campbell Fork, a tributary to Kanawha River, in Kanawha County.
Coal; river, a left-hand branch of Monongahela River in Marion County.
Coal; run, a large left-hand branch of Kanawha River, rising in Raleigh County, and flowing northeastward through Boone County. It forms the boundary line between a portion of Lincoln and Kanawha counties and enters Kanawha River at the town of St. Albans.
Coal; run, a small left-hand tributary to New River in Fayette County.
Coal Bank; branch, a small left-hand tributary to Elkhorn Creek, a branch of Tug Fork of Big Sandy River, in McDowell County.
Coalburg; post village in Kanawha County on the Chesapeake and Ohio Railway and on Kanawha River. Altitude, 623 feet.
Coaldale; post village and railway station in Mercer County on the Norfolk and Western Railway and on South Fork of Elkhorn Creek. Altitude, 2,345 feet.
Cobb; creek, a left-hand tributary to Little Coal River, a branch of Coal River, in Lincoln County.
Cobbs; post village in Boone County.
Coburn; post village in Wetzel County.
Cochran Knob; summit in Lewis County.
Coco; post village in Kanawha County.
Coffin; creek, a small left-hand tributary to Knapp Creek, a branch of Greenbrier River, in Pocahontas County.

Coffman; post village in Greenbrier County.
Cokeleys; village in Ritchie County.
Coketon; post village in Tucker County on the West Virginia Central and Pittsburg Railway.
Colaw Knob; summit of the Allegheny Mountains in Pocahontas County. Altitude, 4,214 feet.
Cold; fork, a small right-hand tributary to Laurel Creek, a branch of Coal River, in Boone County.
Cold Knob; fork, a small left-hand tributary to South Fork of Cherry River in Greenbrier County.
Cold Knob; summit in Greenbrier County. Elevation, 4,318 feet.
Cold Spring; run, a very small right-hand branch of Big Laurel Creek, a tributary to Cherry River, in Greenbrier County.
Coldstream; post village in Hampshire County.
Coldwater; post village in Doddridge County.
Cole; mountain, a short ridge in Greenbrier County south of Greenbrier River.
Colebank; post village in Preston County.
Coleman; creek, a right-hand branch of Guyandot River in Lincoln County.
Colemans; creek, a very small right-hand branch of Tug Fork of Big Sandy River, a tributary to Ohio River, in Logan County.
Coles; mountain, a short ridge in Greenbrier County. Elevation, 2,500 feet.
Colfax; post village in Marion County on the Baltimore and Ohio Railroad.
Colic; mountain, a short ridge west of South Fork of Potomac River in Pendleton County.
Colliers; post village in Brooke County.
Collins; branch, a very small right-hand tributary to Paint Creek, a branch of Kanawha River, in Kanawha County.
Collins; run, a right-hand branch of Stewart's Creek in Gilmer County.
Collison; creek, a small left-hand tributary to Gauley River in Nicholas County.
Columbia Sulphur Springs; post village in Greenbrier County located on Anthony Creek.
Columbus; post village in Clay County.
Comer; branch, a small right-hand tributary to Barker Creek, a branch of Guyandot River, in Wyoming County.
Comfort; post village in Boone County,
Conally; run, a small right-hand tributary to Valley River in Randolph County.
Conaway; post village in Tyler County.
Concord; post village in Hampshire County.
Concord Church; village in Mercer County. Altitude, 2,620 feet.
Confidence; post village in Putnam County.
Confluence; post village in Lewis County.
Conger; fork, a small right-hand branch of Old Lick Creek, a tributary to Holly River, in Webster County.
Congo; post village in Hancock County on the Pittsburg, Cincinnati, Chicago and St. Louis Railway.
Conings; post village in Gilmer County.
Conley; branch, a small right-hand tributary to Island Creek, a branch of Guyandot River, in Logan County.
Connelly; branch, a very small left-hand tributary to Mud River, a branch of Guyandot River, in Lincoln County.
Conyer; fork, a right-hand branch of Cedar Creek, in Gilmer and Braxton counties.
Cool; branch, a very small right-hand tributary to Huff Creek, a branch of Guyandot River, in Wyoming County.
Cool Spring Knob; Summit in Webster County.

GAZETTEER OF WEST VIRGINIA.

Coon; branch, a very small left-hand branch of Coal River, a tributary to Kanawha River, in Boone County.

Coon; branch, a very small left-hand tributary to Laurel Branch, a tributary to Clear Fork of Guyandot River, in Wyoming County.

Coon; branch, a very small left-hand tributary to Clear Fork, a branch of Tug Fork of Big Sandy River, in McDowell County.

Coon; branch, a small left-hand tributary to Dry Fork, a branch of Tug Fork of Big Sandy River, in McDowell County.

Coon; creek, a very small right-hand tributary to Gauley River, in Webster County.

Coon; creek, a small left-hand branch of Meadow Creek, a tributary to New River, in Summers County.

Coon; creek, a right-hand tributary of Hurricane Creek in Putnam County.

Coon; creek, a left-hand tributary to Elk River in Braxton County.

Coon; fork, a small left-hand branch of Rock Castle Creek, a tributary to Guyandot River, in Wyoming County.

Coon; run, a right-hand branch of Cove Lick, a tributary to Sand Fork, in Lewis County.

Coon; run, a right-hand branch of West Fork River in Harrison and Marion counties.

Cooney Otter; creek, a left-hand branch of Barker Creek, a tributary to Guyandot River, in Wyoming County.

Coon Knob; summit in Braxton County. Altitude, 1,725 feet.

Coon Knob; triangulation station in Mingo County.

Coonskin; branch, a very small left-hand tributary to Elk River in Kanawha County.

Coon Tree; branch, a small left-hand tributary to Spice Creek, a branch of Tug Fork of Big Sandy River, in McDowell County.

Cooper; creek, a small right-hand tributary to Glade Creek, a branch of New River, in Raleigh County.

Cooper; creek, a right-hand tributary to Elk River in Kanawha County.

Cooper; rock, a summit in Monongalia County. Elevation, 2,000 feet.

Cooper; run, a small left-hand tributary to North Fork of Greenbrier River in Pocahontas County.

Cooper Knob; Summit of Brown Mountain in Tucker County.

Coopers; post village in Mercer County on the Norfolk and Western Railway and on Bluestone River. Altitude, 2,266 feet.

Copeland; branch, a small right-hand tributary to Big Creek, a small branch of Gauley River, in Fayette County.

Copeland; knob in Taylor County.

Copen; post village in Braxton County.

Copen; run, a small right-hand tributary to Little Kanawha River in Braxton County.

Copenhaver; fork, a small left-hand tributary to Little Sandy Creek, a small branch of Elk River, in Kanawha County.

Copenhaver; post village in Kanawha County.

Copper; run, a left-hand tributary to Little Kanawha River in Gilmer and Braxton counties.

Copperas Mine; fork, a small left-hand branch of Trace Fork of Guyandot River, a tributary to Ohio River, in Logan County.

Copperhead; branch, a very small right-hand tributary to Pinnacle Creek, a branch of Guyandot River, in Wyoming County.

Copper Snake; run, a small left-hand branch of Steer Run in Gilmer County.

Corbin; branch, a right-hand branch of Booths Creek in Taylor County.

Corcoran; post village in Randolph County.

Core; post village in Monongalia County.

Corinth; post village in Preston County on the Baltimore and Ohio Railroad.
Cork; post village in Tyler County.
Corley; post village in Braxton County.
Corliss; post village in Fayette County.
Corn; post village in Mason County.
Cornstalk; post village in Greenbrier County.
Cornwallis; post village in Ritchie County on the Baltimore and Ohio Railroad.
Cortland; post village in Tucker County.
Cos; post village in Upshur County.
Cosner Gap; height in Grant County. Elevation, 1,325 feet.
Cottageville; post village in Jackson County on the Baltimore and Ohio Railroad.
Cottle Glades; marsh in Nicholas County.
Cottle Knob; summit in Nicholas County. Altitude, 3,120 feet.
Cottonhill; post village in Fayette County on New River and on the Chesapeake and Ohio Railway. Altitude, 792 feet.
Cotton Hill; short ridge south of Kanawha River in Fayette County.
Couger; fork, tributary to Holly River.
Coulter; run, a right-hand branch of Middle Wheeling Creek in Ohio County.
Counterfeit; branch, a small left-hand branch of Witchers Creek, a tributary to Kanawha River, in Kanawha County.
Countsville; post village in Roane County.
Courtney; run, a left-hand branch of Monongahela River in Monongalia County.
Cove; creek, a small left-hand tributary to Marsh Fork of Coal River in Raleigh County.
Cove; creek, a small right-hand branch of East Fork of Twelvepole Creek, a tributary to Ohio River, in Wayne County.
Cove; mount, a summit in Lincoln County. Altitude, 1,308 feet.
Cove; mountain, a short ridge in Monroe County. Elevation, 3,000 to 3,420 feet, the latter being the height of one of its peaks.
Covecreek; post village in Wayne County.
Covegap; post village in Wayne County.
Cove Lick; right-hand branch of Sand Fork in Lewis County.
Cow; creek, a small right-hand tributary to Clear Fork, a branch of Guyandot River, in Wyoming County.
Cow; creek, a small left-hand branch of Poplar Fork of Kanawha River in Putnam County.
Cow; creek, a small left-hand branch of Pond Fork of Little Coal River in Boone County.
Cow; creek, a left-hand tributary to Island Creek, a branch of Guyandot River in Logan County.
Cow; run, a very small left-hand tributary to Buffalo Creek, a branch of Elk River, in Clay County.
Cowen; town in Webster County on the Baltimore and Ohio Railroad. Population, 257.
Cow Skin; fork, a small left-hand branch of Lower Sleith Fork, in Braxton County.
Coxs Landing; post village in Cabell County on the Baltimore and Ohio Railroad.
Coxs Mills; post village in Gilmer County.
Crabapple Knob; summit in Kanawha County. Altitude, 1,380 feet.
Crab Orchard; creek, a small left-hand tributary to Piney Creek, a branch of New River, in Raleigh County.
Craig; run, a small left-hand tributary to Williams River in Webster County.
Craigmoor; post village in Harrison County.
Craigsville; post village in Nicholas County.
Crammeys; run, a left-hand branch of Cheat River in Monongalia County.

Cranberry; creek, a small left-hand tributary to Piney Creek, a branch of New River, in Raleigh County.
Cranberry; mountain, a short ridge in Pocahontas County. Elevation, 3,500 to 4,000 feet.
Cranberry; river, a large left-hand tributary to Gauley River. It rises in Cranberry Mountain in Pocahontas County and flows northwestward through Webster and Nicholas counties to its junction with the Gauley.
Cranberry Flat; short ridge between Laurel Branch and Stone Coal Run in the central part of Randolph County.
Cranberry Glades; marsh at the head of Cranberry River in Pocahontas County.
Crane; creek, a small right-hand tributary to Dry Fork, a branch of Tug Fork of Big Sandy River, in McDowell County.
Crane; creek, a small left-hand tributary to Bluestone River in Mercer County.
Crane; fork, a small right-hand tributary to Clear Fork, a branch of Guyandot River, in Wyoming County.
Crane Camp; run, a small right-hand tributary to West Fork of Monongahela River in Lewis County.
Cranesville; post village in Preston County.
Crane Trace; branch, a small left-hand tributary to Clear Fork, a branch of Tug Fork of Big Sandy River, in McDowell County.
Crany; post village in Wyoming County.
Craven; run, a small right-hand tributary to Valley River in Randolph County.
Crawford; run, a small left-hand tributary to Gauley River in Nicholas County.
Crawford; run, a small right-hand tributary to Valley River in Randolph County.
Crawford; post village in Lewis County.
Crawley; creek, a small left-hand tributary to Guyandot River, a branch of Ohio River, in Logan County.
Crawley; post village in Greenbrier County.
Crescent; post village in Fayette County on Kanawha River and on the Chesapeake and Ohio Railway. Altitude, 638 feet.
Creston; post village in Wirt County.
Crickard; post village in Randolph County.
Crickmer; post village in Fayette County.
Crimson Springs; post village in Monroe County.
Crisp; post village in Pleasants County.
Crook; post village in Boone County.
Crooked; creek, a left-hand branch of Scary Creek, a tributary to Kanawha River, in Putnam County.
Crooked; creek, a small right-hand branch of Guyandot River, a tributary to Ohio River, in Logan County.
Crooked; creek, a small right-hand tributary to Coal River, a branch of Kanawha River, in Kanawha County.
Crooked; fork, a left-hand branch of Sand Fork in Lewis County.
Crooked; fork, a right-hand branch of Right Fork of Steer Creek in Gilmer and Braxton counties.
Crooked; fork, a right-hand tributary to the head of Big Sycamore Creek, a small branch of Elk River, in Clay County.
Crooked; run, a small left-hand tributary to North River, a branch of Cacapon River, in Hampshire County.
Crooked; run, a small left-hand branch of Cedar Creek in Gilmer County.
Crooked; run, a small left-hand branch of Wolf Creek, a tributary to New River, in Fayette County.
Crooked Ridge; short spur in Fayette County.
Crossroads; post village in Monongalia County.

Crouch Knob; summit in Randolph County.
Crow; post village in Raleigh County.
Crow; run, a left-hand branch of Fishing Creek in Wetzel County.
Crownhill; post village in Kanawha County on the Chesapeake and Ohio Railway.
Crow Summit; post village in Jackson County on the Baltimore and Ohio Railroad.
Crump; branch, a very small left-hand tributary to Cabin Creek, a branch of Kanawha River, in Kanawha County.
Crumps Bottom; post village in Summers County.
Cub; branch, a very small right-hand tributary to Run Creek, a branch of Guyandot River, in Logan County.
Cub; branch, a small right-hand tributary to Panther Creek, a branch of Tug Fork of Big Sandy River, in McDowell County.
Cub; run, a right-hand tributary of Right Fork of Steer Creek in Gilmer County.
Cuba; post village in Jackson County.
Cubana; post village in Randolph County.
Cucumber; creek, an indirect right-hand tributary to Dry Fork, a branch of Tug Fork of Big Sandy River, in McDowell County.
Culler; run, a left-hand tributary to Lost River in Hardy County.
Culloden; town in Cabell County on the Chesapeake and Ohio Railway. Population, 99.
Culverson; creek, a small creek rising and sinking in Greenbrier County.
Cummings; creek, a small left-hand branch of Knapp Creek, a tributary to Greenbrier River, in Pocahontas County.
Cunningham; fork, a left-hand branch of Big Buffalo Creek in Braxton County.
Cunningham Knob; summit of the Allegheny Mountains in Randolph County. Altitude, 4,485 feet.
Cupboard; run, a small left-hand tributary to Oil Creek in Lewis County.
Curran Knob; summit in Randolph County.
Curry; post village in Logan County.
Curry Ridge; a short spur between Plummer and Lost rivers in Taylor County.
Curtin; post village in Nicholas County on the Baltimore and Ohio Railroad.
Curtis; run, a left-hand tributary of Castleman Run in Ohio County.
Cutlip; fork, a right-hand branch of Little Otter Creek in Braxton County.
Cutlips; post village in Braxton County.
Cutwright; run, a small left-hand tributary to Buckhannon River in Upshur County.
Cuzzart; post village in Preston County.
Cyclone; post village in Logan County. Altitude, 854 feet.
Cyrus; creek, a very small left-hand tributary to Mud River, a branch of Guyandot River, in Cabell County.
Cyrus; post village in Roane County.
Daddy; run, a left-hand branch of Cedar Creek in Gilmer County.
Dahmer; post village in Pendleton County.
Dailey; village in Jefferson County on the West Virginia Central and Pittsburg Railway.
Daisy; village in Wood County.
Dakon; post village in Wetzel County.
Dale; post village in Tyler County.
Dallas; post village in Marshall County.
Dallison; post village in Wood County.
Dam; creek, a very small right-hand branch of Marrowbone Creek, a tributary to Tug Fork of Big Sandy River, in Logan County.
Dameron; post village in Raleigh County.

GAZETTEER OF WEST VIRGINIA. 45

Dan; branch, a small left-hand tributary to Elkhorn Creek, a branch of Tug Fork of Big Sandy River, in McDowell County.
Dan Harman; branch, a small right-hand tributary to Dry Fork, a branch of Tug Fork of Big Sandy River, in McDowell County.
Daniels; post village in Raleigh County.
Danstown; post village in Jackson County.
Danville; post village in Boone County.
Darkesville; post village in Berkeley County on the Cumberland Valley Railroad.
Darnell; hollow in Monongalia County.
Dartmoor; post village in Barbour County on the West Virginia Central and Pittsburg Railway.
Daubenspeck Knob; summit in Nicholas County. Altitude, 3,020 feet.
Dave; branch, a very small left-hand tributary to Big Huff Creek, a branch of Guyandot River, in Logan and Wyoming counties.
Dave Green; branch, a small right-hand tributary to Pond Fork of Little Coal River, a branch of Coal River, in Boone County.
Daves; fork, a small right-hand branch of Brush Creek, a tributary to Bluestone River, in Mercer County.
David; branch, a very small right-hand tributary to Guyandot River in Wyoming County.
Davis; creek, a small left-hand tributary to Guyandot River, a branch of Ohio River, in Cabell County.
Davis; creek, a left-hand tributary to Kanawha River in Kanawha County.
Davis; fork, a very small right-hand tributary to Sycamore Creek, a branch of Clear Fork of Coal River, in Raleigh County.
Davis; run, a small left-hand tributary to Birch River in Braxton County.
Davis; town in Tucker County on the West Virginia Central and Pittsburg Railway. Altitude, 1,077 feet. Population, 2,391.
Davis Knob; summit in Braxton County. Altitude, 1,565 feet.
Davis, Mount; triangulation station in Cabell County. Altitude, 1,077 feet.
Davis Trace; branch, a very small right-hand tributary to Middle Fork of Mud River in Lincoln County.
Davisville; post village in Wood County, on the Baltimore and Ohio Railroad.
Davy; branch, a small right-hand tributary to Tug Fork of Big Sandy River in McDowell County.
Davy; branch, a very small left-hand tributary to Buffalo Creek, a branch of Guyandot River, in Logan County.
Davy; station in McDowell County on the Norfolk and Western Railway and on Tug Fork of Big Sandy River.
Davy Fork; creek, a right-hand branch of Buffalo Creek in Marion County.
Davy; run, a small left-hand branch of Spice Run, a tributary to Greenbrier River, in Greenbrier County.
Davy Cook; branch, a very small right-hand tributary to Toney Fork of Clear Fork, a branch of Guyandot River, in Wyoming County.
Davys; creek, a small left-hand tributary to Greenbrier River in Greenbrier County.
Dawson; post village in Greenbrier County.
Day; mountain, a short spur in Pocahontas County. Elevation, 3,000 to 3,500 feet.
Day; run, a small right-hand tributary to Williams River in Pocahontas County.
Daybrook; post village in Monongalia County.
Day Camp; branch, a small right-hand tributary to Clear Fork, a branch of Tug Fork of Big Sandy River, in McDowell County.
Dayton; post village in Harrison County. Altitude, 925 feet.
Dean; post village in Wetzel County.

Debby; post village in Mason County.

Deckers; creek, a small right-hand branch of Monongahela River in Preston and Monongalia counties.

Decota; post village in Kanawha County.

Deep; run, a small right-hand tributary to North Fork of Potomac River in Mineral County.

Deep; run, a small left-hand tributary to Elk River in Webster County.

Deep; run, a small left-hand tributary to Holly River in Webster County.

Deep Ford; branch, a very small left-hand tributary to Guyandot River, a branch of Ohio River, in Mingo County.

Deep Hole; creek, a very small right-hand branch of West Fork of Twelvepole Creek, a tributary to Ohio River, in Wayne County.

Deepvalley; post village in Tyler County.

Deepwater; post village in Fayette County on Kanawha River and on the Chesapeake and Ohio Railway. Altitude, 645 feet.

Deer; creek, a right-hand branch of North Fork of Greenbrier River in Pocahontas County.

Deer; creek, a right-hand tributary to Hominy Creek, a branch of Gauley River, in Nicholas County.

Deer; run, a small right-hand tributary to Little Birch River in Braxton County.

Deer; run, a small right-hand tributary to South Branch of Potomac River in Pendleton County.

Deer Knob; summit in Upshur County.

Deerlick; post village in Mason County.

Deerrun; post village in Pendleton County.

Deerskin; branch, a small left-hand tributary to Panther Creek, a branch of Tug Fork of Big Sandy River, in McDowell County.

Deerwalk; post village in Wood County.

Defeat; branch, a small right-hand tributary to Little Huff Creek, a branch of Guyandot River, in Wyoming County.

Deitz; post village in Fayette County.

Dekalb; post village in Gilmer County, situated on Little Kanawha River.

Delancy; post village in Wood County.

Delashmeet; creek, a very small left-hand tributary to Bluestone River in Mercer County.

Delila; post village in Webster County.

Dell; post village in Upshur County.

Dellslow; post village in Monongalia County on the Morgantown and Kingwood Railroad.

Delong; post village in Pleasants County.

Delorme; railway station in Logan County on the Norfolk and Western Railway and on Tug Fork of Big Sandy River.

Delphi; post village in Nicholas County.

Delray; post village in Hampshire County.

Delta; post village in Braxton County.

Dempsey; branch, a left-hand branch of Laurel Creek, a tributary to New River, in Fayette County.

Dempsey; mountain, a short ridge north of Greenbrier River in Summers County. Elevation, 2,500 feet.

Dempsey; post village in Fayette County.

Dennis; post village in Greenbrier County.

Dennis; run, a small right-hand branch of Laurel Creek, a tributary to Elk River, in Webster County.

Dennison; fork, a small left-hand branch of Laurel Fork, a tributary to Spruce Fork of Little Coal River, in Boone County.
Dennison; fork, a left-hand tributary of Mud River in Lincoln County.
Dent; post village in Barbour County.
Desert; branch, a small left-hand tributary to North Fork of Cherry River in Nicholas County.
Desert; fork, a right-hand head fork of Holly River in Webster County.
Deskins; fork, a small left-hand branch of Rich Creek, a tributary to East Fork of Twelvepole Creek, in Wayne County.
Deuls; run, a left-hand branch of Buffalo Creek in Marion County.
Devil; creek, a small right-hand branch of Second Creek, a tributary to Greenbrier River, in Monroe County.
Devil; run, a very small right-hand tributary to Little Kanawha River in Braxton County.
Devil; run, a small right-hand tributary to Middle Fork of Tygarts Valley River in Barbour and Randolph counties.
Devil Nose; summit in Clay County.
Devils; fork, a small left-hand tributary to Guyandot River in Raleigh County.
Devils Den; branch, a small right-hand branch of Leatherwood Creek, a tributary to Elk River, in Clay County.
Dewey; post village in Mercer County.
De Witt; post village in Wyoming County.
Dexter; post village in Roane County.
Dial; post village in Kanawha County.
Diamond; post village in Kanawha County on the Chesapeake and Ohio Railway.
Diana; post village in Webster County on the Holly River and Addison Railway.
Diatter; run, a small right-hand tributary to Birch River in Braxton County.
Dick; creek, a very small right-hand tributary to Little Coal River, a branch of Coal River and tributary to Kanawha River, in Boone County.
Dickerson; branch, a very small right-hand tributary to Kanawha River in Kanawha County.
Dick Ridge; spur in Nicholas County.
Dickson; post village in Wayne County on the Norfolk and Western Railway.
Dick Trace; small right-hand branch of Dingus Run, a tributary to Guyandot River, in Logan County.
Dicy; post village in Wayne County.
Difficult; creek, a small right-hand tributary to North Branch of Potomac River in Grant County.
Dilley; run, a small left-hand branch of Strange Creek, a tributary to Elk River, in Nicholas County.
Dilleys Mill; post village in Pocahontas County.
Dillon; branch, a small right-hand tributary to Sand Lick Creek, a branch of Marsh Fork of Coal River, in Raleigh County.
Dillon; run, a small left-hand tributary to Cacapon River in Hampshire County.
Dillons Run; post village in Hampshire County.
Dimmock; post village in Fayette County on the Chesapeake and Ohio Railway and on New River. Altitude, 1,045 feet.
Dingess; branch, a very small left-hand tributary to Buffalo Creek, a branch of Guyandot River, in Logan County.
Dingess; branch, a very small left-hand tributary to Elk Creek, a branch of Guyandot River, in Logan County.
Dingess; branch, a small right-hand tributary to Marsh Fork of Coal River in Raleigh County.

Dingess; fork, a very small left-hand branch of Big Huff Creek, a tributary to Guyandot River, in Wyoming County.

Dingess; post village in Mingo County.

Dingess; station in Logan County on the Norfolk and Western Railway and on Right Fork of Twelvepole Creek.

Dingess Trace; very small right-hand branch of Right Fork of Twelvepole Creek, a tributary to Ohio River, in Logan County.

Dingus; run, a small right-hand branch of Guyandot River in Logan County.

Divide; post village in Fayette County.

Dixie; post village in Fayette County.

Dixon; run, a right-hand branch of Pyles Fork of Buffalo Creek in Marion County.

Doak; post village in Doddridge County.

Doane; post village in Wayne County, on the Norfolk and Western Railway.

Dobbin; post village in Grant County on North Fork of Potomac River and on the West Virginia Central and Pittsburg Railway. Altitude, 2,593 feet.

Dobbin Ridge; short, broken, mountainous country in Tucker and Grant counties.

Doctor; branch, a very small right-hand tributary to Elk River, a large branch of Kanawha River, in Kanawha County.

Dodd; post village in Roane County.

Doddridge; county, situated in the northwestern part of the State on the Allegheny plateau. Area, 344 square miles. Population, 13,689—white, 13,663;. negro, 25; foreign born, 129. County seat, West Union. The mean magnetic declination in 1900 was 2° 30′. The mean annual rainfall is 40 to 50 inches, and the mean annual temperature, 50° to 55°. The county is traversed by the Baltimore and Ohio Railroad.

Dodrill; post village in Calhoun County.

Dodson; run, a small right-hand tributary to Valley River in Randolph County.

Doe; branch, a small left-hand tributary to Bluestone River, a branch of New River, in Mercer County.

Doe; run, a left-hand branch of Tygarts Valley River in Taylor County.

Dogbone; branch, a small left-hand tributary to Left Fork of Mud River, a branch of Guyandot River, in Lincoln County.

Dogway; fork, a small left-hand tributary to Cranberry River in Webster and Pocahontas counties.

Dogwood; creek, a small left-hand branch of Meadow River, a tributary to Gauley River, in Fayette County.

Dola; post village in Harrison County on the Baltimore and Ohio Railroad.

Dolan Knob; summit on boundary line between Cabell and Wayne counties. Altitude, 1,090 feet.

Doman; post village in Hardy County.

Dombey; village in Wood County.

Donald; post village in Nicholas County.

Donlan; post village in Gilmer County.

Donnelly; branch, a very small left-hand tributary to Kanawha River in Kanawha County.

Donohue; post village in Ritchie County.

Dorcas; post village in Grant County.

Dority; post village in Preston County.

Dorr; post village in Monroe County.

Dorsey; branch, a very small left-hand branch of Twentymile Creek, a tributary to Gauley River, in Nicholas County.

Dorsey; knob in Monongalia County. Elevation, 1,438 feet.

Dotson; post village in McDowell County.

GAZETTEER OF WEST VIRGINIA. 49

Double Camp; branch, a very small right-hand tributary to Guyandot River in Wyoming County.
Dougher Knob; summit in Greenbrier County. Altitude, 2,818 feet.
Doughertys; creek, a small right-hand tributary to Cheat River in Preston County.
Douglas; fork, a small right-hand tributary to Elk River in Randolph County.
Douglas; post village in Calhoun County on the West Virginia Central and Pittsburg Railway.
Dovener; post village in Lewis County.
Dowdy; creek, a very small right-hand tributary to New River in Fayette County.
Doyle; post village in Wood County.
Dragstone; creek, a very small right-hand branch of Tug Fork of Big Sandy River, a tributary to Ohio River, in Wayne County.
Drake; run, a right-hand branch of Pyles Fork of Buffalo Creek in Marion County.
Drawdy; creek, a small left-hand branch of Coal River, a tributary to Kanawha River, in Boone County.
Drews; creek, a left-hand branch of Peachtree Creek, a tributary to Marsh Fork of Coal River, in Raleigh County.
Drift; branch, a very small right-hand tributary to West Fork of Twelvepole Creek, a branch of Ohio River, in Wayne County.
Driftwood; post village in Pocahontas County.
Driscol; post village in Pocahontas County.
Droop; mountain, a short spur in Greenbrier and Pocahontas counties. One of its peaks has an altitude of 3,634 feet.
Dropping Lick; creek, a small left-hand tributary to Indian Creek, a branch of New River, in Monroe County.
Dry; branch, a very small left-hand branch of Davis Creek, a tributary to Kanawha River, in Kanawha County.
Dry; branch, a small right-hand tributary to Campbell Creek, a branch of Kanawha River, in Kanawha County.
Dry; branch, a small right-hand branch of Witchers Creek, a tributary to Kanawha River, in Kanawha County.
Dry; branch, a right-hand tributary to Cabin Creek, a branch of Kanawha River, in Kanawha County.
Dry; branch, a small right-hand tributary to Clear Fork, a branch of Guyandot River, in Wyoming County.
Dry; branch, a very small right-hand tributary to Indian Creek, a branch of Guyandot River, in Wyoming County.
Dry; branch, a very small right-hand tributary to Pond Fork of Little Coal River in Boone County.
Dry; branch, a very small right-hand tributary to Tug Fork of Big Sandy River in McDowell County.
Dry; creek, a small right-hand branch of Rich Creek, a tributary to New River, in Monroe County.
Dry; creek, a small right-hand branch of Spring Creek, a tributary to Greenbrier River, in Greenbrier County.
Dry; creek, a small right-hand tributary to Greenbrier River in Pocahontas County.
Dry; creek, a small right-hand tributary to Marsh Fork of Coal River in Raleigh County.
Dry; creek, a very small left-hand tributary to Mud River, a branch of Guyandot River, in Cabell County.
Dry; creek, a left-hand tributary to Howards Creek, a branch of Greenbrier River, in Greenbrier County. Its headwater is known locally as Tuckahoe Creek.

Dry; fork, a left-hand branch of Lower Bull Run, a small right-hand tributary to Cedar Creek, in Gilmer County.
Dry; fork, a right-hand fork of Cheat River in Tucker and Randolph counties.
Dry; fork, a small right-hand tributary to Elk River in Pocahontas County.
Dry; fork, a large right-hand tributary to Tug Fork of Big Sandy River in McDowell County.
Dry; run, a small left-hand tributary to South Branch of Potomac River in Pendleton County.
Dry; run, a small left-hand tributary to Little Kanawha River in Gilmer County.
Dry; run, a right-hand tributary to North Fork of Potomac River in Pendleton County.
Dry; run, a small right-hand tributary to Valley River in Randolph County.
Dry; run, a small right-hand tributary to Left Fork of Buckhannon River in Randolph County.
Dry; run, a small right-hand tributary to South Branch of Potomac River in Pendleton County.
Dry; run, a small right-hand branch of Second Creek, a tributary to Greenbrier River, in Monroe County.
Dry; run, a left-hand branch of Tanner Creek in Gilmer County.
Dry; run, a right-hand branch of Lost Run in Taylor County.
Drybranch; post village in Kanawha County on the Chesapeake and Ohio Railway.
Drycreek; post village in Raleigh County. Altitude, 1,342 feet.
Dryfork; post village in Randolph County on the Dry Fork Railroad.
Dryrun; hollow in Horse Ridges in Morgan County.
Dryrun; post village in Pendleton County.
Dubree; post village in Fayette County.
Duck; creek, a small left-hand tributary to Little Kanawha River in Gilmer County.
Duck; creek, a small right-hand branch of Elk River in Braxton County.
Duckworth; post village in Doddridge County on the Baltimore and Ohio Railroad.
Dudley; fork, a left-hand tributary of Pyles Fork of Buffalo Creek in Marion County.
Dudley; post village in Cabell County.
Duffields; post village in Jefferson County on the Baltimore and Ohio Railroad. Altitude, 562 feet.
Duffy; post village in Lewis County.
Dugout; post village in Raleigh County.
Duhring; post village in Mercer County on the Norfolk and and Western Railway and on Bluestone River. Altitude, 2,333 feet.
Duke; post village in Kanawha County on the Baltimore and Ohio Railroad.
Dulin; post village in Wirt County.
Dull; creek, a small right-hand tributary to Elk River, a large branch of Kanawha River, in Clay County.
Dumpling; run, a small left-hand tributary to South Branch of Potomac River in Hampshire and Hardy counties.
Duncan; post village in Jackson County on the Baltimore and Ohio Railroad.
Duncan; run, a small left-hand branch of Deer Creek, a tributary to North Fork of Greenbrier River, in Pocahontas County.
Dunham Lick; run, a right-hand branch of Prichett Creek in Marion County.
Dunkard; creek, a left-hand branch of Monongahela River, heading in Monongalia County in North, South, and Middle forks.
Dunkard Mill; run, a left-hand branch of Buffalo Creek in Marion County.
Dunleith; post village in Wayne County.
Dunloup; creek, a small left-hand tributary to New River in Fayette and Raleigh counties.

GAZETTEER OF WEST VIRGINIA. 51

Dunlow; post village in Wayne County on the Norfolk and Western Railway.
Dunmore; post village in Pocahontas County.
Dunns; post village in Mercer County.
Duo; post village in Greenbrier County.
Durbin; post village in Pocahontas County on the Chesapeake and Ohio and on the West Virginia Central and Pittsburg railways.
Dust Camp; run, a small left-hand tributary to Little Kanawha River in Gilmer County.
Dutch; fork, a very small left-hand tributary to Pocahontas River in Kanawha County.
Dyers; run, a small left-hand tributary to Elk River in Webster County.
Eads Ridge; summit in Monroe County. Altitude, 2,854 feet.
Eagle; branch, a small right-hand tributary to Greenbrier River in Summers County.
Eagle; post village in Fayette County on Kanawha River and on the Chesapeake and Ohio Railway.
Eagle Mills; post village in Doddridge County.
Earl; post village in Nicholas County.
Earnshaw; post village in Wetzel County.
East; fork, a right-hand branch of Fourteenmile Creek, a tributary to Guyandot River, in Lincoln County.
East; river, a left-hand tributary to New River in Mercer County.
East; run, a right-hand branch of Buffalo Creek in Marion County.
Eastbank; town in Kanawha County on the Chesapeake and Ohio Railway and on Kanawha River. Altitude, 623 feet. Population, 468.
East Lynn; post village in Wayne County.
Easton; post village in Monongalia County on the Baltimore and Ohio Railroad. Altitude, 967 feet.
East River; mountain, a ridge extending along boundary line between Mercer County, West Va., and Bland County, Va.
East River; station in Mercer County on the Norfolk and Western Railway and on East River.
East Sewell; station in Fayette County on the Chesapeake and Ohio Railway and on New River.
Easy; run, a small left-hand tributary to Back Fork of Elk River in Webster County.
Eatons; post village in Wood County.
Eby; post village in Taylor County.
Echart; post village in Boone County. Altitude, 1,424 feet.
Echo; post village in Wayne County on the Norfolk and Western Railway.
Eckman; post village in McDowell County on the Norfolk and Western Railway and on Elkhorn Creek.
Eden; post village in Calhoun County.
Edens; fork, a small left-hand branch of Right Fork of Twomile Creek, a tributary to Elk River, in Kanawha County.
Edgar; post village in Jackson County.
Edgarton; post village in Mingo County.
Edgington; post village in Brooke County on the Pittsburg, Cincinnati, Chicago and St. Louis Railway. Altitude, 702 feet.
Edith; post village in Wyoming County.
Edmiston; post village in Lewis County.
Edmond; post village in Fayette County.
Edmonds; branch, a small right-hand tributary to Mud River, a branch of Guyandot River, in Cabell County.
Edray; post village in Pocahontas County.
Edwin; post village in Webster County.

Efaw; knob in Monongalia County.
Effie; post village in Wayne County.
Egeria; post village in Raleigh County.
Eggleton; post village in Putnam County.
Eglon; post village in Preston County.
Egypt; post village in Wayne County.
Eighteenmile; fork, a small right-hand branch of Campbell Creek, a tributary to Kanawha River, in Kanawha County.
Eighteen Mile; small left-hand tributary to Ohio River in Putnam County.
Eldora; post village in Marion County.
Elgood; post village in Mercer County. Altitude, 2,870 feet.
Eli, post village in Wood County.
Elijah; creek, a small right-hand tributary to Big Clear Creek, a branch of Meadow River, in Greenbrier County.
Eliza; run, a left-hand tributary of Buffalo Creek in Marion County.
Elizabeth; county seat of Wirt County on the Little Kanawha Railroad. Population, 657.
Elk; creek, a small branch of Monongahela River in Harrison County.
Elk; creek, a small right-hand tributary to Guyandot River in Logan County.
Elk; fork, a small right-hand tributary to Pigeon Creek, a branch of Tug Fork of Big Sandy River, in Logan County.
Elk; mountain, a ridge between Elk and Holly rivers in Webster County. Elevation, 1,500 to 2,500 feet.
Elk; mountain, a short ridge near the head of North Fork of Potomac River.
Elk; mountain, a summit in Randolph County. Elevation, 4,000 feet.
Elk; mountain, a ridge lying east of Dry Fork of Elk River in Randolph County.
Elk; village in Tucker County.
Elk; river, a right-hand branch of Kanawha River in Webster, Braxton, Clay, and Kanawha counties.
Elk; run, a small right-hand tributary to North Branch of Potomac River in Grant County.
Elk Garden; town in Mineral County on the West Virginia Central and Pittsburg Railroad. Altitude, 2,300 feet; population, 581.
Elkhorn; creek, a right-hand tributary to Tug Fork of Big Sandy River in McDowell County.
Elkhorn; post village in McDowell County on the Norfolk and Western Railway and on South Fork of Elkhorn Creek. Altitude, 1,885 feet.
Elkhorn Rock; summit on South Fork Mountain in Hardy County.
Elkins; branch, a very small right-hand tributary to Left Fork of Mud River in Lincoln County.
Elkins; branch, a small left-hand tributary to Laurel Branch, a tributary to Clear Fork of Guyandot River, in Wyoming County.
Elkins; county seat of Randolph County on the West Virginia Central and Pittsburg Railroad. Population, 2,016.
Elkins Gap; triangulation station in Wyoming County. Elevation, 1,944 feet.
Elk Knob; post village in Summers County.
Elklick; branch, a very small left-hand tributary to Clear Fork, a branch of Guyandot River, in Wyoming County.
Elklick; branch, a very small left-hand tributary to Buffalo Creek, a branch of Guyandot River, in Logan County.
Elk Lick; branch, a small left-hand branch of Blue Creek, a tributary to Elk River, in Kanawha County.
Elk Lick; left-hand head fork of Laurel Fork of Cheat River in Randolph County.
Elk Lick; small left-hand tributary to Oil Creek in Lewis County.

Elklick; run, a small right-hand tributary to Greenbrier River in Pocahontas County.
Elk Trace; small left-hand tributary to Big Huff Creek, a branch of Guyandot River, in Logan and Wyoming counties.
Elk Trace; small right-hand branch of Big Tub Creek, a tributary to Guyandot River, in Wyoming County.
Elk Twomile; creek, a left-hand tributary to Elk River in Kanawha County.
Elk water; left-hand tributary to Valley River in Randolph County.
Elkwater; post village in Randolph County.
Ella; post village in Marshall County.
Elleber; run, a small left-hand tributary to North Fork of Greenbrier River in Pocahontas County.
Elleber Ridge; summit between Elleber Run and Tackey Fork in Pocahontas County. Elevation, 4,000 to 4,500 feet.
Ellenboro; post village in Ritchie County.
Elliot; post village in Fayette County.
Ellis; creek, a small right-hand tributary to Marsh Fork of Coal River in Raleigh County.
Ellis; creek, a right-hand branch of Sand Fork and tributary to Little Kanawha River in Gilmer County.
Ellis; post village in Gilmer County on Ellis Creek.
Ellison; post village in Summers County.
Ellsworth; post village in Ritchie County.
Elm; fork, a left-hand tributary to Buffalo Creek, a branch of Elk River, in Nicholas and Clay counties.
Elmgrove; town in Ohio County on the Baltimore and Ohio Railroad. Altitude, 681 feet; population, 768.
Elmira; post village in Braxton County.
Elmo; post village in Fayette County on the Chesapeake and Ohio Railway and on New River. Altitude, 860 feet.
Elmwood; post village in Mason County on the Chesapeake and Ohio Railway.
Eloise; post village in Wayne County.
Elton; post village in Summers County.
Elverton; post village in Fayette County.
Elwell; post village in Mason County on the Baltimore and Ohio Railroad.
Ely; fork, a small left-hand tributary to Little Coal River, a branch of Coal River, in Lincoln County.
Emanuel; hill, a summit in Fayette County. Altitude, 2,360 feet.
Emma; post village in Putnam County.
Emory; post village in Mineral County.
Endicott; post village in Wetzel County.
England; run, a small left-hand tributary to Little Kanawha River in Braxton County.
Ennis; post village in McDowell County on the Norfolk and Western Railway and on South Fork of Elkhorn Creek. Altitude, 1,990 feet.
Enoch; branch, a small left-hand tributary to Gauley River in Nicholas and Webster counties.
Enoch; post village in Clay County.
Enoch; run, a small right-hand branch of Muddlety Creek, a tributary to Gauley River, in Nicholas County.
Enon; post village in Nicholas County.
Enterprise; post village in Harrison County on the Baltimore and Ohio Railroad.
Entry; mountain, a summit in Pendleton County.
Ephraim; creek, a very small right-hand tributary to New River in Fayette County.

Erbacon; post village in Webster County on the Baltimore and Ohio Railroad.
Erie; post village in Wayne County on the Baltimore and Ohio Railroad.
Ernest; post village in Roane County.
Etam; post village in Preston County.
Ethel; post village in Boone County.
Euclid; post village in Calhoun County.
Eugene; post village in Mingo County.
Eureka; post village in Pleasants County on the Baltimore and Ohio Railroad.
Eva; post village in Ritchie County.
Evans; branch, a very small left-hand tributary to Barker Creek, a branch of Guyandot River, in Wyoming County
Evans; fork, a small left-hand branch of Falling Rock Creek, a tributary to Elk River, in Kanawha County.
Evans; post village in Jackson County on the Baltimore and Ohio Railroad.
Evans; run, a left-hand tributary of Buffalo Creek in Marion County.
Evansville; post village in Preston County.
Evelyn; post village in Wirt County.
Everett; post village in Tyler County.
Evergreen; post village in Upshur County.
Everson; post village in Marion County on the Baltimore and Ohio Railroad.
Ewing; fork, a small right-hand tributary to Clear Fork of Coal River in Raleigh County.
Extra; post village in Putnam County.
Extract; post village in Hampshire County.
Eye; post village in Nicholas County.
Eyes; run, a small right-hand tributary to Thorn Run of South Branch of Potomac River in Pendleton County.
Fabius; post village in Hardy County.
Faily; creek, a very small left-hand tributary to New River in Raleigh County.
Fairfax; post village in Mingo County on the West Virginia Central and Pittsburg Railroad.
Fairfield; post village in Kanawha County on the Chesapeake and Ohio Railway.
Fairmont; county seat of Marion County on the Baltimore and Ohio Railroad. Altitude, 888 feet. Population, 5,655.
Fairplain; post village in Jackson County.
Fairview; village in Hancock County. Population, 407.
Falkner; branch, a small right-hand branch of Muddlety Creek, a tributary to Gauley River, in Nicholas County.
Fall; creek, a small left-hand branch of Coal River, a tributary to Kanawha River, in Kanawha and Lincoln counties.
Fall; run, a right-hand branch of Little Kanawha River in Braxton County.
Fall; run, a small right-hand branch of Back Fork of Holly River in Webster County.
Fall; run, a small left-hand branch of Right Fork of Holly River in Braxton County.
Fallen Timber; run, a small right-hand tributary to Little Kanawha River in Lewis County.
Fallen Timber; short ridge in the western part of Pocahontas County. Elevation, 4,000 feet.
Falling Rock; creek, a left-hand tributary to Elk River in Kanawha and Clay counties.
Falling Spring; mountain, a short ridge north of Greenbrier River in Greenbrier County. Elevation, 2,500 feet.
Falling Spring; post village in Greenbrier County located on Greenbrier River.
Falling Spring; run, a small right-hand tributary to Elk River in Randolph County.

Falling Waters; post village in Berkeley County on the Cumberland Valley Railroad.
Fall Rock; branch, a very small left-hand tributary to Guyandot River in Wyoming County.
Falls; branch, a very small left-hand tributary to Beech Fork of Twelvepole Creek, a branch of Ohio River, in Wayne County.
Falls; creek, a small left-hand tributary to Kanawha River in Fayette County.
Falls; creek, a very small left-hand tributary to Guyandot River, a branch of Ohio River, in Lincoln County.
Falls; post village in Grant County.
Fallsmill; post village in Braxton County.
Fanlight; post village in Wetzel County.
Far; post village in Wetzel County.
Farley; branch, a small left-hand tributary to Cabin Creek, a branch of Guyandot River, in Wyoming County.
Farley; branch, an indirect right-hand tributary to Tommy Creek, a head fork of Guyandot River, in Raleigh County.
Farley; branch, a very small right-hand tributary to Pond Fork of Little Coal River in Boone County.
Farley; branch, a very small right-hand tributary to Mud River, a branch of Guyandot River, in Lincoln County.
Farmington; post village in Marion County on the Baltimore and Ohio Railroad.
Farnum; post village in Harrison County.
Fat; creek, a small right-hand tributary to Piney Creek, a branch of New River, in Raleigh County.
Faulkner; post village in Randolph County on the West Virginia Central and Pittsburg Railroad.
Fayette; county, situated a little south of the central part of the State on the Alleghany Plateau. It is drained by the Kanawha, New, and Gauley rivers. Area, 775 square miles. Population, 31,987—white, 26,130; negro, 5,857; foreign born, 975. County seat, Fayetteville. The mean magnetic declination in 1900 was 1° 30′. The mean annual rainfall is 50 to 60 inches, and the mean annual temperature 55° to 55°. The county is traversed by the Chesapeake and Ohio and by the Kanawha and Michigan railways.
Fayette; post village in Fayette County on New River and on the Chesapeake and Ohio Railway. Altitude, 900 feet.
Fayetteville; county seat of Fayette County about three miles west of New River. Altitude, 1,750 feet. Population, 413.
Federal; post village in Pleasants County.
Feed Trough; run, a small right-hand tributary to Birch River in Nicholas County.
Fellowsville; post village in Preston County.
Felt; run, a small left-hand tributary to Left Fork of Steer Creek in Gilmer County.
Ferguson; post village in Wayne County.
Fern; creek, a small right-hand tributary to New River in Fayette County.
Fern; post village in Pleasants County.
Ferris; post village in Fayette County.
Ferrum; village in Jefferson County.
Ferry; branch, a very small left-hand tributary to Kanawha River in Kanawha County.
Ferry; run, a right-hand tributary of Buffalo Creek in Brooke County.
Festus; village in Marion County.
Fetterman; town in Taylor County on the Baltimore and Ohio Railroad. Altitude, 984 feet. Population, 796.

Fez; creek, a very small left-hand tributary to Mud River, a branch of Guyandot River, in Lincoln County.

Fields; creek, a small left-hand tributary to Kanawha River in Kanawha County.

Fifteenmile; creek, a small left-hand tributary to Paint Creek, a branch of Kanawha River, in Fayette County.

Fifteenmile; fork, a left-hand branch of Cabin Creek, a tributary to Kanawha River, in Kanawha County.

Files; creek, a right-hand branch of Valley River in Randolph County.

Finch; post village in Ritchie County.

Finlow; post village in Fayette County.

Finney; branch, a small right-hand tributary to Kanawha River in Kanawha County.

Finster; post village in Lewis County.

Fire; creek, a very small right-hand tributary to New River in Fayette County.

Firecreek; post village in Fayette County on the Chesapeake and Ohio Railway and on New River. Altitude, 1,029 feet.

Fish; creek, a small left-hand branch of Ohio River in Marshall County.

Fisher; fork, a right-hand branch of Rocky Fork of Pocotaligo River, a tributary to Kanawha River, in Kanawha County.

Fisher Knob; summit in Braxton County. Elevation, 1,710 feet.

Fishhook; fork, a small left-hand tributary to Blake Branch of Smithers Creek, a tributary to Kanawha River, in Fayette County.

Fishing; creek, a left-hand branch of Ohio River heading in North and South Forks in Wetzel County.

Fishing Hawk; small left-hand tributary to Shavers Fork of Cheat River in Randolph County.

Fishpot; run, a right-hand branch of Little Kanawha River in Gilmer County.

Fitz; run, a small left-hand tributary to Sand Fork in Lewis County.

Fitzwater; branch, a small right-hand branch of Peter Creek, a tributary to Gauley River, in Nicholas County.

Fitzwater; run, a small right-hand branch of Buffalo Creek, a tributary to Elk River, in Clay County.

Five Lick; run, a small right-hand tributary to Laurel Fork of Cheat River in Randolph County.

Five Mile; creek, a small left-hand tributary to East River, a branch of New River, in Mercer County.

Fivemile; fork, a left-hand branch of Kelly Creek, a tributary to Kanawha River, in Kanawha County.

Fivemile; fork, a very small left-hand branch of Smithers Creek, a tributary to Kanawha River, in Fayette County.

Fivemile; fork, a small right-hand branch of Campbell Creek, a tributary to Kanawha River, in Kanawha County.

Fivemile; fork, a small right-hand branch of Cooper Creek, a tributary to Kanawha River, in Kanawha County.

Fivemile; post village in Mason County.

Flag; run, a small left-hand tributary to Cheat River in Preston County.

Flaggy Meadow; run, a right-hand branch of Buffalo Creek in Marion County.

Flat; fork, a small right-hand branch of Buffalo Creek, a tributary to Elk River, in Clay County.

Flat; run, a right-hand branch of Tygart Valley River in Taylor County.

Flat; run, a small left-hand branch of Sycamore Creek in Gilmer County.

Flat; run, a left-hand branch of Pyles Fork of Buffalo Creek in Marion County.

Flatfork; post village in Roane County.

Flatrock; post village in Mason County.

Flat Top; mountain, a ridge in Wyoming, Mercer, Raleigh, and Summers counties. Average altitude, 3,375 feet.
Flat Top; mountain, a summit in Monroe County. Altitude, 3,375 feet.
Flattop; post village in Mercer County. Altitude, 3,180 feet.
Flat Top; summit in Nicholas County.
Flatwoods; post village in Braxton County, on the Baltimore and Ohio and the West Virginia Central and Pittsburg railroads. Altitude, 1,223 feet.
Flatwoods; run, a small right-hand tributary to Elk River in Braxton County.
Flaxton; post village in Mason County.
Fleming; fork, a right-hand branch of Buffalo Creek in Marion County.
Fleming; run, a small left-hand tributary to Anthony Creek, a branch of Greenbrier River, in Greenbrier County.
Flemington; post village in Taylor County on the Baltimore and Ohio Railroad.
Fleshy; run, a small right-hand tributary to Little Kanawha River in Braxton County.
Fletcher; post village in Jackson County.
Flinn; post village in Jackson County.
Flint; post village in Doddridge County.
Flint; run, a small left-hand branch of The Creek and tributary to Back Fork of Elk River in Randolph County.
Flint; run, a small left-hand tributary to Ohio River in Doddridge County.
Flipping; creek, a small left-hand tributary to Bluestone River in Mercer County.
Flippins Ridge; mountains in Mercer County.
Floding; post village in Cabell County.
Flora; post village in Barbour County.
Floyd; branch, a very small right-hand tributary to Coal River, a branch of Kanawha River, in Boone County.
Folsom; post village in Wetzel County.
Foltz; post village in Berkeley County.
Fonda; post village in Harrison County.
Foote; post village in Mineral County.
Ford; post village in Wood County.
Ford Knob; summit of Big Sewell Mountain in Fayette County. Altitude, 3,330 feet.
Ford Knob; summit in Fayette County. Altitude, 2,860 feet.
Fore Knobs; summits in Allegheny Front in Grant County.
Foresthill; post village in Summers County.
Fork; creek, a small left-hand branch of Coal River, a tributary to Kanawha River, in Boone County.
Fork; mountain, a short ridge in Webster County.
Fork; mountain, a ridge on the south side of Cranberry River, separating it from the headwaters of the Greenbrier.
Fork; mountain, a short ridge near the head of Greenbrier River.
Fork Ridge; mountains in Mercer County.
Fork Ridge; short spur of Middle Fork Mountains.
Forksburg; village in Marion County.
Forks of Capon; post village in Hampshire County.
Forks of Little Sandy; post village in Kanawha County.
Fort: branch, a small right-hand tributary to Indian Creek, a branch of Guyandot River, in Wyoming County.
Fort Gay; post village in Wayne County.
Fort Laurel; creek, a small right-hand tributary to New River in Fayette County, called Laurel Creek at its mouth.
Fort Seybert; post village in Pendleton County.

Fort Spring; post village in Greenbrier County on Greenbrier River and on the Chesapeake and Ohio Railway. Altitude, 1,626 feet.

Forty Weight; branch, a small head tributary to Laurel Fork, a tributary to Clear Fork of Guyandot River, in Raleigh County.

Foss; post village in Summers County.

Foster; post village in Boone County.

Foster Chapel; post village in Jackson County.

Fountain Spring; post village in Wood County.

Fourmile; creek, a small left-hand branch of Lens Creek, a tributary to Kanawha River, in Kanawha County.

Fourmile; creek, a small left-hand tributary to Guyandot River, a branch of Ohio River, in Lincoln County.

Fourmile; fork, a very small left-hand branch of Smithers Creek, a tributary to Kanawha River, in Fayette County.

Fourmile; fork, a very small left-hand branch of Kelly Creek, a tributary to Kanawha River, in Kanawha County.

Fourmile; fork, a small left-hand branch of Paint Creek, a tributary to Kanawha River, in Kanawha County.

Fourmile; fork, a small right-hand branch of Whiteoak Creek, a tributary to Coal River, in Boone County.

Fourmile; fork, a right-hand branch of Cooper Creek, a tributary to Elk River, in Kanawha County.

Fourmile; run, a right-hand branch of North Fork of Fishing Creek in Wetzel County.

Four Pole; creek, a very small right-hand branch of Tug Fork of Big Sandy River in Mingo County.

Fourpole; creek, a small left-hand tributary to Ohio River in Wayne and Cabell counties.

Fourteen; post village in Lincoln County.

Fourteenmile; creek, a small left-hand branch of Guyandot River, a tributary to Ohio River, in Lincoln County.

Fowlerknob; post village in Nicholas County.

Fox; post village in Braxton County.

Fox Knob; summit in Nicholas County.

Fox Tree; run, a small left-hand tributary to Cranberry River in Webster County.

Frame; run, a left-hand branch of Strange Creek in Braxton County.

Frame Knob; summit in Braxton County. Elevation, 1,563 feet.

Frametown; post village in Braxton County.

Frances; creek, a small right-hand branch of Kiah Fork, a tributary to Twelvepole Creek, in Wayne County.

Frank; branch, a small left-hand branch of Lilly Fork of Buffalo Creek, a tributary to Elk River, in Clay County.

Frank; fork, a very small right-hand branch of Blue Creek, a tributary to Elk River, in Kanawha County.

Frank; fork, a very small right-hand branch of Laurel Fork, a tributary to Clear Fork of Guyandot River, in Wyoming and Raleigh counties.

Frank; post village in Putnam County.

Frankford; town in Greenbrier County. Population, 138.

Franklin; branch, a small right-hand branch of Twomile Creek, a tributary to Guyandot River, in Lincoln County.

Franklin; county seat of Pendleton County on the Baltimore and Ohio Railroad. Population, 205.

Frazier; run, a small left-hand tributary to Cheat River in Preston County.

Fraziers Bottom; post village in Putnam County.

Freed; post village in Calhoun County.
Freeman; post village in Mercer County, on the Norfolk and Western Railway. Altitude, 2,258 feet.
Freemansburg; post village in Lewis County.
Freeport; post village in Wirt County.
Freeze; fork, a head fork of Dingus Run, a tributary to Guyandot River, in Logan County.
French; creek, a left-hand branch of Buckhannon River in Upshur County.
Frenchcreek; post village in Upshur County.
Frenchton; post village in Upshur County.
Frew; post village in Tyler County.
Friarshill; post village in Greenbrier County.
Friendly; town in Tyler County, on the Baltimore and Ohio Railroad. Population, 253.
Friends; run, a small left-hand tributary to South Branch of Potomac River in Pendleton County.
Frisco; village in Marion County.
Front Hills; summits in Grant County.
Frost; post village in Pocahontas County.
Frozen; branch, a very small left-hand branch of Kelly Creek, a tributary to Kanawha River, in Kanawha County.
Frozencamp; post village in Jackson County.
Fry; post village in Kanawha County.
Fudge; branch, a very small left-hand tributary to Little Sandy Creek, a small branch of Elk River, in Kanawha County.
Fudger; creek, a small left-hand tributary to Mud River, a branch of Guyandot River, in Cabell County.
Fudges Creek; post village in Cabell County.
Fullen; post village in Monroe County.
Fulton; creek, a very small right-hand tributary to Clear Fork of Coal River in Raleigh County.
Fuqua; creek, a small right-hand branch of Coal River, a tributary to Kanawha River, in Lincoln County.
Furber; run, a right-hand branch of Proctor Creek in Wetzel County.
Furnace; post village in Mineral County.
Furnett; branch, a very small left-hand tributary to Big Ugly Creek, a branch of Guyandot River, in Lincoln County.
Furnett; creek, a small right-hand tributary to Guyandot River, a branch of Ohio River, in Lincoln County.
Fury Knob; summit in Nicholas County.
Gad; post village in Nicholas County.
Gaines; post village in Upshur County.
Galfred; run, a small left-hand branch of Suttleton Creek, a tributary to Greenbrier River, in Pocahontas County.
Gallatin; branch, a very small left-hand tributary to Kanawha River in Kanawha County.
Galletin; village in Marion County.
Gandeeville; post village in Roane County.
Gandy; creek, a right-hand head fork of Dry Fork of Cheat River in Randolph County.
Gandy; run, a small right-hand tributary to Red Creek in Tucker County.
Ganotown; post village in Berkeley County.
Gap; mountain in Monroe County.
Gapmills; post village in Monroe County.

Garden Gap; branch, a very small left-hand tributary to Little Huff Creek, a branch of Guyandot River, in Wyoming County.
Garden Ground; mountain in Fayette County.
Gardner; branch, a very small right-hand tributary to Clear Fork of Coal River in Raleigh County.
Garfield; post village in Jackson County.
Garland; fork, a small right-hand tributary to Spruce Fork of Little Coal River in Logan County.
Garland; post village in Barbour County.
Garnet; post village in Kanawha County.
Garrett; creek, a small left-hand branch of Twelvepole Creek, a tributary to Ohio River, in Wayne County.
Garretts Bend; post village in Lincoln County.
Garrison; run, a left-hand branch of Castleman Run in Ohio County.
Gary; post village in Webster County on the Norfolk and Western Railway.
Gashell; run, a right-hand branch of Little Wheeling Creek in Ohio County.
Gaston; post village in Lewis County on the West Virginia Central and Pittsburg Railroad. Altitude 1,040 feet.
Gate; fork, a right-hand tributary of Left Fork of Steer Creek in Braxton and Gilmer counties.
Gates; post village in Monroe County.
Gatewood; branch, a small right-hand tributary to Cabin Creek, a branch of Kanawha River, in Kanawha County.
Gatewood; post village in Fayette County.
Gath; village in Marion County.
Gauley; mountain, a ridge in Randolph and Pocahontas counties. Elevation, 4,000 feet.
Gauley; mountain, a ridge between Gauley and New rivers, forks of Kanawha River, in Fayette County. Elevation, 1,500 to 2,000 feet.
Gauley; river, a right-hand branch of Kanawha River, entering it about 20 miles above Charleston. Length, 109 miles.
Gauley Bridge; post village in Fayette County on Gauley River and on the Chesapeake and Ohio Railway.
Gay; post village in Jackson County.
Gay Knob; summit in Pocahontas County.
Gazil; post village in Kanawha County.
Geho; post village in Calhoun County.
Gem; post village in Braxton County.
Geneva; post village in Roane County.
Genoa; post village in Wayne County on the Norfolk and Western Railway.
George; branch, a small left-hand tributary to Laurel Creek, a branch of Coal River, in Boone County.
George; branch, a small right-hand tributary to Panther Creek, a branch of Tug Fork of Big Sandy River, in McDowell County.
George; branch, a very small left-hand tributary to Barker Creek, a branch of Guyandot River, in Wyoming County.
George; run, a left-hand tributary of Ohio River in Ohio County.
Georges; creek, a small right-hand tributary to Kanawha River in Kanawha County.
Georgetown; post village in Monongalia County.
Georgie; post village in Wood County.
German; post village in Braxton County.
Gerrardstown; post village in Berkeley County.
Get Out; run, a tributary to Little Kanawha River in Upshur County.
Giatto; post village in Mercer County.

GAZETTEER OF WEST VIRGINIA. 61

Gibson; branch, a small right-hand tributary to Fifteenmile Fork of Cabin Creek, a branch of Kanawha River, in Kanawha County.
Gibson; post village in Pleasants County on the Norfolk and Western Railway.
Gibson Knob; summit in Pocahontas County. Altitude, 4,360 feet.
Gibsons Mill; post village in Fayette County.
Gilbert; creek, a left-hand tributary to Guyandot River, a branch of Ohio River, in Mingo County.
Gilbert; post village in Mingo County. Altitude, 832 feet.
Gilboa; post village in Nicholas County.
Gilkerson; post village in Wayne County.
Gilliam; post village in McDowell County on the Norfolk and Western Railway.
Gillespie; run, a left-hand branch of Middle Wheeling Creek in Ohio County.
Gilmer; county situated in the central part of the county, on the Allegheny Plateau. It is here deeply dissected. It is traversed and drained by Little Kanawha River. Area, 367 square miles. Population, 11,762—white, 11,726; negro, 36; foreign born, 18. County seat, Glenville. The mean magnetic declination in 1900 was 1° 20′. The mean annual rainfall is 40 to 50 inches, and the mean annual temperature, 50° to 55°.
Girta; post village in Ritchie County.
Girty; run, a left-hand tributary of Ohio River in Brooke County.
Given; branch, a very small right-hand tributary to Elk River in Kanawha County.
Given; post village in Jackson County.
Glade; creek, a left-hand branch of New River in Raleigh County.
Glade; creek, a small left-hand branch of Meadow River, a tributary to Gauley River, in Fayette County.
Glade; creek, a small left-hand branch of Muddlety Creek, a tributary to Gauley River, in Nicholas County.
Glade; creek, a small right-hand tributary to New River in Fayette County.
Glade; run, a left-hand tributary of Pawpaw Creek in Marion County.
Glade; run, a right-hand tributary of Cheat River in Monongalia County.
Glade; run, a small right-hand tributary to Blackwater River in Tucker County.
Glade; run, a small left-hand branch of Laurel Creek, a tributary to Elk River, in Webster County.
Glade; station in Fayette County on the Chesapeake and Ohio Railway and on New River. Altitude, 1,236 feet.
Gladefarms; post village in Preston County.
Gladesville; post village in Preston County.
Gladwin; post village in Tucker County, on the Dry Fork Railroad.
Glady; creek, a right-hand branch of Little Kanawha River in Lewis County.
Glady; creek, a right-hand branch of Tygarts Valley River in Marion County.
Glady; creek, a small right-hand tributary to Laurel Creek, a branch of Valley River, in Barbour County.
Glady; fork, a large left-hand branch of Dry Fork, one of the head forks of Cheat River, in Randolph and Tucker counties.
Glady; fork, a small left-hand tributary to Right Fork of Stone Coal Creek in Upshur County.
Glady; fork, a left-hand tributary to Brush Creek, a branch of Bluestone River, in Mercer County.
Glady; post village in Randolph County, on the West Virginia Central and Pittsburg Railway.
Glass Lick; small right-hand tributary to Beech Fork of Twelvepole Creek, a branch of Ohio River, in Wayne County.
Glebe; post village in Hampshire County.
Glenalum; post village in Mingo County on the Norfolk and Western Railway.

Glencoe; post village in Greenbrier County.
Glen Easton; post village in Marshall County.
Glen Falls; post village in Harrison County.
Glengary; post village in Berkeley County.
Glenns; run, a left-hand branch of Ohio River in Ohio County.
Glenville; county seat of Gilmer County on Little Kanawha River. Population, 398. Altitude, 738 feet.
Glenwood; post village in Mason County.
Glomera; post village in Raleigh County.
Glover; branch, a very small right-hand branch of Guyandot River, a branch of Ohio River, in Lincoln County.
Glovergap; post village in Marion County on the Baltimore and Ohio Railroad. Altitude, 1,146 feet.
Gluck; run, a very small right-hand tributary to Little Kanawha River in Gilmer County.
Gnat; run, a small right-hand tributary to Gauley River in Webster County.
Godby Knob; summit in Logan County.
Godfrey; branch, a small right-hand tributary to Wide Mouth Creek, a branch of Bluestone River, in Mercer County.
Godfrey; post village in Mercer County.
Goffs; post village in Ritchie County.
Golden; post village in Marshall County.
Goldtown; post village in Jackson County.
Gomez; post village in Calhoun County.
Goodhope; post village Harrison County.
Goodwill; post village in Mercer County on the Norfolk and Western Railway.
Goose; creek, a right-hand branch of Tygarts Valley River in Marion County.
Goosecreek; post village in Ritchie County.
Goose Lick; left-hand branch of Indian Fork in Lewis County.
Gooseneck; post village in Ritchie County.
Gordon; post village in Boone County on the Norfolk and Western Railway.
Gormania; post village in Grant County on North Branch of Potomac River and on the West Virginia Central and Pittsburg Railway.
Gough; run, a right-hand branch of Potomac River in Morgan County.
Gould; post village in Clay County.
Grace; post village in Roane County on the Baltimore and Ohio Railroad.
Grady; post village in Wood County.
Grafton; county seat of Taylor County on the Baltimore and Ohio Railroad. Altitude, 997 feet. Population, 5,650.
Graham Mines; post village in Kanawha County.
Graham Station; post village in Mason County on the Baltimore and Ohio Railroad.
Grand Camp; run, a right-hand branch of French Creek, a tributary to Buckhannon River, in Upshur County.
Grand Camp; run, a small right-hand branch of Cedar Creek in Gilmer County.
Granddaddy; run, a left-hand branch of Left Fork of Steer Creek in Braxton County.
Grandstaff; run, a right-hand branch of Wheeling Creek in Marshall County.
Grandview; post village in Raleigh County.
Grangeville; village in Marion County.
Granny; creek, a right-hand tributary to Elk River in Braxton County.
Grant; county, situated in the northeastern part of the State. Its surface consists of a close alternation of ridges and valleys. It is traversed from northeast to northwest by branches of the Potomac, by which it is drained. Area, 483 square miles. Population, 7,275—white, 7,023; negro, 252; foreign born, 95. County

seat, Petersburg. The mean magnetic declination in 1900 was 3° 45′. The mean annual rainfall is 50 to 60 inches, and the mean annual temperature 40° to 50°. The county is traversed by the West Virginia Central and Pittsburg Railway.

Grants; branch, a very small right-hand branch of Tug Fork of Big Sandy River, a tributary to Ohio River, in Logan County.

Grantsville; county seat of Calhoun County. Population, 225.

Grape Island; post village in Pleasants County, on the Baltimore and Ohio Railroad.

Grapevine; branch, a small left-hand tributary to Pond Fork of Little Coal River in Boone County.

Grapevine; branch, a small left-hand tributary to Dry Fork, a branch of Tug Fork of Big Sandy River, in McDowell County.

Grapevine; branch, a right-hand branch of Fourpole Creek in Cabell County.

Grapevine; branch, a very small right-hand tributary to Tug Fork of Big Sandy River in McDowell County.

Grapevine; creek, a small right-hand branch of Tug Fork of Big Sandy River, a tributary to Ohio River, in Logan County.

Grapevine Knob; summit in Kanawha County.

Grass; run, a left-hand branch of Little Kanawha River in Gilmer County.

Grass; run, a right-hand branch of Saltlick Creek in Braxton County.

Grasshopper; run, a right-hand branch of Potomac River in Morgan County.

Grassland; post village in Harrison County.

Grass Lick; head fork of left fork of Steer Creek in Braxton County.

Grassy; branch, a very small left-hand tributary to Bluestone River in Mercer County.

Grassy; creek, a left-hand tributary to Holly River in Webster County.

Grassy; creek, a small right-hand branch of Hominy Creek, a tributary to Gauley River, in Nicholas County.

Grassy; fork, a left-hand tributary to Big Sycamore Creek, a small branch of Elk River, in Clay County.

Grassy; fork, a small left-hand tributary to Little Coal River, a branch of Coal River, in Lincoln County.

Grassy; mountain, a summit west of North Branch of the Potomac in Pendleton County.

Grassy; run, a small right-hand tributary to Buckhannon River in Upshur County.

Grassy; run, a very small right-hand branch of Buffalo Creek, a tributary to Elk River, in Clay County.

Grassy; run, a small right-hand branch of Stewart Creek in Gilmer County.

Grassy; run, a small left-hand tributary to North River in Hampshire and Hardy counties.

Grassy; run, a left-hand branch of Prickett Run in Marion County.

Grassy Knob; summit in Greenbrier County. Elevation, 4,391 feet.

Grassy Meadows; post village in Greenbrier County.

Graux; post village in Roane County.

Grave; fork, a small right-hand branch of Slab Fork, a tributary to Guyandot River, in Raleigh County.

Gravel Lick; small right-hand branch of Morris Fork of Blue Creek, a tributary to Elk River, in Kanawha County.

Gray; run, a right-hand branch of Buffalo Creek in Marion County.

Gray; station in Logan County on the Norfolk and Western Railway and on Tug Fork of Big Sandy River.

Graydon; post village in Fayette County.

Graysflat; village in Marion County.

Gray Sulphur; springs, situated in Monroe County near Peterstown.

Graysville; post village in Marshall County on the Baltimore and Ohio Railroad.

Great Backbone; mountain, a narrow ridge in Tucker and Preston counties. Elevation, 2,500 to 3,500 feet.

Great Cacapon; post village in Morgan County on the Baltimore and Ohio Railroad.

Great Flat Top; mountain, a ridge extending along the boundary lines between McDowell, Wyoming, and Mercer counties.

Great House; branch, a very small right-hand tributary to Buffalo Creek, a branch of Elk River, in Clay County.

Great North; (See Shenandoah Mountains.)

Green; branch, a very small left-hand tributary to Big Huff Creek, a branch of Guyandot River, in Logan County.

Green; valley in Stony Ridge, Mercer County.

Greenbank; post village in Pocahontas County.

Green Bay; branch, a very small right-hand branch of Indian Creek, a tributary to New River, in Monroe County.

Greenbottom; post village in Cabell County.

Greenbrier; county, situated in the southeastern part of the State. Area, 1,051 square miles. Population, 20,683—white, 18,854; negro, 1,829; foreign born, 121. County seat, Lewisburg. The mean magnetic declination in 1900 was 1° 30'. The mean annual rainfall is 50 to 60 inches, and the mean annual temperature 50° to 55°. The county is traversed by the Chesapeake and Ohio Railway.

Greenbrier; creek, a small left-hand branch of West Fork of Twelvepole Creek, a tributary to Ohio River, in Wayne County.

Greenbrier; fork, a small left-hand tributary to Panther Creek, a branch of Tug Fork of Big Sandy River, in McDowell County.

Greenbrier; mountain, a ridge west of Greenbrier River in Greenbrier County. Elevation, 2,000 to 3,359 feet, the latter being the height of one peak.

Greenbrier; post village in Greenbrier County on the Chesapeake and Ohio Railway.

Greenbrier; river, a large right-hand branch of New River, entering it at Hinton.

Greencastle; post village in Wirt County.

Greenhill; post village in Wetzel County.

Green Knob; summit near the boundary line of Randolph and Pendleton counties. Elevation, 4,500 feet.

Greenland; post village in Grant County, situated on New Creek Mountain. Altitude, 1,443 feet.

Greenland Gap; height in New Creek Mountain, Grant County.

Greenmont; town in Monongalia County. Population, 349.

Greens; branch, a small right-hand tributary to Cabin Creek, a branch of Kanawha River, in Kanawha County.

Greens; run, a left-hand branch of Buffalo Creek in Brooke County.

Green Shoal; branch, a small right-hand tributary to Guyandot River, a branch of Ohio River, in Lincoln County.

Greenshoal; post village in Lincoln County.

Greenspring; post village in Hampshire County on the Baltimore and Ohio Railroad.

Green Sulphur Springs; post village in Summers County.

Greenville; post village in Monroe County.

Greenwood; post village in Doddridge County on the Baltimore and Ohio Railroad. Altitude, 880 feet.

Gregg Knob; summit in the Allegheny Mountains in Randolph County. Altitude, 4,310 feet.

Greggs; post village in Ohio County.

Griffith; branch, a very small left-hand tributary to Piney Creek, a branch of New River, in Raleigh County.

Griffith; creek, a small right-hand tributary to Greenbrier River in Summers County.

Griffithsville; post village in Lincoln County.
Grimms Landing; post village in Mason County.
Grog; run, a left-hand branch of Buffalo Creek in Brooke County.
Groomer; creek, a small left-hand tributary to Greenbrier River in Summers and Monroe counties.
Groundhog; branch, a very small right-hand tributary to Little Huff Creek, a branch of Guyandot River, in Wyoming County.
Grove; creek, a left-hand branch of Elk River in Clay County.
Grove; post village in Doddridge County.
Gulf; branch, a small left-hand tributary to Rock Castle Creek, a branch of Guyandot River, in Wyoming County.
Gunville; post village in Mason County.
Guseman; post village in Preston County.
Guy; run, a small right-hand branch of Knapp Creek, a tributary to Greenbrier River, in Pocahontas County.
Guyandot; mountain, a ridge of mountains in Raleigh and Wyoming counties.
Guyandot; river, a left-hand branch of Ohio River. It turns in the summit of the Allegheny Plateau and flows nearly northwest to its mouth at Huntington. It is navigable for 100 miles.
Guyandotte; town in Cabell County on the Baltimore and Ohio and the Chesapeake and Ohio railroads. Altitude, 558 feet. Population, 1,450.
Guyses; run, a right-hand branch of Tygarts Valley River in Marion County.
Gwin Flats; narrow summit in Webster County south of Cranberry River.
Gwinn; post village in Cabell County.
Gwins; run, a small right-hand branch of Laurel Creek, a tributary to Elk River, in Webster County.
Gypsy; post village in Harrison County on the Baltimore and Ohio Railroad.
Hacker Camp; run, a small left-hand tributary to Little Kanawha River in Lewis County.
Hacker Valley; post village in Webster County.
Haddicks; run, a small left-hand tributary to Shavers Fork of Cheat River in Tucker and Randolph counties.
Hagans; post village in Monongalia County.
Haggle; branch, a very small right-hand tributary to Coal River, a branch of Kanawha River, in Boone County.
Haines Knob; summit in the Alleghenies in Randolph County. Altitude, 4,130 feet.
Hale; branch, a very small right-hand tributary to Davis Creek, a branch of Kanawha River, in Kanawha County.
Hales; branch, a small left-hand tributary to Five Mile Creek, a branch of East River, in Mercer County.
Hall; post village in Barbour County.
Hall; run, a right-hand tributary of Middle Wheeling Creek in Ohio County.
Halleck; post village in Monongalia County.
Halls Mills; post village in Wetzel County.
Hallsville; post village in McDowell County located on or near Tug Fork of Big Sandy River.
Halltown; post village in Jefferson County on the Baltimore and Ohio Railroad.
Hambleton; post village in Tucker County on the West Virginia Central and Pittsburg Railway.
Hambleton; station in Grant County on the West Virginia Central and Pittsburg Railway and on North Branch of Potomac River.
Hamilton; branch, a very small left-hand tributary to Loop Creek, a branch of Kanawha River, in Fayette County.

Hamilton; branch, a small right-hand tributary to Dunloup Creek, a branch of New River, in Fayette County.

Hamilton; creek, a small right-hand tributary to Guyandot River, a branch of Ohio River, in Lincoln County.

Hamlin; county seat of Lincoln County.

Hammer; run, a small left-hand tributary to South Branch of Potomac River in Pendleton County.

Hammick; fork, a small left-hand branch of Buffalo Creek, a tributary to Elk River, in Clay County.

Hammick Hill; summit in Kanawha County.

Hammond; post village in Marion County on the Baltimore and Ohio Railroad.

Hammond Ridge; short spur of Big Ridge in Greenbrier County.

Hampshire; county, situated in the northeastern part of the State. It is traversed by Great Cacapon and Little Cacapon rivers and the South Branch of the Potomac. The surface consists mainly of an alternation of ridges and valleys, the former of no great height. The average elevation is not far from 1,000 feet. Area, 662 square miles. Population, 11,806—white, 11,344; negro, 461; foreign born, 51. County seat, Romney. The mean magnetic declination in 1900 was 3° 45′. The mean annual rainfall is 50 to 60 inches, and the mean annual temperature 45° to 50°. The county is traversed by the Baltimore and Ohio Railroad.

Hamrick Knob; summit in Webster County.

Hamrick Ridge; short spur separating Turkey Creek and Big Run, in Webster County.

Hancock; county, situated in the Panhandle, bordering on the Ohio River. Area, 86 square miles. Population, 6,693—white, 6,646; negro, 46; foreign born, 380. County seat, New Cumberland. The mean magnetic declination in 1900 was 3° 5′. The mean annual rainfall is 30 to 40 inches, and the mean annual temperature 50° to 55°. The county is traversed by the Pittsburg, Cincinnati, Chicago and St. Louis Railway.

Handley; post village in Kanawha County on the Chesapeake and Ohio Railway. Altitude, 632 feet.

Haney Hollow; short right-hand tributary to Kanawha River, in Kanawha County.

Hanging; run, a small right-hand tributary to Middle Fork of Tygarts Valley River, in Barbour County.

Hanging Rock; branch, a small right-hand tributary to North Fork of Cherry River, in Greenbrier County.

Hanging Rock; post village in Hampshire County on the Baltimore and Ohio Railroad.

Hanging Rock; summit at the junction of Nicholas, Webster, and Granbury counties.

Hanging Rock Mills; post village in Hardy County.

Hannahsville; post village in Tucker County.

Hanover; post village in Wyoming County.

Hans; creek, a small left-hand branch of Indian Creek, a tributary to New River, in Monroe County.

Hardesty; post village in Preston County.

Harding; post village in Randolph County on the West Virginia Central and Pittsburg Railway.

Hardman; fork, a right-hand branch of Grass Run, in Gilmer County.

Hard Scrabble; summit at head of North Fork of the Potomac, in Pendleton County. Altitude, 4,500 feet.

Hardway; branch, a small left-hand branch of Twentymile Creek, a tributary to Gauley River, in Nicholas County.

GAZETTEER OF WEST VIRGINIA.

Hardy; county, situated in the northeastern part of the State. It is traversed by Lost River and South Branch of Potomac River. The surface consists of alternation ridges trending northeast and southwest. The elevation ranges from 800 to 3,000 feet. Area, 594 square miles. Population, 8,449—white, 7,992; negro, 457; foreign born, 23. County seat, Moorefield. The mean magnetic declination in 1900 was 3° 15′. The mean annual rainfall is 50 to 60 inches, and the mean annual temperature 45° to 50°.

Hardy; post village in Mercer County.

Hardy; run, a small right-hand branch of Wolf Creek, a tributary to Greenbrier River in Monroe County.

Harewood; post village in Fayette County on Kanawha River and on the Kanawha and Michigan Railway.

Harker; run, a left-hand branch of Long Drain in Wetzel County.

Harless; fork, a small left-hand branch of Fourmile Creek, a tributary to Guyandot River, in Lincoln County.

Harman; branch, a small left-hand tributary to Tug Fork of Big Sandy River, in McDowell County.

Harman; post village in Randolph County on the Dry Fork Railroad.

Harmon; branch, a small left-hand tributary to East River in Mercer County.

Harmond; creek; a small right-hand branch of Pocahontas River, a tributary to Kanawha River, in Putnam County.

Harper; branch, a small right-hand tributary to Blue Creek, a branch of Elk River, in Kanawha County.

Harpers Ferry; town in Jefferson County on the Baltimore and Ohio Railroad; population, 896.

Harris; branch, a very small right-hand tributary to Tug Fork of Big Sandy River, in McDowell County.

Harrison; county, situated in the northwestern part of the State on the slope of the Alleghany Plateau, and drained northward by the Monongahela River. Area, 431 square miles. Population, 27,690—white, 26,435; negro, 1,252; foreign born, 821; county seat, Clarksburg. The mean magnetic declination in 1900 was 2° 45′. The mean annual rainfall is 40 to 50 inches, and the mean annual temperature 50°. The county is traversed by the Baltimore and Ohio Railroad.

Harrison; post village in Clay County on the West Virginia Central and Pittsburg Railway.

Harrisville; county seat of Ritchie County. Population, 472.

Harrow Knob; summit in Braxton County; elevation, 1,622 feet.

Harry; branch, a very small right-hand tributary to Guyandot River in Mingo County.

Hart; post village in Lincoln County on the Baltimore and Ohio Railroad.

Hartford; village in Mason County on the Baltimore and Ohio Railroad. Population, 515.

Hartley; post village in Ritchie County.

Hartley; run, a right-hand branch of Little Fishing Creek in Wetzel County.

Hartmonsville; post village in Mineral County.

Harts; run, a small left-hand branch of Howards Creek, a tributary to Greenbrier River, in Greenbrier County.

Harvey; creek, a right-hand branch of Trace Fork in Putnam and Lincoln counties.

Harvey; post village in Raleigh County on the Ohio Central Lines. Altitude, 2,030 feet.

Harvey; run, a left-hand branch of Paw Paw Creek in Marion and Monongalia counties.

Hatcher; post village in Mercer County.

Hateful; creek, a small left-hand tributary to Williams River, in Webster and Pocahontas counties.

Hatfield; branch, a small left-hand tributary to Big Cub Creek, a branch of Guyandot River, in Wyoming County.

Hatfield; branch, a very small right-hand tributary to Tug Fork of Big Sandy River, a branch of Ohio River, in Logan County.

Hatfield; post village in Mingo County.

Hathaway; post village in Calhoun County.

Hawes; run, a small right-hand tributary to South Fork of Potomac River in Pendleton County.

Haw Flat; run, a small right-hand tributary to North Fork of Potomac River in Pendleton County.

Hawflat Knob; summit in Randolph County.

Hawksnest; town in Fayette County on the Chesapeake and Ohio Railway and on New River. Altitude, 827 feet. Population, 109.

Haw Ridge; summit at head of Buffalo Fork of Greenbrier River in Pocahontas County.

Hayden; post village in Preston County.

Hayes; gap in Pendleton County.

Haymond; post village in Nicholas County.

Haynes; branch, a right-hand branch of Twelvepole Creek in Wayne County.

Haynes; post village in Webster County.

Hays; creek, a small left-hand tributary to Marsh Fork of Coal River in Raleigh County.

Hazel; post village in Wetzel County.

Hazelgreen; post village in Ritchie County.

Hazelton; post village in Preston County.

Hazy; gap in Raleigh County.

Headsville; post village in Mineral County.

Heaters; fork, a branch of Rocky Fork of Ellis Creek in Gilmer County.

Heaters; post village in Braxton County on the Baltimore and Ohio Railroad. Altitude, 853 feet.

Heath; creek, a small left-hand tributary to Guyandot River, a branch of Ohio River, in Cabell County.

Hebron; post village in Pleasants County.

Hecla; post village in Raleigh County.

Hedges; mountain in Berkeley County. Elevation, 1,100 feet.

Hedgesville; post village in Berkeley County. Population, 342.

Heights; post village in Mason County.

Heldreth; post village in Doddridge County.

Hell; run, a small right-hand tributary to Middle Fork of Tygarts Valley River in Barbour and Randolph counties.

Helvetia; post village in Randolph County.

Hemlock; post village in Upshur County on the Norfolk and Western Railway.

Hemp Knob; summit in Wayne County. Altitude, 1,190 feet.

Hemp Patch; run, a small left-hand branch of Fall Run, a tributary to Little Kanawha River, in Braxton County.

Henderson; village in Mason County on the Baltimore and Ohio Railroad. Population, 304.

Hendricks; creek, a small left-hand branch of Meadow River, a tributary to Gauley River, in Fayette County.

Hendricks; post village in Tucker County. Population, 317.

Henrietta; post village in Calhoun County.

Henry; post village in Grant County on the West Virginia Central and Pittsburg Railway. Population, 339.
Hensley Knob; triangulation station in McDowell County.
Herbert; post village in Wayne County.
Hereford; post village in Jackson County.
Hern; post village in Mason County.
Herndon; post village in Wyoming County.
Hernshaw; post village in Kanawha County.
Herold; post village in Braxton County.
Herring; post village in Preston County.
Hershman; run, a small right-hand branch of Buckeye Fork of Little Skin Creek in Lewis County.
Hettie; post village in Braxton County.
Hevener Knobs; summits in Pocahontas County.
Hewett; creek, a small left-hand branch of Spruce Fork of Little Coal River in Boone and Logan counties.
Hewett; post village in Boone County. Altitude, 853 feet.
Hewitt; creek, a small right-hand tributary to Little Coal River, a branch of Coal Creek, in Boone County.
Hibbs; run, a left-hand tributary of Buffalo Creek in Marion County.
Hickman; ridge in Webster County.
Hickman; run, a right-hand branch of Monongahela River in Marion County.
Hickman; run, a right-hand branch of Fish Creek in Marshall County.
Hickory; branch, a very small right-hand tributary to Pinnacle Creek, a branch of Guyandot River, in Wyoming County.
Hickory; branch, a small right-hand tributary to Dunloup Creek, a branch of New River, in Fayette County.
Hickory; fork, a small left-hand tributary to Buffalo Creek, a branch of Elk River, in Clay County.
Hickory; post village in Mason County.
Hickory Camp; branch, a very small right-hand tributary to Paint Creek, a branch of Kanawha River, in Fayette County.
Hickory Flat; run, a small right-hand tributary to Buckhannon River in Upshur County.
Hickory Knob; summit in the Allegheny Front on the boundary line between Greenbrier County, W. Va., and Alleghany County, Va. Altitude, 3,357 feet.
Hickory Knob; summit in Gilmer County. Altitude, 1,570 feet.
Hickory Knob; summit in Kanawha County. Altitude, 1,450 feet.
Hickory Knob; summit in Putnam County.
Hickory Lick; small left-hand tributary to Greenbrier River in Pocahontas County.
Hico; post village in Fayette County.
Hicumbotom; post village in Kanawha County.
Hidden Hollow; short left-hand tributary to Elk River in Kanawha County.
Higby; post village in Roane County.
Higginbotham; run, a right-hand branch of Fish Creek in Marshall County.
Higgins; run, a right-hand tributary of Potomac River in Berkeley County.
Higginsville; post village in Hampshire County.
High Knob; one of the southernmost summits of Little Middle Mountain, in the Alleghenies in Randolph County. Altitude, 4,710 feet.
High Knob; summit in Braxton County. Altitude, 1,720 feet.
High Knob; summit in Nicholas County.
High Knob; summit of Mill Creek Mountain in Hardy and Hampshire counties.
Highland; mountain ridge in Morgan County. Elevation, 990 feet.

Highland; post village in Ritchie County on the Baltimore and Ohio Railroad.
Highview; post village in Hampshire County.
Hill; creek, a small left-hand branch of Muddlety Creek, a tributary to Gauley River, in Nicholas County.
Hill; post village in Boone County.
Hillebert; post village in Doddridge County.
Hillsboro; village in Pocahontas County. Population, 204.
Hill Top; town in Fayette County. Population, 263.
Hinch; post village in Mingo County.
Hiner; post village in Pendleton County.
Hinkle; branch, a very small right-hand tributary to Gauley River in Webster and Nicholas counties.
Hinkle; post village in Upshur County.
Hinkleville; post village in Upshur County.
Hinton; county seat of Summers County on the Chesapeake and Ohio Railway. Population, 3,763. Altitude, 1,372 feet.
Hiram; post village in Taylor County.
Hite; fork, an indirect left-hand tributary to Dry Fork, a branch of Tug Fork of Big Sandy River, in McDowell County.
Hoard; post village in Monongalia County on the Baltimore and Ohio Railroad.
Hodam; mountain, a broken mountainous ridge in the central part of Webster County. Elevation, 2,000 to 2,500 feet.
Hodge Knob; summit of Paint Mountain on the boundary between Raleigh and Fayette counties.
Hodges; branch, a left-hand branch of Hurricane Creek in Putnam County.
Hodges; post village in Cabell County.
Hodom; post village in Webster County.
Hog; fork, a small right-hand branch of Tate Creek, a tributary to Elk River, in Braxton County.
Hog; run, a left-hand branch of Little Fishing Creek in Wetzel County.
Hogback; mountain ridge in Morgan County.
Hog Camp; run, a very small left-hand branch of Big Laurel Creek, a tributary to Cherry River, in Greenbrier County.
Hogg; post village in Putnam County.
Hog Hollow; small branch of Skin Creek, tributary to Monongahela River, in Lewis County.
Hog Pen; run, a small right-hand branch of Robinson Fork of Buffalo Creek, a tributary to Elk River, in Nicholas County.
Hogsett; post village in Mason County on the Baltimore and Ohio Railroad
Hogtan; run, a left-hand branch of Buffalo Creek in Brooke County.
Holbrook; post village in Ritchie County.
Holcomb; post village in Nicholas County.
Hollidays Cove; post village in Hancock County on the Pittsburg, Cincinnati, Chicago and St. Louis Railway. Altitude, 719 feet.
Holly; post village in Braxton County on the Holly River and Addison Railway.
Holly; river, a right-hand branch of Elk River in Braxton County.
Holly Bush; fork, a very small left-hand branch of Fourmile Creek, a tributary to Guyandot River, in Lincoln County.
Hollygrove; post village in Upshur County.
Hollin; branch, a very small left-hand tributary to Guyandot River, a branch of Ohio River, in Cabell County.
Hollywood; post village in Monroe County.
Holman; post village in Monongalia County.

Holmes; branch, a small left-hand branch of the Right Fork of Twomile Creek, a tributary to Kanawha River, in Kanawha County.
Holmes Knob; summit in Kanawha County. Altitude, 1,334 feet.
Holt; run, a small right-hand branch of Little Kanawha River in Gilmer County.
Holton; post village in Morgan County.
Hominy; creek, a left-hand tributary to Gauley River in Nicholas and Greenbrier counties.
Hominyfalls; post village in Nicholas County.
Honey; run, a right-hand branch of Little Fishing Creek in Wetzel County.
Honey Camp; branch, a small right-hand tributary to Spice Creek, a branch of Tug Fork of Big Sandy River, in McDowell County.
Honey Camp; run, a small right-hand tributary to Right Fork of Middle Fork of Little Kanawha River in Upshur County.
Honey Trace; creek, a small left-hand branch of Milam Creek, a tributary to East Fork of Twelvepole Creek, in Wayne County.
Honsocker; knob in Wetzel County.
Hoodsville; village in Marion County.
Hookersville; post village in Nicholas County. Altitude, 1,877 feet.
Hooks Mills; post village in Hampshire County.
Hoover; post village in Braxton County.
Hope; post village in Braxton County.
Hopeville; post village in Grant County, situated on North Fork of Potomac River.
Hopkins; branch, a very small right-hand tributary to Little Coal River, a branch of Coal River, in Boone County.
Hopkins; fork, a right-hand tributary to Laurel Creek, a branch of Coal River, in Boone County.
Hopkins; mountain in Greenbrier County. Altitude, 3,356 feet.
Horner; fork, a right-hand branch of Big Laurel Creek, a tributary to Elk River, in Clay County.
Horner; post village in Lewis County.
Horner; run, a left-hand branch of Booths Creek in Harrison County.
Horse; branch, a very small left-hand branch of Coal River, a tributary to Kanawha River, in Boone County.
Horse; creek, a left-hand tributary to Little Coal River, a branch of Coal River, in Boone County.
Horse; creek, a very small left-hand tributary to Guyandot River in Wyoming County.
Horse; creek, a small left-hand tributary to Tug Fork of Big Sandy River in McDowell County.
Horse; creek, a small right-hand tributary to Marsh Fork of Coal River in Raleigh County.
Horse; creek, a very small right-hand branch of Paint Creek, a tributary to Kanawha River, in Fayette County.
Horse; fork, a small left-hand branch of Falling Rock Creek, a tributary to Elk River, in Kanawha County.
Horse; fork, a very small left-hand tributary to New River in Summers County.
Horse; mountain ridge in Morgan County.
Horse Camp; run, a small right-hand tributary to Dry Fork of Cheat River in Randolph County.
Horse Mill; branch, a small right-hand branch of Kelly Creek, a tributary to Kanawha River, in Kanawha County.
Horseneck; post village in Pleasants County.
Horsepen; fork, a left-hand tributary to Gilbert Creek, a branch of Guyandot River, in Mingo County.

Horse Pen; ridge, mountains in Wyoming and Raleigh counties.
Horse Ridge; short spur east of Gauley River in Webster County.
Horse Ridge; short, curved spur between Cherry and Cranberry rivers in Nicholas County. Altitude, 2,500 feet.
Horse Shoe; run, a right-hand branch of Cheat River in Tucker and Preston counties.
Horseshoe Run; post village in Preston County.
Horton; post village in Randolph County on the Dry Fork Railroad.
Hoult; post village in Marion County on the Baltimore and Ohio Railroad.
Hound; fork, a very small left-hand tributary to Guyandot River in Wyoming County.
House; branch, a left-hand branch of Wolf Creek, a tributary to New River, in Fayette County.
House Place; branch, a very small left-hand tributary to Pinnacle Creek, a branch of Guyandot River, in Wyoming County.
Houston; run, a small left-hand tributary to Elk River in Braxton and Webster counties.
Hovatter; post village in Tucker County.
Howard; fork, a right-hand branch of Rocky Fork of Pocatalico River, a tributary to Kanawha River, in Kanawha County.
Howard; post village in Marshall County on the Chesapeake and Ohio Railway.
Howards; creek, a left-hand branch of Greenbrier River in Greenbrier County. It is known locally as Jericho Draft at its head.
Howards Lick; left-hand tributary to Lost River in Hardy County.
Howards Lick; post village in Hardy County.
Howell; fork, a small right-hand tributary to Right Fork of Middle Fork of Little Kanawha River in Upshur County.
Howell; post village in Cabell County.
Howell; run, a small right-hand tributary to North Branch of Potomac River in Mineral County.
Howesville; post village in Preston County on the West Virginia Northern Railroad.
Hoyt; post village in Roane County.
Hubbard; fork, a small right-hand tributary to Rock Creek, a branch of Little Coal River, in Boone County.
Hubbardstown; post village in Wayne County.
Huddleston; knob in Cabell County. Elevation, 1,021 feet.
Hudson; hollow, in Cabell County.
Hudson; post village in Preston County.
Huey; run, a right-hand branch of Buffalo Creek in Marion County.
Huff; broken mountainous country in Wyoming County, the highest peak reaching an altitude of 2,716 feet.
Huff; post village in Randolph County.
Huff; run, a right-hand branch of North Fork of Short Creek in Ohio County.
Huff Knob; summit of Flat Top Mountain on the boundary line between Mercer and Raleigh counties.
Huffman; post village in Barbour County.
Huggins; branch, a small right-hand tributary to Big Clear Creek, a branch of Meadow River, in Greenbrier County.
Hughart; post village in Greenbrier County.
Hughes; creek, a small right-hand tributary to Kanawha River in Kanawha County.
Hughes; fork, a small right-hand tributary to Salt Lick Fork of Little Kanawha River in Braxton County.
Hughes; fork, a small right-hand tributary to Skin Creek in Lewis County.

GAZETTEER OF WEST VIRGINIA.

Hughes; fork, a right-hand branch of Bell Creek, a tributary to Gauley River, in Kanawha County.
Hughes; river, a left-hand tributary to Ohio River, formed by two forks—North and South—in Ritchie and Wirt counties.
Hughes; run, a small right-hand tributary to Gauley River in Webster County.
Hughes Knob; summit in Lincoln County.
Hugo; post village in Putnam County.
Hukiel; run, a left-hand branch of Buffalo Run in Brooke County.
Humphreys; run, a very small left-hand tributary to Indian Creek a branch of New River, in Monroe County.
Hundred; town in Wetzel County on the Baltimore and Ohio Railroad. Population, 261.
Hungry; creek, a right-hand branch of Trace Creek in Lincoln County.
Hunter; post village in Mingo County.
Hunters Springs; post village in Monroe County.
Huntersville; post village in Pocahontas County.
Huntsville; post village in Jackson County.
Hungards; creek, a small right-hand tributary to Greenbrier River in Summers County.
Hunter; branch, a small right-hand tributary to Spruce Fork of Little Coal River, a branch of Coal River, in Boone County.
Hunter; branch, a small right-hand tributary to North Fork of Cherry River in Nicholas County.
Hunter Place; summit in Nicholas County. Altitude, 3,738 feet.
Hunting; creek, a small right-hand tributary to Cherry River, a branch of Gauley River, in Nicholas County.
Hunting Camp; run, a left-hand tributary to Spruce Run, a small branch of Cheat River, in Preston County.
Hunting Ground; broken, mountainous country in Pendleton County west of North Fork of the Potomac.
Hunting Shirt; branch, a very small left-hand tributary to Tug Fork of Big Sandy River, in McDowell County.
Huntington; county seat of Cabell County on the Baltimore and Ohio Railroad and the Chesapeake and Ohio Railway. Altitude, 567 feet. Population, 11,923.
Hunt Road; run, a small left-hand tributary to Left Fork of Steer Creek in Gilmer County.
Hur; post village in Calhoun County.
Hurricane; branch, a small left-hand tributary to Paint Creek, a branch of Kanawha River, in Kanawha County.
Hurricane; branch, a very small left-hand branch of Kiah Fork, a tributary to Twelvepole Creek, in Wayne County.
Hurricane; branch, a small right-hand tributary to Dry Fork, a branch of Tug Fork of Big Sandy River, in McDowell County.
Hurricane; branch, a very small right-hand tributary to Laurel Branch, a tributary to Clear Fork of Guyandot River, in Wyoming County.
Hurricane; branch, a small right-hand tributary to Panther Creek, a branch of Tug Fork of Big Sandy River, in McDowell County.
Hurricane; creek, a left-hand tributary to Kanawha River in Putnam County.
Hurricane; fork, a left-hand branch of Kelly Creek, a tributary to Kanawha River, in Kanawha County.
Hurricane; village in Putnam County on the Chesapeake and Ohio Railway. Altitude, 687 feet. Population, 240.
Hurricane Ridge; mountains in Mercer County.

Hurst; post village in Lewis County.
Husted; creek, a right-hand tributary of Booths Creek in Taylor County.
Hutchinson; post village in Marion County on the Baltimore and Ohio Railroad.
Hutchison; branch, a very small right-hand branch of Peter Creek, a tributary to Gauley River, in Nicholas County.
Hutton; run, a small left-hand tributary to South Branch of Potomac River in Hardy County.
Huttons Knob; summit of Cheat Mountain in Randolph County. Altitude, 4,260 feet.
Huttonsville; post village in Randolph County on the West Virginia Central and Pittsburg Railway.
Hyar; run, a small left-hand tributary to Little Kanawha River in Braxton County.
Hyer; post village in Braxton County.
Hypes; post village in Fayette County.
Iaeger; post village in McDowell County on the Norfolk and Western Railway and on Tug Fork of Big Sandy River.
Ida; post village in Putnam County.
Ike Lick; small left-hand branch of Lilly Fork of Buffalo Creek, a tributary to Elk River, in Nicholas County.
Imans; run, a small right-hand branch of South Mill Creek, a tributary to South Branch of Potomac River, in Grant County.
Imboden; post village in Fayette County.
Improvement Lick; small left-hand tributary to Greenbrier River in Pocahontas County.
Incline; post village in McDowell County.
Independence; post village in Preston County on the Baltimore and Ohio Railroad. Altitude, 1,156 feet.
Indian; creek, a small left-hand branch of Coal River, a tributary to Kanawha River, in Boone County.
Indian; creek, a left-hand tributary to Guyandot River in Wyoming County. It rises in Indian Ridge.
Indian; creek, a small left-hand tributary to Elk River, a large branch of Kanawha River, in Kanawha County.
Indian; creek, a right-hand branch of New River in Summers and Monroe counties.
Indian; fork, a large left-hand branch of Sand Fork in Gilmer and Lewis counties.
Indian; fork, a small right-hand tributary to Mud River, a branch of Guyandot River, in Cabell and Putnam counties.
Indian; gap in Raleigh County caused by Drews Creek.
Indian; gap at head of Spice Creek in McDowell County.
Indian; triangulation station in Indian Ridge on boundary line between Wyoming and McDowell counties.
Indiancamp; post village in Upshur County.
Indian Camp; run, a small left-hand tributary to Buckhannon River, in Upshur County.
Indian Draft; small right-hand tributary to Greenbrier River in Pocahontas County.
Indian Draft; small right-hand branch of Indian Creek, a tributary to New River, in Monroe County.
Indian Grave; branch, a small right-hand tributary to Tug River in McDowell County.
Indian Mills; post village in Summers County.
Indian Ridge; mountains on boundary between Wyoming and McDowell counties.
Industry; post village in Calhoun County.
Inez; post village in Cabell County on the Chesapeake and Ohio Railway.

Ingleside; post village in Mercer County on the Norfolk and Western Railway and on East River. Altitude, 1,945 feet.
Ingram; branch, a very small left-hand tributary to Loop Creek, a branch of Kanawha River, in Fayette County.
Inkerman; post village in Hardy County.
Institute; post village in Kanawha County.
Inwood; post village in Berkeley County on the Cumberland Valley Railroad.
Iola; post village in Roane County.
Ira; post village in Clay County.
Ireland; post village in Lewis County.
Irewood; creek, a small left-hand branch of Meadow River, a tributary to Gauley River, in Fayette County.
Irona; post village in Preston County.
Irontown; post village in Taylor County.
Isaac; run, a left-hand branch of Carney Fork of Rock Run in Wetzel County.
Island; creek, a small left-hand tributary to New River in Mercer and Summers counties.
Island; creek, a small left-hand tributary to Coal Creek, a branch of Kanawha River, in Lincoln County.
Island; creek, a small left-hand tributary to Guyandot River, a branch of Ohio River, in Logan County.
Islandbranch; post village in Kanawha County.
Island Ford; run, a small left-hand tributary to Greenbrier River, in Pocahontas County.
Isners; run, a small right-hand tributary to Valley River in Randolph County.
Iuka; post village in Tyler County.
Ivanhoe; post village in Upshur County.
Ivy; creek, a small left-hand tributary to Little Coal River, a branch of Coal River, in Lincoln County.
Ivy; post village in Upshur County. Altitutde, 3,593 feet.
Ivy Knob; triangulation station on boundary line between Raleigh and Wyoming counties. Altitude, 3,693 feet.
Jack; branch, a small left-hand tributary to Pond Fork of Little Coal River in Boone County.
Jack; mountain, a short ridge in Pendleton County. Elevation, 3,500 feet.
Jack; post village in Webster County.
Jack; run, a left-hand branch of Lost Run in Taylor County.
Jackson; branch, a very small left-hand tributary to West Fork of Twelvepole Creek, a branch of Ohio River, in Wayne County.
Jackson; county, situated in the western part of the State, on the Allegheny Plateau, and bordering on the Ohio River. Area, 455 square miles. Population, 22,987—white, 22,872; negro, 115; foreign born, 91. County seat, Ripley. The mean magnetic declination in 1900 was 1° 30′. The mean annual rainfall is 40 to 50 inches, and the mean annual temperature 50° to 55°. The county is traversed by the Ohio River Railroad.
Jackson; fork, a small right-hand branch of Right Fork of Middle Fork of Tygarts Valley River in Upshur and Randolph counties.
Jackson Ridge; short spur in Pocahontas County.
Jacksonville; post village in Lewis County.
Jacky; fork, a very small right-hand tributary to Indian Creek, a branch of Guyandot River, in Wyoming County.
Jaco; post village in Monongalia County.
Jacob; fork, a right-hand tributary to Dry Fork, a branch of Tug Fork of Big Sandy River, in McDowell County.

Jacob Cook; branch, a very small right-hand tributary to Clear Fork, a branch of Guyandot River, in Wyoming County.

Jacox; post village in Pocahontas County.

Jacox Knob; summit in Pocahontas County.

Jake; branch, a very small right-hand tributary to Coal River, a branch of Kanawha River, in Boone County.

Jake; run, a small right-hand branch of Ellis Creek in Gilmer County.

Jake; run, a left-hand tributary of Wheeling Creek in Marshall County.

James; branch, a very small right-hand tributary to Pond Fork of Little Coal River in Boone County.

James; creek, a small right-hand tributary to West Fork, a branch of Pond Fork of Little Coal River, in Boone County.

James Knob; summit in Braxton County.

Janelew; post village in Lewis County on the West Virginia Central and Pittsburg Railway.

Jarrell; branch, a small right-hand tributary to West Fork, a branch of Pond Fork of Little Coal River, in Boone County.

Jarrett; branch, a very small right-hand tributary to Kanawha River in Fayette County.

Jarrett; post village in Kanawha County.

Jarrolds Valley; post village in Raleigh County.

Jarvisville; post village in Harrison County.

Jasper Workman; branch, a small left-hand tributary to Pond Fork of Little Coal River in Boone County.

Jed; branch, a small right-hand tributary to Tug Fork of Big Sandy River in McDowell County.

Jefferson; county, situated in the northeastern part of the State, limited on the east by Potomac River and the Blue Ridge. With the exception of the slopes of the Blue Ridge its surface is rolling, with an average altitude of about 500 feet. Area, 213 square miles. Population, 15,935—white, 11,994; negro, 3,941; foreign born, 96. County seat, Charlestown. The mean magnetic declination in 1900 was 4°. The mean annual rainfall is 40 to 50 inches, and the mean annual temperature 50° to 55°. The county is traversed by the Baltimore and Ohio and the Norfolk and Western railways.

Jeffery; post village in Boone County.

John; branch, a small left-hand tributary to Millers Camp Branch, a fork of Marsh Fork of Coal River, in Raleigh County.

Jenk; fork, a small left-hand branch of Right Fork of Middle Fork of Tygarts Valley River in Upshur County.

Jenkins; fork, a small left-hand branch of Armstrong Creek, a tributary to Kanawha River, in Fayette County.

Jenks; post village in Lincoln County.

Jennie; creek, a small right-hand branch of Tug Fork of Big Sandy River, a tributary to Ohio River, in Wayne and Logan counties.

Jenny; gap in Guyandot Mountain, caused by Skinner Fork, in Raleigh County.

Jericho; post village in Hampshire County.

Jericho Draft; the name applied locally to the headwaters of Howards Creek, a tributary to Greenbrier River, in Greenbrier County.

Jerry; fork, a very small right-hand branch of Peter Creek, a tributary to Gauley River, in Nicholas County.

Jerry; run, a right-hand branch of Simpson Creek in Taylor County.

Jerrys Run; post village in Wood County.

Jersey; run, a small left-hand tributary to Right Fork of Middle Fork of Little Kanawha River in Webster County.

Jerseywood; run, a right-hand tributary to Ellis Creek in Gilmer County.
Jesse; post village in Wyoming County.
Jetsville; post village in Greenbrier County.
Jigly; branch, a small indirect right-hand tributary to Laurel Fork, a branch of Spruce Fork of Little Coal River, in Boone County.
Jim; branch, a very small left-hand tributary to Clear Fork, a branch of Guyandot River, in Wyoming County.
Jim; branch, a small right-hand tributary to Clear Fork, a branch of Tug Fork of Big Sandy River, in McDowell County.
Jim; branch, a very small right-hand tributary to Cooney Otter Creek, an indirect left-hand tributary to Guyandot River, in Wyoming County.
Jim; branch, a very small right-hand tributary to Guyandot River in Wyoming County.
Jim; branch, a very small right-hand tributary to Slab Fork, a branch of Guyandot River, on boundary between Raleigh and Wyoming counties.
Jimmy; fork, a right-hand branch of Wilderness Fork of Fork Creek, a tributary to Coal River, in Boone County.
Jim Spring; run, a small right-hand tributary to Gauley River in Webster County.
Jimtown; post village in Harrison County.
Job; post village in Randolph County on the Dry Fork Railroad.
Job; run, a right-hand branch of Little Kanawha River in Gilmer County.
Job Knob; fork, a small right-hand branch of South Fork of Big Clear Creek, a tributary to Meadow River, in Greenbrier County.
Job Knob; summit in Greenbrier County. Altitude, 4,359 feet.
Joblin; branch, a very small left-hand tributary to Kanawha River in Kanawha County.
Joe; branch, a very small left-hand tributary to Guyandot River in Wyoming County.
Joe; branch, a very small right-hand tributary to Coal River, a branch of Kanawha River, in Boone County.
Joe; creek, a head fork of Williams Fork, a tributary to Trace Fork of Mud River, in Lincoln County.
Joe; creek, a small right-hand tributary to Coal River, a branch of Kanawha River, in Boone County.
Joe; fork, a head fork of Right Fork of Steer Creek, in Braxton County.
Joe; run, a left-hand branch of Sand Fork in Gilmer County.
Joe; run, a right-hand branch of Buffalo Creek in Marion County.
Joebranch; post village in Wyoming County.
Joe Hollow; short left-hand tributary to Elk River in Kanawha County.
Joe Knob; summit in Greenbrier County. Altitude, 3,939 feet.
Joel; branch, a very small left-hand tributary to West Fork of Twelvepole Creek, a branch of Ohio River, in Wayne County.
Joel; run, a small right-hand tributary to Gauley River in Webster County.
Joe Ridge; mountains in Raleigh County.
Johithan; run, a small left-hand tributary to Williams River in Webster County.
John; branch, a very small right-hand tributary to Mud River, a branch of Guyandot River, in Cabell County.
John; branch, a very small indirect right-hand tributary to Dry Fork, a branch of Tug Fork of Big Sandy River, in McDowell County.
John; post village in Monongalia County.
Johnniecake; run, a left-hand branch of Pyles Fork of Buffalo Creek in Marion County.
Johnnycake; branch, a small right-hand tributary to Tug Fork of Big Sandy River in McDowell County.

John O; branch, a very small right-hand tributary to Laurel Branch, a tributary to Guyandot River, in Wyoming County.

Johnson; fork, a small left-hand branch of Falling Rock Creek, a tributary to Elk River, in Kanawha County.

Johnson; fork, a small left-hand tributary to Loop Creek, a branch of Kanawha River, in Fayette County.

Johnson; hollow in Monongalia County.

Johnson; post village in Barbour County.

Johnson; run, a small right-hand tributary to Gauley River in Webster County.

Johnson Knob; summit in Kanawha County. Altitude 2,200 feet.

Johnsons Crossroads; post village in Monroe County.

Johnstown; post village in Harrison County.

Jones; branch, a small right-hand tributary to Paint Creek, a branch of Kanawha River, in Kanawha County.

Jones; fork, a very small right-hand branch of Peter Creek, a tributary to Gauley River, in Nicholas County.

Jones; post village in Putnam County.

Jones; run, a very small left-hand branch of Big Laurel Creek, a tributary to Cherry River, in Greenbrier County.

Jones Springs; post village in Berkeley County.

Jordan; creek, a small right-hand tributary to Elk River, a branch of Kanawha River, in Kanawha County.

Jordan; post village in Kanawha County.

Jordanrun; post village in Grant County.

Joseph Mills; post village in Tyler County.

Joshua; creek, a small left-hand tributary to Greenbrier River in Pocahontas County.

Joshua; run, a very small left-hand tributary to New River in Summers County.

Josiah; post village in Tyler County.

Joy; post village in Doddridge County.

Joy; run, a left-hand tributary of North Fork of Dunkard Creek in Monongalia County.

Jud; branch, a very small left-hand tributary to Indian Creek, a branch of Guyandot River, in Wyoming County.

Judson; post village in Summers County.

Judyton; post village in Greenbrier County.

Jule Webb; fork, a head fork of Horse Creek, a tributary to Little Coal River, in Boone County.

Julia; post village in Greenbrier County.

Jumbo; post village in Webster County.

Jump; branch, a small right-hand tributary to South Fork of Tug River in McDowell County.

Jumping; branch, a left-hand tributary to Little Bluestone Creek, a branch of Bluestone River, in Summers County.

Jumping Branch; post village in Summers County.

Jumping Gut; small left-hand tributary to Elk River in Clay County.

Junction; post village in Hampshire County.

Junior; town in Barbour County on the West Virginia Central and Pittsburg Railway. Population, 335.

Kabletown; post village in Jefferson County.

Kalamazoo; post village in Barbour County.

Kanawha; county, situated in the western part of the State, on the Allegheny Plateau. It is here deeply dissected. It is traversed by Kanawha River, which, with its branches, the principal of which are Coal Creek and Elk River, drains its area. Area, 872 square miles. Population, 54,696—white, 50,711; negro,

3,983; foreign born, 744. County seat, Charleston. The mean magnetic declination in 1900 was 2°. The mean annual rainfall is 40 to 50 inches, and the mean annual temperature 50° to 55°. The county is traversed by the Charleston, Clendennin and Sutton, the Chesapeake and Ohio, the Ohio Central Lines, and the Kanawha and Michigan railways.

Kanawha; fork, a small right-hand tributary to Davis Creek, a branch of Kanawha River, in Kanawha County.

Kanawha; river, a large left-hand branch of Ohio River, heading, under the name of New River, in western North Carolina, and flowing north and northwest to its mouth opposite Gallipolis. Its chief branches are Gauley and Elk rivers, the former joining it at Kanawha Falls and the latter at Charleston. The drainage area, including New River, is 16,690 square miles. Length, 400 miles. Navigable to Kanawha Falls.

Kanawha; run, a right-hand branch of Holly River, a tributary to Elk River, in Braxton County.

Kanawha City; post village in Kanawha County on the Chesapeake and Ohio Railway.

Kanawha Falls; post village in Fayette County on Kanawha River and on the Chesapeake and Ohio and the Ohio Central railroads. Altitude, 665 feet.

Kanawha Head; post village in Upshur County.

Kanawha Station; post village in Wood County. Altitude, 611 feet.

Karn; post village in Monroe County.

Kasson; post village in Barbour County.

Kate Knob; summit in Lincoln County.

Kates; branch, a very small right-hand tributary to Glade Creek, a branch of New River, in Raleigh County.

Kates; mountain, a ridge in Greenbrier County. Altitude, 2,500 to 3,000 feet.

Katly; village in Marion County.

Katyslick; village in Harrison County.

Kausooth; post village in Marshall County.

Kearneysville; post village in Jefferson County. Altitude, 589 feet.

Kedron; post village in Upshur County.

Keenan; post village in Monroe County.

Keenan; branch, a very small left-hand branch of Peter Creek, a tributary to Gauley River, in Nicholas County.

Keeney; creek, a small right-hand tributary to New River in Fayette County.

Keeney; mountain, a ridge in Summers County north of Greenbrier River. Elevation, 2,000 to 3,500 feet.

Keeney; creek, a small right-hand tributary to New River in Fayette County.

Keeney Knob; summit of Keeney Mountain in Summers County. Altitude, 3,945 feet.

Kegley; post village in Mercer County.

Keith; fork, a small left-hand tributary to Skin Creek in Lewis County.

Keith; post village in Fayette County.

Keller; post village in Jefferson County.

Kelleys; creek, a small left-hand tributary to Greenbrier River in Summers and Monroe counties.

Kellogg; post village in Wayne County on the Chesapeake and Ohio Railway.

Kelly; creek, a very small right-hand branch of Pocotaligo River, a tributary to Kanawha River, in Putnam County.

Kelly; creek, a right-hand tributary to Kanawha River in Kanawha County.

Kelly; post village in Doddridge County.

Kelley Knob; summit in Randolph County.

Kendalia; post village in Kanawha County.

Kenna; post village in Jackson County.

Kenna Ridge; mountains in the southwestern part of Braxton County, ranging in elevation from 1,000 to 1,600 feet.

Kennison; mountain, a short ridge in the western part of Pocahontas County. Elevation, 3,500 to 4,000 feet.

Kenova; village in Wayne County on the Baltimore and Ohio, the Chesapeake and Ohio, and the Norfolk and Western railways. Altitude, 581 feet. Population, 863.

Kenton; post village in Doddridge County.

Kentuck; fork, a very small left-hand branch of Fourmile Creek, a tributary to Guyandot River, in Lincoln County.

Kentuck; post village in Jackson County.

Kerens; post village in Randolph County on the West Virginia Central and Pittsburg Railway.

Kerless Knob; summit in Greenbrier County. Altitude, 3,441 feet.

Kern; run, a small stream in Lewis County.

Keslers Crosslanes; post village in Nicholas County.

Kester; post village in Roane County.

Ketterman; post village in Grant County, located on South Branch of Potomac River.

Kettle; post village in Roane County.

Kettle; run, a small right-hand branch of Left Fork of Middle Fork of Tygarts Valley River in Randolph County.

Kueths; run, a right-hand branch of Fall Run in Braxton County.

Kewee; creek, a small left-hand tributary to Dry Fork, a branch of Tug Fork of Big Sandy River, in McDowell County.

Key; run, a small left-hand tributary to Greenbrier River in Pocahontas County.

Keyser; town and county seat of Mineral County on the Baltimore and Ohio and the West Virginia Central and Pittsburg railroads. Altitude, 802 feet. Population, 2,536.

Keystone; town in McDowell County on the Norfolk and Western Railway and on Elkhorn Creek. Population, 1,088.

Kiah; fork, a right-hand branch of East Fork of Twelvepole Creek, a tributary to Ohio River, in Wayne County.

Kiahsville; post village in Wayne County.

Kidwell; post village in Tyler County.

Kieffer; post village in Greenbrier County.

Kile Knob; summit in Pendleton County.

Kilgore; creek, a small right-hand tributary to Mud River, a branch of Guyandot River, in Cabell County.

Kimball; station in McDowell County on the Norfolk and Western Railway and on Elkhorn Creek.

Kimlin; run, a left-hand branch of Buffalo Creek in Brooke County.

Kimsey; run, a left-hand tributary to Lost River in Hardy County.

Kincaid; knob in Marion County.

Kincaid; post village in Fayette County.

Kincaid; run, a small left-hand tributary to Greenbrier River in Greenbrier County.

King; post village in Wetzel County.

Kings; run, a small right-hand tributary to Valley River in Randolph County.

Kingsbury; post village in Wood County.

King Shoal; branch, a small left-hand tributary to Guyandot River, a branch of Ohio River, in Logan County.

Kingsville; post village in Randolph County.

GAZETTEER OF WEST VIRGINIA.

Kingwood; town and county seat of Preston County on the West Virginia Northern Railroad. Altitude, 1,778 feet. Population, 700.
Kirby; post village in Hampshire County.
Kirt; post village in Barbour County.
Kline; gap in New Creek Mountain caused by New Creek in Grant County.
Kline; post village in Pendleton County.
Knapp; creek, a left-hand tributary to Greenbrier River in Pocahontas County.
Knawl; post village in Braxton County.
Knight; post village in Doddridge County.
Knob; branch, a very small right-hand tributary to Paint Creek, a branch of Kanawha River, in Fayette County.
Knob; fork, a very small right-hand tributary to Clear Fork, a branch of the Guyandot River, in Wyoming County.
Knob; fork, a left-hand branch of Middle Wheeling Creek in Ohio County.
Knobley; post village in Mineral County.
Knobly; mountain, a long narrow ridge in Grant and Mineral counties. Altitude, 1,500 feet.
Knottsville; post village in Taylor County.
Knoxville; post village in Marshall County.
Kodol; post village in Wetzel County.
Krise; post village in Fayette County.
Kyger; post village in Roane County on the Baltimore and Ohio Railroad.
Kyle; post village in McDowell County on the Norfolk and Western Railway.
Lacey; branch, a small left-hand tributary to Pond Fork of Little Coal River in Boone County.
Laclede; post village in Cabell County.
Ladley; run, a left-hand branch of Middle Wheeling Creek in Ohio County.
Lahmansville; post village in Grant County.
Lake; post village in Logan County.
Lambert; branch, a small left-hand tributary to Pinnacle Creek, a branch of Guyandot River, in Wyoming County.
Lambert; creek, a very small right-hand branch of West Fork of Twelvepole Creek, a tributary to Ohio River, in Wayne County.
Lambert; branch, a small right-hand tributary to Barker Creek, a branch of Guyandot River, in Wyoming County.
Lamont; post village in Marshall County.
Lanark; post village in Raleigh County.
Landes; post village in Grant County.
Landgraff; post village in McDowell County on the Norfolk and Western Railway.
Lane; post village in Mason County.
Lanes Bottom; post village in Webster County.
Lanham; post village in Putnam County.
Lankey; mountain, a short ridge west of South Branch of Potomac River in Pendleton County.
Lansing; post village in Fayette County.
Lantz; post village in Barbour County.
Larew; post village in Taylor County.
Larkin Hollow; right-hand tributary to Kanawha River in Kanawha County.
Lashmeet; post village in Mercer County, located near Bluestone River on Delashmeet Creek. Altitude, 2,588 feet.
Latonia; post village in Gilmer County.
Lattimer; post village in Roane County.
Launa; post village in Raleigh County.

Laurel; branch, a small left-hand tributary to Marrowbone Creek, a branch of Tug Fork of Big Sandy River, in Logan County.

Laurel; branch, a small left-hand tributary to South Fork of Tug River in McDowell County.

Laurel; branch, a small left-hand tributary to Bluestone River, a branch of New River, in Mercer County.

Laurel; branch, a very small left-hand tributary to Piney Creek, a branch of New River, in Raleigh County.

Laurel; branch, a small left-hand tributary to Millers Camp Branch, a branch of Marsh Fork of Coal River, in Raleigh County.

Laurel; branch, a very small left-hand tributary to Pinnacle Creek, a branch of Guyandot River, in Wyoming County.

Laurel; branch, a left-hand tributary to Clear Fork, a branch of Guyandot River, in Wyoming County.

Laurel; branch, a left-hand branch of Left Fork of Armstrong Creek, a tributary of Kanawha River, in Fayette County.

Laurel; branch, a very small right-hand tributary to Guyandot River in Logan County.

Laurel; branch, a very small right-hand tributary to Clear Fork of Coal River in Raleigh County.

Laurel; branch, a very small right-hand tributary to Bluestone River in Mercer County.

Laurel; branch, a small right-hand tributary to Elkhorn Creek, a branch of Tug Fork of Big Sandy River, in McDowell County.

Laurel; branch, a very small right-hand branch of Tug Fork of Big Sandy River, a tributary to Ohio River, in Logan County.

Laurel; branch, a small right-hand tributary to Hominy Creek, a branch of Gauley River, in Nicholas County.

Laurel; branch, a very small right-hand tributary to Powellton Fork of Armstrong Creek, a branch of Kanawha River, in Fayette County.

Laurel; creek, a small right-hand tributary to Middle Fork of Tygarts Valley River in Randolph County.

Laurel; creek, a left-hand branch of Coal River, a tributary to Kanawha River, in Boone County.

Laurel; creek, a very small left-hand tributary to Mud River, a branch of Guyandot River, in Lincoln County.

Laurel; creek, a left-hand tributary to New River in Fayette County.

Laurel; creek, a small left-hand tributary to Greenbrier River in Greenbrier County.

Laurel; creek, a small left-hand branch of Knapp Creek, a tributary to Greenbrier River, in Pocahontas County.

Laurel; creek, a small left-hand branch of Peter Creek, a tributary to Gauley River, in Nicholas County.

Laurel; creek, a left-hand tributary to Elk River in Braxton and Webster counties.

Laurel; creek, a small right-hand tributary to New River in Summers County.

Laurel; creek, a small right-hand tributary to Williams River in Pocahontas County.

Laurel; creek, a small right-hand tributary to Gauley River in Webster County.

Laurel; creek, a small right-hand tributary to Mud River, a branch of Guyandot River, in Lincoln County.

Laurel; creek, a very small right-hand tributary to Guyandot River, a branch of Ohio River, in Lincoln County.

Laurel; creek, a right-hand branch of Big Ugly Creek, a tributary to Guyandot River, in Lincoln County.

Laurel; creek, a small right-hand branch of East Fork of Twelvepole Creek, a tributary to Ohio River, in Wayne County.

Laurel; creek, a small right-hand tributary to Gauley River, a large branch of Kanawha River, in Nicholas County.
Laurel; creek, a small right-hand branch of Second Creek, a tributary to Greenbrier River, in Monroe County.
Laurel; creek, a small right-hand branch of Meadow River, a tributary to Gauley River, in Greenbrier County.
Laurel; creek, a small right-hand branch of Brush Creek, a tributary to Bluestone River, in Mercer County.
Laurel; creek, a small right-hand tributary to New River in Fayette County.
Laurel; creek, a right-hand tributary to Valley River in Barbour County.
Laurel; creek, a right-hand tributary to Indian Creek, a branch of New River, in Monroe County.
Laurel; fork, a head fork of Holly River in Webster County.
Laurel; fork, a head fork of Williams Fork, a branch of Trace Fork of Mud River, in Lincoln County.
Laurel; fork, a left-hand branch of Horse Creek, a tributary to Little Coal River, in Lincoln County.
Laurel; fork, a small left-hand branch of Big Creek, a tributary to Mud River, in Lincoln County.
Laurel; fork, a small left-hand tributary to Elk River in Pocahontas County.
Laurel; fork, a small left-hand branch of Lilly Fork of Buffalo Creek, a tributary to Elk River, in Clay County.
Laurel; fork, a small left-hand branch of Big Sycamore Creek, a tributary to Elk River, in Clay County.
Laurel; fork, a left-hand branch of Right Fork of Peters Creek, a tributary to Gauley River, in Nicholas County.
Laurel; fork, a small left-hand branch of Witchers Creek, a tributary to Kanawha River, in Kanawha County.
Laurel; fork, a small left-hand tributary to Long Bottom Creek, a branch of Cabin Creek, in Kanawha County.
Laurel; fork, an indirect left-hand tributary to Clear Fork, a branch of Guyandot River, in Wyoming County.
Laurel; fork, a small left-hand tributary to Right Fork of Steer Creek in Gilmer County.
Laurel; fork, a small left-hand branch of Granny Creek in Braxton County.
Laurel; fork, a left-hand branch of Grove Creek in Clay County.
Laurel; fork, a large left-hand branch of Dry Fork, a head fork of Cheat River, in Randolph County.
Laurel; fork, a right-hand branch of Sand Creek, a tributary to Guyandot River, in Lincoln County.
Laurel; fork, a small right-hand branch of Little Hart Creek, a tributary to Guyandot River, in Lincoln County.
Laurel; fork, a small right-hand tributary to Twentymile Creek, a branch of Gauley River, in Nicholas County.
Laurel; fork, a small right-hand branch of Blue Creek, a tributary to Elk River, in Kanawha County.
Laurel; fork, a right-hand branch of Bell Creek, a tributary to Gauley River, in Kanawha County.
Laurel; fork, a right-hand branch of Coal Fork of Cabin Creek, a tributary to Kanawha River, in Kanawha County.
Laurel; fork, a right-hand branch of Spruce Fork of Little Coal River in Boone and Logan counties.
Laurel; fork, a small right-hand tributary to Birch River, a branch of Elk River, in Webster County.

Laurel; fork, a right-hand branch of Tanner Fork and tributary to Little Kanawha River in Gilmer County.

Laurel; fork, a small right-hand tributary to Pigeon Creek, a branch of Tug Fork of Big Sandy River, in Logan County.

Laurel; fork, a right-hand tributary to French Creek in Upshur County.

Laurel; hill, a ridge separating Cheat and Valley rivers. Altitude, 3,000 feet.

Laurel; hills, a long, narrow ridge in Preston, Barbour, and Tucker counties. Altitude, 2,000 to 2,500 feet.

Laurel; post village in Barbour County.

Laurel; run, a small left-hand tributary to Little Kanawha River in Upshur County.

Laurel; run, a small left-hand tributary to the Middle Fork of Tygarts Valley River in Upshur County.

Laurel; run, a small left-hand tributary to Left Fork of Middle Fork of Tygarts Valley River in Randolph County.

Laurel; run, a small left-hand tributary to North Fork of Potomac River in Pendleton County.

Laurel; run, a small left-hand tributary to Little Kanawha River in Braxton County.

Laurel; run, a small left-hand tributary to Meadow Creek in the western part of Greenbrier County.

Laurel; run, a small left-hand tributary to Little Birch River in Braxton County.

Laurel; run, a small right-hand branch of Duck Creek, a right-hand tributary to Elk River, in Braxton County.

Laurel; run, a small right-hand tributary to Dry Fork of Cheat River in Tucker County.

Laurel; run, a small right-hand tributary to West Fork of Monongahela River in Lewis County.

Laurel; run, a small right-hand tributary to Williams River in Webster County.

Laurel; run, a small right-hand tributary to Greenbrier River in Pocahontas County.

Laurel; run, a small branch of Youghiogheny River in Preston County.

Laurel Branch; post village in Monroe County.

Laureldale; post village in Mineral County. Altitude, 1,326 feet.

Laurel Patch; run, a right-hand branch of Left Fork of Holly River in Braxton County.

Lavalette; post village in Wayne County on the Norfolk and Western Railway.

Lavender; fork, a small right-hand tributary to Horse Creek, a branch of Little Coal River, in Boone County.

Lavinia; fork, a small left-hand branch of Hopkins Fork of Laurel Creek, tributary to Coal River, in Boone County.

Lawford; post village in Ritchie County.

Lawson; post village in Raleigh County. Altitude, 1,055 feet.

Lawton; post village in Fayette County.

Laywell; branch, a right-hand tributary to Trace Fork in Putnam County.

Lazearville; post village in Brooke County on the Pennsylvania Railroad.

Leachtown; post village in Wood County.

Leading; creek, a right-hand branch of Little Kanawha River in Gilmer County.

Leading; creek, a small right-hand tributary to Valley River in Randolph County.

Leading Creek; post village in Lewis County.

Leadmine; post village in Tucker County.

League; post village in Ritchie County.

Leander; post village in Fayette County.

Leatherbark; run, a left-hand branch of Cedar Creek in Gilmer County.

Leather Bark; run, a small right-hand tributary to Greenbrier River in Pocahontas County.

Leatherwood; creek, a left-hand tributary to Elk River in Clay, Nicholas, and Kanawha counties.
Leatherwood; creek, a small right-hand tributary to Guyandot River in Mingo County.
Leatherwood; fork, a left-hand tributary to Elk River in Webster County.
Leatherwood; town in Ohio County. Population, 123.
Lecta; post village in Wirt County.
Lee; branch, a very small left-hand tributary to Kanawha River in Fayette County.
Lee; creek, a right-hand tributary to Indian Fork of Mud River in Cabell County.
Lee; post village in Wirt County.
Leebell; post village in Randolph County.
Leetown; post village in Jefferson County.
Leewood; post village in Kanawha County.
Lefthand; post village in Roane County.
Legg; post village in Kanawha County.
Lehew; post village in Hampshire County.
Leiter; post village in Randolph County on the Roaring Creek and Belington Railroad.
Leivasy; post village in Nicholas County.
Lem; fork, a very small right-hand tributary to Sycamore Creek, a branch of Clear Fork of Coal River, in Raleigh County.
Lenox; post village in Preston County.
Lens; creek, a left-hand tributary to Kanawha River in Kanawha County.
Leo; post village in Roane County.
Leon; village in Mason County on the Ohio Central Lines. Population, 250.
Leonard; fork, a small left-hand tributary to Right Fork of Middle Fork of Tygarts Valley River in Upshur County.
Leonard; post village in Greenbrier County.
Leopard; run, a small right-hand tributary to Left Fork of Steer Creek in Braxton County.
Leopold; post village in Doddridge County.
Lerona; post village in Mercer County.
Leroy; post village in Jackson County on the Baltimore and Ohio Railroad.
Lesage; post village in Cabell County on the Baltimore and Ohio Railroad.
Leslie; branch, a small right-hand tributary to Tug Fork of Big Sandy River in McDowell County.
Lester; post village in Raleigh County.
Letart; post village in Mason County on the Baltimore and Ohio Railroad.
Letch; post village in Braxton County.
Letherbark; post village in Calhoun County.
Lettergap; post village in Gilmer County.
Levels; post village in Hampshire County.
Levisee; creek, a right-hand branch of Wolf Creek, a tributary to New River, in Fayette County.
Lewis; county, situated in the central part of the State, on the Allegheny Plateau, drained northward by tributaries of the Monongahela. Area, 414 square miles. Population, 16,980—white, 16,792; negro, 178; foreign born, 265. County seat, Weston. The mean magnetic declination in 1900 was 2° 45′. The mean annual rainfall is 40 to 50 inches, and the mean annual temperature 50° to 55°. The county is traversed by the Baltimore and Ohio Railroad.
Lewis; fork, a very small left-hand branch of Laurel Fork, a tributary to Clear Fork of Guyandot River, in Wyoming County.
Lewis; post villlage in Harrison County.
Lewis; run, a small right-hand tributary to Tygarts Valley River, in Barbour County.

Lewisburg; county seat of Greenbrier County. Population, 872.

Lewis Queen; branch, a small left-hand branch of Kiah Fork, a tributary to Twelvepole Creek, in Wayne County.

Lewiston; post village in Kanawha County.

Liberty; post village in Putnam County.

Lick; branch, a very small left-hand tributary to Beech Fork of Twelvepole Creek, a branch of Ohio River, in Wayne County.

Lick; branch, a very small left-hand tributary to Tug Fork of Big Sandy River in McDowell County.

Lick; branch, a small left-hand tributary to Fourteenmile Creek, a branch of Guyandot River, in Lincoln County.

Lick; branch, a left-hand branch of Open Fork of Bell Creek, a tributary to Gauley River, in Nicholas County.

Lick; branch, a very small left-hand tributary to Kanawha River in Kanawha County.

Lick; branch, a very small left-hand tributary to Brier Creek, a branch of Coal River, in Kanawha County.

Lick; branch, a small right-hand branch of Little Sandy Creek, a tributary to Elk River, in Kanawha County.

Lick; branch, a small right-hand tributary to Tug Fork of Big Sandy River in McDowell County.

Lick; branch, a small right-hand tributary to Pond Fork of Little Coal River in Boone County.

Lick; branch, a small right-hand tributary to Cranberry River in Webster County.

Lick; branch, a very small right-hand tributary to Paint Creek, a branch of Kanawha River, in Fayette County.

Lick; branch, a very small right-hand branch of Tug Fork of Big Sandy River, a tributary to Ohio River, in Logan County.

Lick; branch, a very small right-hand tributary to Bluestone River in Mercer County.

Lick; branch, a very small right-hand tributary to North Fork of Elkhorn Creek in McDowell County.

Lick; branch, a very small right-hand tributary to South Fork of Elkhorn Creek in McDowell County.

Lick; branch, a very small right-hand tributary to Indian Creek, a branch of Guyandot River, in Wyoming County.

Lick; creek, a small left-hand tributary to Laurel Creek in Braxton County.

Lick; creek, a small left-hand tributary to Little Coal River, a branch of Coal River, in Boone County.

Lick; creek, a small left-hand tributary to New River in Mercer and Summers counties.

Lick; creek, a small right-hand tributary to Trace Fork of Mud River, a branch of Guyandot River, in Putnam County.

Lick; creek, a small right-hand tributary to Coal River, a branch of Kanawha River, in Boone County.

Lick; creek, a small right-hand tributary to East Fork of Twelvepole Creek, a branch of Ohio River, in Wayne County.

Lick; creek, a small right-hand tributary to New River in Summers County.

Lick; fork, a very small left-hand tributary to Clear Fork of Coal River in Raleigh County.

Lick; fork, a left-hand tributary to Grass Run in Gilmer County.

Lick; fork, a small right-hand branch of Mossy Creek, a tributary to Paint Creek, in Fayette County.

Lick; fork, a small right-hand tributary to Steer Run in Gilmer County.

Lick; mountain, a short spur in Greenbrier County.
Lick; run, a small left-hand tributary to Cheat River, in Preston County.
Lick; run, a small right-hand tributary to Left Fork of Right Fork of Buckhannon River in Randolph County.
Lick; run, a right-hand tributary to South Fork of Potomac River in Pendleton County.
Lick Hollow; branch, a very small right-hand branch of Tug Fork of Big Sandy River, a tributary to Ohio River, in Logan County.
Lick Hollow; creek, a small right-hand tributary to Little Creek, a branch of Anthonys Creek, in Greenbrier County.
Licking; creek, a small left-hand tributary to Cheat River in Tucker County.
Lick Knob; triangulation station situated on Paint Mountain, on boundary line between Raleigh and Fayette counties. Altitude, 3,268 feet.
Licklog; branch, a very small right-hand tributary to West Fork of Twelvepole Creek, a branch of Ohio River, in Wayne County.
Lightburn; post village in Lewis County.
Lile; post village in Greenbrier County.
Lilly; branch, a small left-hand branch of Twentymile Creek, a tributary to Gauley River, in Nicholas County.
Lilly; fork, a left-hand branch of Buffalo Creek, a tributary to Elk River, in Clay County.
Lilly; post village in Summers County.
Lillydale; post village in Monroe County.
Lima; post village in Tyler County.
Limestone; branch, a very small right-hand tributary to Guyandot River, a branch of Ohio River, in Lincoln County.
Limestone; mountain, a short ridge in Tucker County. Altitude, 1,500 to 3,000 feet.
Limestone; post village in Marshall County.
Limestone; run, a small right-hand tributary to O'Brien Fork in Braxton County.
Lincoln; county, situated in the western part of the State on the lower slopes of the Allegheny Plateau and drained by tributaries of Guyandot River. Area, 441 square miles. Population, 15,434—white, 15,371; negro, 63; foreign born, 7. County seat, Hamlin. The mean magnetic declination in 1900 was 1°. The mean annual rainfall is 40 to 50 inches, and the mean annual temperature 50° to 55°.
Lincoln; post village in Wyoming County.
Linden; post village in Roane County.
Lindside; post village in Monroe County.
Line; creek, a small right-hand branch of Peters Creek, a tributary to Gauley River, in Nicholas County.
Link; post village in Braxton County.
Linn; post village in Gilmer County.
Linwood; post village in Pocahontas County.
Lisle; branch, a left-hand branch of Guyandot River in Cabell County.
Little; branch, a very small left-hand tributary to Clear Fork, a branch of Guyandot River, in Wyoming County.
Little; creek, a small left-hand branch of Slaughter Creek, a tributary to Kanawha River, in Kanawha County.
Little; creek, a left-hand tributary to Island Creek, a branch of Guyandot River, in Logan County.
Little; creek, a small right-hand branch of Muddlety Creek, a tributary to Gauley River, in Nicholas County.

Little; creek, a right-hand branch of Anthony Creek, a tributary to Greenbrier River, in Greenbrier County.

Little; creek, a right-hand branch of North Fork of Tug River in McDowell County.

Little; fork, a small left-hand branch of Meadow Creek, a tributary to Meadow River, in Greenbrier County.

Little; fork, a small left-hand tributary to Williams River in Webster County.

Little; fork, a small right-hand tributary to South Fork of Potomac River in Pendleton County.

Little; fork, a very small right-hand tributary to South Fork of Elkhorn Creek, in McDowell and Mercer counties.

Little; mountain, a short ridge in Monroe County. Altitude, 2,500 feet.

Little; mountain, a short ridge between North Fork of Greenbrier River and Greenbrier River in Pocahontas County. Altitude, 3,000 feet.

Little; mountain, a ridge in Monroe County.

Little; mountain, a short spur of Big Mountain, west of South Branch of Potomac River, in Pendleton County.

Little; mountain, a short spur of New Creek Mountains in Grant County. Altitude, 1,500 to 2,000 feet.

Little; mountain, a short ridge in Monroe County. Altitude, 2,000 feet.

Little; post village in Tyler County.

Little; river, a left-hand tributary to East Fork of Greenbrier River in Pocahontas County.

Little; river, a small left-hand branch of West Fork of Greenbrier River in Randolph County.

Little Beaver; creek, a right-hand tributary to Piney Creek, a branch of New River, in Raleigh County.

Little Beech; mountain, a short ridge east of Shavers Mountain, between East and West forks of Glady Fork, in Randolph County.

Little Beech Knob; summit in Greenbrier County.

Little Beechy; creek, a very small left-hand tributary to Elk River in Clay County.

Little Beechy; run, a small left-hand tributary to Williams River in Webster County.

Littlebirch; post village in Braxton County.

Little Birch; river, a right-hand branch of Birch River in Braxton and Webster counties.

Little Black; fork, a small right-hand tributary to Shavers Fork of Cheat River in Randolph County.

Little Blackwater; river, a small right-hand branch of Blackwater River in Tucker County.

Little Bluestone; creek, a small left-hand tributary to Bluestone River, a branch of New River, in Summers County.

Little Brier; creek, a small right-hand tributary to Coal River, a branch of Kanawha River, in Kanawha County.

Little Briery Knob; summit in Nicholas County.

Little Buffalo; creek, a small left-hand tributary to Elk River in Braxton County.

Little Buffalo; creek, a very small left-hand tributary to Mud River, a branch of Guyandot River, in Lincoln County.

Little Buffalo; creek, a left-hand branch of Big Buffalo River in Preston County.

Little Cabell; creek, a small right-hand tributary to Mud River, a branch of Guyandot River, in Cabell County.

Little Cacapon; river, a left-hand tributary to North Branch of Potomac River in Hampshire County.

Little Clear; creek, a right-hand branch of Meadow River in Greenbrier County.

Little Clear Creek; mountain, a ridge between Big Clear Creek and Little Clear Creek in Greenbrier County.

Little Coal; run, a large left-hand branch of Coal River, a tributary to Kanawha River, in Lincoln and Boone counties.

Little Crooked; run, a small left-hand tributary to Cedar Creek in Gilmer County.

Little Cub; branch, a very small left-hand tributary to Tug Fork of Big Sandy River in McDowell County.

Little Cub; creek, a small left-hand tributary to Guyandot River, a branch of Ohio River, in Wyoming County.

Little Day Camp; branch, a small right-hand tributary to Spice Creek, a branch of Tug Fork of Big Sandy River, in McDowell County.

Little Dents; run, a left-hand tributary of Buffalo Creek in Marion County.

Little Devil; creek, a small right-hand tributary to Second Creek, a branch of Greenbrier River, in Monroe County.

Little Dry; run, a small right-hand tributary to Left Fork of Buckhannon River in Randolph County.

Little Dunkard Mill; creek, a left-hand tributary to Buffalo Creek.

Little Elk; creek, a small right-hand tributary to Gauley River, a large branch of Kanawha River in Nicholas County.

Little Ellis; creek, a left-hand branch of Ellis Creek in Gilmer County.

Littlefalls; post village in Monongalia County on the Baltimore and Ohio Railroad.

Little Fishing; creek, a small left-hand branch of Ohio River in Wetzel County.

Little Fudger; creek, a right-hand branch of Fudger Creek, a tributary to Mud River, in Cabell County.

Little Gauley; mountains, a long, narrow, broken ridge in Kanawha and Fayette counties. Altitude 1,500 feet.

Little Hart; creek, a very small left-hand tributary to Guyandot River, a branch of Ohio River, in Lincoln County.

Little Hewitt; creek, a very small right-hand tributary to Little Coal River, a branch of Coal River, in Boone County.

Little High Knob; summit in Pocahontas County.

Little Horse; creek, a small left-hand tributary to Little Coal River, a branch of Coal River, in Boone County.

Little Huff; creek, a left-hand tributary to Guyandot River, a branch of Ohio River, in Wyoming County.

Little Hurricane; creek, a small left-hand tributary to Kanawha River in Putnam County.

Little Indian; creek, a small left-hand tributary to Tug Fork of Big Sandy River in McDowell County.

Little Jarrell; fork, a small left-hand branch of Big Jarrell Fork, a tributary to Hopkins Fork of Coal River, in Boone County.

Little Jenny; branch, a very small right-hand tributary to Tug Fork of Big Sandy River in McDowell County.

Little Jonathan; run, a small left-hand tributary to Cheat River in Tucker County.

Little Kanawha; river, a left-hand branch of Ohio River, rising in Upshur County and flowing northwest through Calhoun, Wirt, and Wood counties. It is navigable to Glenville.

Little Knob; summit in Greenbrier County.

Little Laurel; creek, a small left-hand tributary to Cherry River, a branch of Gauley River, in Nicholas and Greenbrier counties.

Little Laurel; creek, a small right-hand branch of Laurel Creek, a tributary to Coal River, in Boone County.

Little Laurel; creek, a small right-hand branch of Kiah Fork of Twelvepole Creek in Wayne County.

Little Laurel; creek, a small right-hand tributary to Williams River in Pocahontas County.
Little Laurel; creek, an indirect right-hand tributary to Hominy Creek, a branch of Gauley River, in Nicholas County.
Little Laurel; creek, a very small right-hand tributary to Brush Creek, a branch of Bluestone River, in Mercer County.
Little Laurel; run, a left-hand branch of Buffalo Creek in Marion County.
Little Laurel; run, a very small left-hand branch of Blue Creek, a tributary to Elk River, in Kanawha County.
Little Laurel; run, a left-hand tributary to Fish Creek in Wetzel and Marshall counties.
Little Locust Knob; summit in Webster County.
Little Lynn; creek, a small right-hand tributary to East Fork of Twelvepole Creek, a branch of Ohio River, in Wayne County.
Little Marsh; fork, a small right-hand branch of Marsh Fork, the left-hand head fork of Coal River, in Raleigh County.
Little Middle; mountain, a short ridge between Gandy Creek and Dry Fork of Cheat River in Randolph County.
Little Milam; creek, a small right-hand branch of Milam Creek, a tributary to East Fork of Twelvepole Creek, in Wayne County.
Little Mod; run, a right-hand branch of Buffalo Creek in Marion County.
Little Naul; creek, a left-hand branch of Naul Creek in Braxton County.
Little Ninemile; fork, a small left-hand branch of Campbell Creek, a tributary to Kanawha River, in Kanawha County.
Little Otter; creek, a small right-hand branch of Elk River in Braxton County.
Littleotter; post village in Braxton County.
Little Paw Paw; creek, left-hand tributary to Monongahela River, in Mineral County.
Little Ridge; short range of mountains in Greenbrier County.
Little Right; fork, a very small left-hand branch of Loop Creek, a tributary to Kanawha Kiver, in Fayette County.
Little Rush; run, a right-hand tributary to Fish Creek in Wetzel County.
Little Sand; run, a small right-hand tributary to Buckhannon River in Upshur County.
Little Sandy; creek, a small right-hand branch of Elk River in Kanawha County.
Little Sandy; creek, a right-hand branch of Big Sandy Creek in Preston County.
Littlesburg; post village in Mercer County.
Little Sevenmile; creek, a small left-hand branch of Sevenmile Creek, a tributary to Ohio River, in Cabell County.
Little Sewell; creek, a small left-hand tributary to Meadow River in Greenbrier County.
Little Sewell; mountain, a short broken mountainous country in the western part of Greenbrier County. Altitude, 3,000 feet.
Little Sewell Mountain; post village in Greenbrier County.
Little Skin; creek, a right-hand branch of Skin Creek in Lewis County.
Little Slate; creek, a left-hand tributary to Dry Fork, a branch of Tug Fork of Big Sandy River, in McDowell County.
Little Spruce; summit in Pocahontas County.
Little Spruce Knob; summit in Pocahontas County. Altitude, 4,360 feet.
Little Staunch; branch, a small right-hand tributary to Dry Fork, a branch of Tug Fork of Big Sandy River, in McDowell County.
Little Stony; creek, a very small left-hand tributary to New River in Fayette County.

GAZETTEER OF WEST VIRGINIA. 91

Little Sugar; creek, a right-hand branch of Sugar Creek, a tributary to Back Fork of Elk River, in Webster and Randolph counties.
Little Sycamore; creek, a very small left-hand tributary to Elk River in Clay County.
Little Twomile; creek, a right-hand branch of Mud River in Cabell County.
Little Ten Mile; creek, a small left-hand tributary to Monongahela River in Harrison County.
Littleton; town in Wetzel County on the Baltimore and Ohio Railroad. Altitude, 930 feet. Population, 509.
Little Twomile; creek, a small right-hand tributary to Mud River, a branch of Guyandot River, in Cabell County.
Little Ugly; creek, a very small right-hand tributary to Guyandot River, a branch of Ohio River, in Lincoln County.
Little Wheeling; creek, a right-hand branch of Wheeling Creek in Ohio County.
Little Whetstone; run, a right-hand tributary of Buffalo Creek in Marion County.
Little Whiteoak; creek, a small left-hand tributary to Pinnacle Creek, a branch of Guyandot River, in Wyoming County.
Little Whiteoak; creek, a very small right-hand tributary to Coal River, a branch of Kanawha River, in Boone County.
Little Whitestick; creek, a small left-hand tributary to Piney Creek, a branch of New River, in Raleigh County.
Little Wolf; creek, a small right-hand tributary to Cheat River in Preston County.
Liverpool; post village in Jackson County on the Baltimore and Ohio Railroad.
Lizard; branch, a very small right-hand tributary to Little Huff Creek, a branch of Guyandot River, in Wyoming County.
Lizemores; post village in Clay County.
Lizzie; post village in Jackson County.
Llewellyn; run, a left-hand tributary of Pyles Fork of Buffalo Creek in Marion County.
Lloyd; post village in Randolph County on the Baltimore and Ohio Railroad.
Lloydsville; post village in Braxton County.
Lobelia; post village in Pocahontas County.
Locke; post village in Tyler County.
Lockhart; post village in Jackson County.
Lockharts Run; post village in Wood County.
Lockney; post village in Gilmer County.
Lock Seven; post village in Kanawha County on the Ohio Central Lines.
Lockwood; post village in Nicholas County.
Locust; fork, a left-hand fork of Fork Creek, a tributary to Coal River, in Boone County.
Locust; post village in Pocahontas County.
Locust Knob; summit in Clay County. Altitude, 1,500 feet.
Locust Knob; summit in Pocahontas County. Altitude, 4,392 feet.
Locust Stump Knob; summit in Braxton County. Altitude, 1,690 feet.
Log; run, a right-hand branch of Sinking Creek, a tributary to Little Kanawha River, in Gilmer County.
Logan; county, situated in the southwestern part of the State, on the Allegheny Plateau. It is here deeply dissected, the surface being an alternation of narrow, sharp ridges and deep, narrow valleys. It is drained by Tug Fork of Big Sandy and Guyandot rivers. Area, 494 square miles. Population, 6,955—white, 6,894; negro, 61; foreign born, 8. County seat, Logan. The mean magnetic declination in 1900 was 45'. The mean annual rainfall is 50 inches, and the mean annual temperature 50° to 55°.
Logan; county seat of Logan County on the Chesapeake and Ohio Railway.

Logan; fork, a small right-hand branch of Hopkins Fork of Laurel Creek, a tributary to Coal River, in Boone County.
Logan; run, a very small right-hand tributary to Valley River in Randolph County.
Logansport; village in Marion County.
Lonecedar; post village in Jackson County on the Baltimore and Ohio Railroad.
Lonetree; post village in Tyler County. Altitude, 3,570 feet.
Lone Tree; summit of Rich Mountain in Randolph County. Altitude, 3,570 feet.
Long; branch, a very small left-hand tributary to Guyandot River in Wyoming County.
Long; branch, a left-hand tributary to Paint Creek, a branch of Kanawha River, in Kanawha County.
Long; branch, a small left-hand tributary to Middle Fork of Davis Creek, a branch of Kanawha River, in Kanawha County.
Long; branch, a small left-hand branch of Sandlick Fork of Laurel Creek, a tributary to Coal River, in Boone County.
Long; branch, an indirect right-hand tributary to Dry Fork, a branch of Tug Fork of Big Sandy River, in McDowell County.
Long; branch, a small right-hand tributary to Fifteen-mile Fork of Cabin Creek, a branch of Kanawha River, in Kanawha County.
Long; branch, a very small right-hand tributary to Clear Fork of Coal River in Raleigh County.
Long; branch, a very small right-hand tributary to Guyandot River in Wyoming County.
Long; branch, a small right-hand tributary to Big Clear Creek, a branch of Meadow River, in Greenbrier County.
Long; branch, a small right-hand tributary to Beech Fork of Twelvepole Creek, a branch of Ohio River, in Wayne County.
Long; branch, a left-hand tributary of Guyandot River in Lincoln County.
Long; branch, a very small right-hand tributary to Mill Creek, a branch of Mud River, in Cabell County.
Long; fork, a left-hand branch of Laurel Patch Run in Braxton County.
Long; post village in Randolph County.
Long; run, a very small left-hand tributary to Elk River, a large branch of Kanawha River, in Clay County.
Long; run, a left-hand branch of Left Fork of Middle Fork of Tygarts Valley River in Randolph County.
Long; run, a small left-hand tributary to Right Fork of Middle Fork of Little Kanawha River in Webster County.
Long; run, a small left-hand tributary to Cheat River in Tucker and Preston counties.
Long; run, a small left-hand branch of Pritchett Creek in Marion County.
Long; run, a small right-hand tributary to Birch River in Braxton County.
Long; run, a left-hand branch of Berkeley Run in Taylor County.
Long; run, a very small right-hand tributary to Left Fork of Buckhannon River in Randolph County.
Longacre; post village in Fayette County on the Ohio Central Lines.
Long Bottom; creek, a small left-hand branch of Cabin Creek, a tributary to Kanawha River, in Kanawha County.
Longdale; post village in Mason County on the Baltimore and Ohio Railroad.
Long Drain; left-hand branch of Fish Creek in Wetzel County.
Long Knob; summit in Braxton County. Altitude, 1,510 feet.
Long Lick; branch, a very small left-hand tributary to Big Huff Creek, a branch of Guyandot River, in Wyoming County.
Long Lick; left-hand branch of Cedar Creek in Gilmer County.

Long Pole; creek, a small right-hand tributary to Tug Fork of Big Sandy River in McDowell County.
Longreach; post village in Tyler County on the Baltimore and Ohio Railroad.
Long Ridge; short range between North and South branches of the Potomac in Pendleton County.
Longrun; post village in Doddridge County on the Baltimore and Ohio Railroad.
Long Run Hill; summit in Randolph County.
Longs; run, a left-hand branch of Castleman Run in Ohio and Brooke counties.
Long Shoal; branch, a very small right-hand tributary to Little Coal River, a branch of Coal River, in Boone County.
Long Shoal; run, a small right-hand tributary to Little Kanawha River.
Longs Ridge; short spur between Turkey and Longs runs, small left-hand branches of Elk River, in Clay County.
Lookout; post village in Fayette County.
Looneyville; post village in Roane County.
Loop; branch, a very small right-hand tributary to North Fork of Elkhorn Creek in McDowell County.
Loop; branch, a very small right-hand tributary to Tug River in McDowell County.
Loop; creek, a right-hand tributary to Kanawha River in Fayette County.
Lorentz; post village in Upshur County on the Baltimore and Ohio Railroad.
Lorton Lick; creek, a small right-hand tributary to Bluestone River in Mercer County.
Lost; branch, a very small right-hand tributary to Guyandot River in Mingo and Wyoming counties.
Lost; river, a head branch of Cacapon River, rising in Hardy County and flowing northeast into the Potomac.
Lost; run, a small left-hand tributary to Left Fork of Middle Fork of Tygarts Valley River in Randolph County.
Lost; run, a right-hand branch of Fish Creek in Wetzel County.
Lost; run, a small right-hand branch of Laurel Creek, a tributary to Elk River, in Webster County.
Lost City; post village in Hardy County.
Lostcreek; post village in Harrison County on the Baltimore and Ohio Railroad. Altitude, 1,013 feet.
Lost Flat; broad summit in Greenbrier County.
Lost River; post village in Hardy County.
Lot; post village in Wetzel County.
Lotta; post village in Wirt County.
Loudenville; post village in Marshall County on the Baltimore and Ohio Railroad.
Loudin; post village in Randolph County.
Louise; post village in Pocahontas County.
Lousecamp; run, a small left-hand tributary to Cheat River in Tucker County.
Louther; post village in Jackson County.
Loveberry; run, a right-hand branch of Sand Fork in Lewis County.
Loveridge; post village in Greenbrier County.
Lowdell; post village in Wood County.
Lowell; branch, a very small right-hand branch of Indian Creek, a tributary to New River, in Monroe and Summers counties.
Lowell; post village in Summers County on the Chesapeake and Ohio Railway. Altitude, 1,512 feet.
Lower; creek, a small right-hand tributary to Mud River, a branch of Guyandot River, in Cabell County.
Lower; gap in Wyoming County.
Lower; mountain, a summit in Pocahontas County.

Lower; run, a very small right-hand tributary to Elk River, a large branch of Kanawha River, in Clay County.
Lower; run, a right-hand branch of South Fork of Fishing Creek in Wetzel County.
Lower Big; run, a right-hand branch of Leading Creek in Gilmer County.
Lower Big; run, a small right-hand tributary to Holly River in Webster County.
Lower Birch; run, a very small left-hand tributary to Elk River in Clay County.
Lower Bull; run, a right-hand tributary to Cedar Creek in Gilmer County.
Lower Cove; head waters of Lost River in Hardy County.
Lower Frame; run, a small left-hand tributary to Elk River in Clay County.
Lower Gap; branch, a small left-hand tributary to Big Huff Creek, a branch of Guyandot River, in Wyoming County.
Lower Hensley; creek, a small right-hand tributary to Tug Fork of Big Sandy River in McDowell County.
Low Gap; branch, a small right-hand tributary to Little Marsh Fork, a branch of Coal River, in Raleigh County.
Low Gap; branch, a small right-hand tributary to Slab Fork, a branch of Guyandot River, in Raleigh County.
Low Gap; creek, a small left-hand tributary to Spruce Fork of Little Coal River, a branch of Coal River, in Boone County.
Lower Level; run, a left-hand branch of Cedar Creek in Gilmer County.
Lower Lick; small left-hand tributary to Laurel Fork, a branch of Spruce Fork of Little Coal River, in Boone County.
Lower Pond Lick; small left-hand tributary to Shavers Fork of Cheat River in Randolph County.
Lower Road; branch, a small right-hand tributary to Clear Fork, a branch of Guyandot River, in Wyoming County.
Lower Rock Camp; run, a small right-hand tributary to Elk River in Braxton County.
Lower Shannon; branch, a small right-hand tributary to Tug Fork of Big Sandy River in McDowell County.
Lower Shant; run, a small right-hand tributary to Back Fork of Elk River in Randolph County.
Lower Shaver; run, a small right-hand tributary to Left Fork of Steer Creek in Braxton County.
Lower Sleith; fork, a left-hand branch of Right Fork of Steer Creek in Braxton County.
Lower Sturgeon; branch, a small right-hand tributary to Big Cub Creek, a branch of Guyandot River, in Wyoming County.
Lower Threemile; fork, a small left-hand branch of Blue Creek, a tributary to Elk River, in Kanawha County.
Lower Tony Camp; run, a small right-hand tributary to Dry Fork of Cheat River in Randolph County.
Lower Two; run, a small left-hand tributary to Left Fork of Steer Creek in Gilmer County.
Lower Two; run, a small left-hand tributary to Cedar Creek in Gilmer County.
Lowman; post village in Wetzel County.
Lowsville; post village in Monongalia County.
Lubeck; post village in Wood County.
Lucerne; post village in Gilmer County.
Lucile; post village in Wirt County.
Lukey; fork, a small left-hand tributary to head of Mud River, a branch of Guyandot River, in Boone County.
Lumberport; post village in Harrison County on the Baltimore and Ohio Railroad.

GAZETTEER OF WEST VIRGINIA.

Lunice; creek, a small left-hand tributary to South Branch of Potomac River in Grant County.
Luray; post village in Pendleton County.
Lurd; post village in Kanawha County.
Luzon; post village in Tyler County.
Lydia; post village in Clay County.
Lykins; creek, a very small right-hand tributary to Paint Creek, a branch of Kanawha River, in Fayette County.
Lynch; post village in Harrison County on the Norfolk and Western Railway.
Lynch; run, a very small right-hand tributary to Little Kanawha River in Gilmer County.
Lynn; creek, a very small left-hand branch of Twelvepole Creek, a tributary to Ohio River, in Wayne County.
Lynncamp; post village in Marshall County.
Lynn Camp; run, a small left-hand tributary to Little Kanawha River in Upshur County.
Lynn Camp; run, a left-hand branch of Fish Creek in Wetzel and Marshall counties.
Lynn Camp; run, a very small left-hand tributary to Gauley River in Webster County.
Lynncamp; run, a right-hand tributary of Left Fork of Steer Creek in Gilmer County.
Lynn Knob; summit in Randolph County.
Lyon; post village in Doddridge County.
Lyons; branch, a right-hand branch of Buch Fork of Twelvepole Creek in Wayne and Cabell counties.
Lytton; post village in Pleasants County on the Baltimore and Ohio Railroad.
Mabie; post village in Randolph County, on the Roaring Creek and Charleston Railroad.
McAlpin; village in Harrison County.
McCauleys; run, a left-hand branch of Oil Creek in Braxton County.
McClains; post village in Jackson County.
McClung; branch, a small left-hand branch of Peter Creek, a tributary to Gauley River, in Nicholas County.
McClungs; post village in Greenbrier County.
McClure; branch, a small right-hand tributary to South Fork of Tug River in McDowell County.
McComas; branch, a very small left-hand tributary to East Fork of Twelvepole Creek, a branch of Ohio River, in Wayne County.
McComas; branch, a right-hand tributary of Mud River in Cabell County.
McComas; post village in Mercer County.
McConkey; village in Taylor County.
McCowans; mount, a spur of Shavers Mountain, between Shavers and Glady forks of Cheat River.
McCoy; run, a right-hand branch of Little Wheeling Creek in Ohio County.
McCue; post village in Upshur County.
McCurdy; post village in Cabell County.
McDonald; fork, a small left-hand branch of Big Cub Creek, a tributary to Guyandot River, in Wyoming County.
MacDonald; station in Fayette County on the Chesapeake and Ohio Railway and on Dunloup Creek, a tributary to New River.
McDonald Mill; creek, a small left-hand tributary to Clear Fork, a branch of Guyandot River, in Wyoming County.
McDowell; branch, a very small left-hand tributary to Clear Fork of Coal River in Raleigh County.

McDowell; county, situated in the southern part of the State on the Allegheny Plateau. It is deeply dissected. The surface is drained in the main by Tug Fork of Big Sandy River.
McDowell; post village in McDowell County on the Norfolk and Western Railway.
McElroy; branch, a small left-hand tributary to Ohio River in Tyler County.
McElroy; creek, a small left-hand tributary to Ohio River in Doddridge County.
MacFarlan; post village in Ritchie County.
McGee; post village in Taylor County.
McGraw; run, a right-hand branch of Little Wheeling Creek in Ohio County.
McGraws; post village in Wyoming County. Altitude, 1,802 feet.
McKee; branch, a small right-hand tributary to Gauley River in Nicholas County.
McKee; mountain, a short ridge in Nicholas County. The highest peak reaches an altitude of 2,365 feet.
McKendree; station in Fayette County on the Chesapeake and Ohio Railway and on New River. Altitude, 1,411 feet.
McKim; creek, a small left-hand tributary to Ohio River in Pleasants County.
McKim; post village in Tyler County.
Macksville; post village in Pendleton County.
McKinley; post village in Wood County.
McMechen; town in Marshall County on the Baltimore and Ohio Railroad. Population, 1,465.
McMellin; post village in Monongalia County.
McMillan; creek, a small left-hand tributary to Big Laurel Creek, a branch of Cherry River, in Greenbrier County.
McMillion; creek, a left-hand branch of Muddlety Creek, a tributary to Gauley River, in Nicholas County.
Mace Knob; summit of Cheat Mountain in Pocahontas County.
Madam; creek, a small left-hand tributary to New River in Summers County.
Madison; county seat of Boone County.
Madison; creek, a left-hand branch of Guyandot River in Cabell County.
Madison; creek, a small left-hand tributary to Guyandot River, a branch of Ohio River, in Wayne County.
Madison; run, a small right-hand tributary to Cheat River in Preston County.
Magazine; branch, a small right-hand tributary to Elk River, a branch of Kanawha River, in Kanawha County.
Maggie; post village in Mason County on the Baltimore and Ohio Railroad.
Magnolia; post village in Morgan County on the Baltimore and Ohio Railroad.
Mahan; run, a left-hand branch of Buffalo Creek in Marion County.
Mahogany; run, a left-hand branch of Muach Run in Monongalia County.
Mahone; creek, a very small left-hand tributary to Mud River, a branch of Guyandot River, in Lincoln County.
Mahone; post village in Ritchie County.
Mahoney; creek, a left-hand branch of Mud River in Lincoln County.
Maidsville; post village in Monongalia County.
Majorsville; post village in Marshall County.
Malden; post village in Kanawha County on the Chesapeake and Ohio and the Ohio Central railroads. Altitude, 606 feet.
Malta; post village in Barbour County.
Mammoth; post village in Kanawha County on the Kellys Creek Railroad.
Man; creek, a small right-hand branch of Glade Creek, a tributary to New River, in Fayette County.
Man; post village in Logan County.
Mandeville; post village in Summers County.
Manganese; post village in Wood County.

GAZETTEER OF WEST VIRGINIA.

Manheim; post village in Preston County.
Manila; post village in Boone County.
Manning; branch, a very small left-hand tributary to Coal River, a branch of Kanawha River, in Kanawha County.
Manning; branch, a very small right-hand tributary to Little Coal River in Boone County.
Manning; run, a small right-hand branch of Big Laurel Creek, a tributary to Cherry River, in Greenbrier County.
Manning Knob; summit in Greenbrier County.
Mannington; town in Marion County on the Baltimore and Ohio Railroad. Altitude, 967 feet. Population, 1,681.
Mann Knob; summit in Wayne County. Altitude, 1,437 feet.
Mann Knob; summit in Greenbrier County.
Manns; creek, a small right-hand tributary to New River in Fayette County.
Manown; post village in Preston County.
Maple; fork, a small right-hand branch of Sand Fork of Paint Creek, a tributary to Kanawha River, in Raleigh County.
Maple; post village in Monongalia County.
Maple; run, a left-hand branch of Cheat River in Monongalia County.
Mapledale; post village in Greenbrier County.
Maple Meadow; creek, a small left-hand tributary to Marsh Fork of Coal River in Raleigh County.
Maplewood; post village in Fayette County.
Marary; branch, a small left-hand tributary to Laurel Creek, a branch of Coal River, in Boone County.
Marcus; post village in Webster County.
Margaret; post village in Harrison County.
Marie; post village in Summers County.
Marion; county, situated in the northern part of the State, on the Allegheny Plateau. It is drained by tributaries to the Monongahela. Area, 357 squares miles. Population, 32,430—white, 31,942; negro, 482; foreign born, 1,769. County seat, Fairmont. The mean magnetic declination in 1900 was 3° 10′. The mean annual rainfall is 40 to 50 inches, and the mean annual temperature 50° to 55°. The county is traversed by the Baltimore and Ohio Railroad.
Marion; post village in Wetzel County on the West Virginia Northern Railroad.
Mark; run, a right-hand tributary of Left Fork of Steer Creek in Gilmer County.
Market; post village in Doddridge County.
Marlin; mountain, a short ridge in Pocahontas County. The highest peak reaches an altitude of 3,198 feet.
Marlin; mountain, a short ridge between Thorny and Browns creeks in Pocahontas County.
Marlin Lick; small left-hand tributary to Greenbrier River in Pocahontas County.
Marlinton; county seat of Pocahontas County on the Chesapeake and Ohio Railway. Population, 171.
Marlowe; village in Berkeley County.
Marmet; post village in Kanawha County on the Chesapeake and Ohio Railway.
Marpleton; post village in Braxton County.
Marquess; post village in Preston County.
Marrowbone; creek, a small right-hand branch of Tug Fork of Big Sandy River, a tributary to Ohio River, in Logan County.
Marrs; branch, a very small left-hand tributary to New River in Fayette County.
Marsh; fork, a stream in Raleigh County, uniting with Clear Fork to form Coal River.

Marsh; fork, a small right-hand branch of Big Hart Creek, a tributary to Guyandot River, in Lincoln County.

Marsh; fork, a small right-hand branch of Slab Fork, a tributary to Guyandot River, in Wyoming County.

Marsh; fork, an indirect left-hand tributary to Indian Creek, a branch of Guyandot River in Wyoming County.

Marshall; county, situated at the base of the Panhandle, bordering upon the Ohio River. Area, 311 square miles. Population, 26,444—white, 25,941; negro, 499; foreign born, 1,264. County seat, Moundsville. The mean magnetic declination in 1900 was 1° 50′. The mean annual rainfall is 40 to 50 inches, and the mean annual temperature 50° to 55°. The county is traversed by the Ohio River and the Baltimore and Ohio railroads.

Marshall; post village in Jackson County.

Marshes; post village in Raleigh County.

Marshville; post village in Harrison County.

Martha; post village in Cabell County.

Marthas Ridge; short spur north of North Fork of Greenbrier River in Pocahontas County. Altitude, 3,500 to 4,000 feet.

Martin; branch, a left-hand tributary to Pocotaligo River, a branch of Kanawha River, in Kanawha County.

Martin; fork, a left-hand branch of Peachtree Creek, a tributary to Marsh Fork of Coal River, in Raleigh County.

Martin; post village in Grant County.

Martinsburg; county seat of Berkeley County on the Baltimore and Ohio and the Cumberland Valley railroads. Population, 7,564.

Marytown; post village in McDowell County.

Mash; branch, a small right-hand tributary to Dingus Run, a branch of Guyandot River, in Logan County.

Mason; county, situated in the western part of the State, bordering on Ohio River at the foot of the Allegheny Plateau. Area, 457 square miles. Population, 24,142—white, 23,604; negro, 537; foreign born, 317. County seat, Point Pleasant. The mean magnetic declination in 1900 was 0° 35′. The mean annual rainfall is 40 to 50 inches, and the mean annual temperature 50° to 55°. The county is traversed by the Ohio Central Lines and the Ohio River Railroad.

Mason; village in Mason County. Population, 904.

Masontown; post village in Preston County on the Morgantown and Kingwood Railroad.

Masonville; post village in Grant County.

Mast Knob; summit in Randolph County.

Matchless; post village in Berkeley County.

Mate; creek, a small right-hand branch of Tug Fork of Big Sandy River, a tributary to Ohio River, in Logan County.

Matewan; post village in Mingo County on the Norfolk and Western Railway.

Matewan; station in Logan County on the Norfolk and Western Railway and on Tug Fork of Chattarawha River.

Mathias; post village in Hardy County.

Mats; creek, a small right-hand tributary to West Fork, a branch of Pond Fork of little Coal River, in Boone County.

Mattie; post village in Roane County.

Matts; creek, a very small left-hand tributary to Greenbrier River in Summers and Monroe counties.

Matville; post village in Raleigh County.

Maud; post village in Wetzel County on the Baltimore and Ohio Railroad.

Maud; run, a right-hand branch of North Fork of Fishing Creek in Wetzel County.

Maxwell; post village in Pleasants County.
Maxwelton; post village in Greenbrier County.
May; post village in Doddridge County.
Maybeury; post village in McDowell County on Norfolk and Western Railway and on South Fork of Elkhorn Creek. Altitude, 2,162 feet.
Maynard; branch, a very small right-hand tributary to East Fork of Twelvepole Creek, a branch of Ohio River, in Wayne County.
Mays; gap in Little Mountain, caused by New Creek, in Grant County.
Maysville; post village in Grant County.
Mayton; post village in Webster County.
Maywood; post village in Fayette County.
Meadland; village in Taylor County.
Meadow; branch, a very small right-hand tributary to Middle Fork of Mud River, a branch of Guyandot River, in Lincoln County.
Meadow; branch, a right-hand branch of Sleepy Creek in Berkeley and Morgan counties.
Meadow; creek, a right-hand branch of Anthony Creek, a tributary to Greenbrier River, in Greenbrier County.
Meadow; creek, a small right-hand tributary to New River in Summers and Fayette counties.
Meadow; creek, a small right-hand branch of Meadow River, a tributary to Gauley River, in Greenbrier County.
Meadow; creek, a small right-hand branch of Muddlety Creek, a tributary to Gauley River, in Nicholas County.
Meadow; fork, a small left-hand branch of Devils Fork, a tributary to Guyandot River, in Raleigh County.
Meadow; fork, a small left-hand branch of Dunloup Creek, a tributary to New River, in Fayette County.
Meadow; fork, a small right-hand branch of Cabin Creek, a tributary to Guyandot River, in Wyoming County.
Meadow; fork, a small right-hand branch of Brier Creek, a tributary to Coal River, in Kanawha County.
Meadow; river, a large left-hand branch of Gauley River, rising in Greenbrier County and flowing northwestward, forming the boundary between Fayette and Nicholas counties, until it enters the Gauley at Carnifax Ferry.
Meadow; run, a right-hand branch of Oil Creek in Braxton County.
Meadow; run, a right-hand branch of Middle Wheeling Creek in Ohio County.
Meadowbluff; post village in Greenbrier County.
Meadowbrook; post village in Harrison County on the Baltimore and Ohio Railroad.
Meadow Creek; mountain, a ridge in Greenbrier County lying nearly parallel to Allegheny Mountains. Altitude, 2,500 to 3,000 feet.
Meadowcreek Station; post village in Summers County on the Chesapeake and Ohio Railway.
Meadowdale; post village in Jackson County on the Baltimore and Ohio Railroad.
Meadowville; post village in Barbour County.
Meadville; post village in Tyler County.
Measle; fork, a small right-hand branch of Slab Fork, a tributary to Guyandot River, in Wyoming County.
Medina; post village in Jackson County.
Medley; post village in Grant County.
Meethouse; branch, a small right-hand tributary to Clear Fork, a branch of Tug Fork of Big Sandy River, in McDowell County.
Meethouse; fork, a right-hand head fork of Panther Creek, a branch of Tug Fork of Big Sandy River, in McDowell County.

Meeting House; branch, a very small left-hand tributary to Elkhorn Creek, a branch of Tug Fork of Big Sandy River, in McDowell County.
Meeting House; run, a left-hand branch of Lost River in Taylor County.
Meighen; post village in Marshall County.
Melissa; post village in Cabell County.
Mentor; post village in Jackson County.
Mercer; county, situated in the southern part of the State bordering on Virginia. It lies on the Allegheny Plateau or East River Mountains, which here form the escarpment which is the southern boundary of the county. Its elevation ranges from 2,000 to 4,000 feet. It is drained by tributaries to New River. Area, 437 square miles. Population, 23,023—white, 20,119; negro, 2,902; foreign born, 269. County seat, Princeton. The mean magnetic declination in 1900 was 1°. The mean annual rainfall is 50 to 60 inches, and the mean annual temperature 50° to 55°. The county is traversed by the Norfolk and Western Railway.
Mercer; post village in Hancock County.
Mercers Bottom; post village in Mason County on the Baltimore and Ohio Railroad.
Mercers Saltworks; post village in Summers County.
Meriden; post village in Barbour County.
Merrick; branch, a small right-hand tributary to Mud River, a branch of Guyandot River, in Cabell County.
Merrick; creek, a very small left-hand tributary to Middle Fork of Mud River in Lincoln County.
Merritt; creek, a small left-hand tributary to Guyandot River, a branch of Ohio River, in Cabell County.
Messer; creek, a very small right-hand branch of Marrowbone Creek, a tributary to Tug Fork of Big Sandy River, in Logan County.
Messer; run, a left-hand tributary of Pyles Fork of Buffalo Creek in Marion County.
Metz; post village in Marion County on the Baltimore and Ohio Railroad.
Micajah Ridge; mountains in Wyoming County.
Michael; mountain, a short ridge in Pocahontas County. Altitude, 3,000 to 3,500 feet.
Middle; branch, a very small right-hand branch of Tug Fork of Big Sandy River, a tributary to Ohio River, in Logan County.
Middle; branch, a small right-hand tributary to Barker Creek, a branch of Guyandot River, in Wyoming County.
Middle; creek, a small left-hand tributary to Elk River in Clay County.
Middle; creek, a left-hand branch of Middle Fork of Mud River in Cabell County.
Middle; fork, a head fork of Back Fork of Elk River in Randolph County.
Middle; fork, a head fork of Cedar Creek in Braxton County.
Middle; fork, a small left-hand branch of Patterson Creek, a tributary to North Branch of Potomac River, in Grant County.
Middle; fork, a left-hand tributary to Williams River in Webster and Pocahontas counties.
Middle; fork, a left-hand branch of Davis Creek, a tributary to Kanawha River, in Kanawha County.
Middle; fork, a small left-hand tributary to Canoe Run in Lewis County.
Middle; fork, an indirect left-hand tributary to Dry Fork, a branch of Tug Fork of Big Sandy River, in McDowell County.
Middle; fork, a small right-hand tributary to Right Fork of Buckhannon River in Randolph County.
Middle; fork, a small right-hand branch of Trace Fork of Guyandot River, a tributary to Ohio River, in Logan County.
Middle; fork, a right-hand branch of Island Creek, a tributary to Guyandot River, in Logan County.

Middle; mountain, a narrow ridge between Gap Mountain and Cove Mountain in Monroe County. Altitude, 2,500 to 3,000 feet.
Middle; mountain, a short ridge in the northern part of Pocahontas County. Altitude, 3,500 feet.
Middle; mountain, a narrow ridge in Pocahontas and Greenbrier counties.
Middle; mountain, a short ridge in Pendleton and Grant counties. Altitude, 2,000 feet.
Middle; run, a small left-hand tributary to Little Kanawha River in Gilmer County.
Middle; run, a small left-hand tributary to Back Fork of Elk River in Webster County.
Middle; run, a small left-hand tributary to Gauley River in Nicholas County.
Middle; run, a small right-hand branch of Big Laurel Creek, a tributary to Cherry River, in Greenbrier County.
Middle; run, a small right-hand tributary to Birch River in Braxton County.
Middlebourne; county seat of Tyler County. Population, 403.
Middle Fork; mountain, a ridge in Webster and Pocahontas counties, between Cranberry and Williams rivers. Altitude, 3,500 to 4,000 feet.
Middlefork; post village in Randolph County on the Baltimore and Ohio Railroad.
Middle Island; creek, a left-hand branch of Ohio River, rising in Tyler County.
Middle Lick; fork, a small right-hand tributary to Davis Creek, a branch of Kanawha River, in Kanawha County.
Middleton; fork, a very small left-hand tributary to Bluestone River, in Mercer County.
Middleway; town in Jefferson County. Population, 466.
Middle Wheeling; creek, a left-hand branch of Little Wheeling Creek, in Ohio County.
Midkiff; post village in Lincoln County.
Midway; post village in Putnam County on the Ohio Central Lines.
Mike; run, a right-hand tributary of Ellis Creek in Gilmer County.
Mike Knob; summit of Yew Mountains in Greenbrier County. Altitude, 4,276 feet.
Milam; branch, a small right-hand tributary to South Fork of Tug River in McDowell County.
Milam; creek, a small left-hand branch of East Fork of Twelvepole Creek, a tributary to Ohio River, in Wayne County.
Milam; post village in Hardy County.
Milam Ridge; mountains in Wyoming County.
Milan; fork, a left-hand branch of Barker Creek, a tributary to Guyandot River, in Wyoming County.
Milan; fork, a left-hand branch of Laurel Fork, a tributary to Clear Fork of Guyandot River, in Wyoming County.
Milburn; branch, a small left-hand tributary to Paint Creek, a branch of Kanawha River, in Kanawha County.
Milburn; creek, a very small left-hand tributary to Paint Creek, a branch of Kanawha River, in Fayette County.
Mile; branch, a very small right-hand tributary to Kanawha River in Kanawha County.
Mile; branch, a very small right-hand tributary to Coal River, a branch of Kanawha River, in Boone County.
Mile; branch, a small right-hand tributary to Whiteoak Creek, a branch of Coal River, in Boone County.
Mile; branch, a very small right-hand tributary to Indian Creek, a branch of Guyandot River, in Wyoming County.
Mile; branch, a very small right-hand tributary to Dry Fork, a branch of Tug Fork of Big Sandy River, in McDowell County.

Mile; creek, a small right-hand tributary to Guyandot River, a branch of Ohio River, in Lincoln County.

Mile; fork, a right-hand branch of Cooper Creek, a tributary to Elk River, in Kanawha County.

Miles; post village in Pendleton County.

Miletus; post village in Doddridge County.

Mill; branch, a very small left-hand tributary to Cherry River, a branch of Gauley River, in Nicholas County.

Mill; branch, a very small left-hand tributary to Fields Creek, a branch of Kanawha River, in Kanawha County.

Mill; branch, a small right-hand tributary to Williams River in Webster County.

Mill; branch, a small right-hand tributary to Guyandot River, a branch of Ohio River, in Lincoln County.

Mill; branch, a very small right-hand tributary to Tug River in McDowell County.

Mill; branch, a small right-hand tributary to Camp Creek, a branch of Bluestone River, in Mercer County.

Mill; branch, a small right-hand tributary to Barker Creek, a branch of Guyandot River, in Wyoming County.

Mill; branch, a very small right-hand tributary to Winding Gulf, a branch of Guyandot River, in Raleigh County.

Mill; creek, a small left-hand tributary to Birch River, a branch of Elk River, in Nicholas County.

Mill; creek, a left-hand tributary to South Branch of Potomac River in Hampshire County.

Mill; creek, a small left-hand branch of Patterson Creek, a tributary to North Branch of Potomac River, in Mineral County.

Mill; creek, a very small left-hand branch of Island Creek, a tributary to Guyandot River, in Logan County.

Mill; creek, a small left-hand tributary to Bluestone River in Mercer County.

Mill; creek, a small left-hand tributary to Tug Fork of Big Sandy River in McDowell County.

Mill; creek, a very small left-hand tributary to New River in Raleigh County.

Mill; creek, a left-hand tributary to Elk River, a large branch of Kanawha River, in Kanawha County.

Mill; creek, a small left-hand branch of Ohio River in Jackson County.

Mill; creek, a left-hand tributary to Elk River in Kanawha County.

Mill; creek, a small left-hand tributary to Valley River in Randolph County.

Mill; creek, a small left-hand tributary to Elk River in Braxton County.

Mill; creek, a small left-hand tributary to Birch River, in Nicholas County.

Mill; creek, a small right-hand tributary to Mud River, a branch of Guyandot River, in Cabell County.

Mill; creek, a small right-hand tributary to Meadow River, a branch of Gauley River, in Greenbrier County.

Mill; creek, a small right-hand tributary to Tygarts Valley River in Barbour County.

Mill; creek, a very small right-hand tributary to Guyandot River, a branch of Ohio River, in Cabell County.

Mill; creek, a very small right-hand tributary to Elkhorn Creek, a branch of Tug Fork of Big Sandy River, in McDowell County.

Mill; creek, a small right-hand tributary to Dunloup Creek, a branch of New River, in Raleigh County.

Mill; creek, a very small right-hand branch of Guyandot River, a tributary to Ohio River, in Logan County.

Mill; creek, a small right-hand branch of Hurricane Creek, a tributary to Kanawha River, in Putnam County.

Mill; creek, a right-hand tributary to New River in Fayette County.
Mill; creek, a right-hand branch of Valley River in Randolph County.
Mill; gap in a spur of the South Fork Mountains, caused by Brushy Run, in Pendleton County.
Mill; mountain, a short ridge on the boundary line between Hardy County, W. Va., and Shenandoah County, Va. Altitude, 3,000 feet.
Mill; run, a small left-hand tributary to Elk River in Webster County.
Mill; run, a small left-hand tributary to Gauley River in Webster County.
Mill; run, a small left-hand tributary to North Fork of Potomac River in Pendleton County.
Mill; run, a small, left-hand tributary to Elk River in Braxton County.
Mill; run, a small right-hand branch of Knapp Creek, a tributary of Greenbrier River, in Pocahontas County.
Mill; run, a small right-hand tributary to Back Fork of Elk River in Webster County.
Mill; run, a small right-hand tributary to Gauley River in Webster County.
Mill; run, a small right-hand tributary to Williams River in Webster County.
Mill; run, a small right-hand tributary to South Branch of Potomac River in Pendleton County.
Mill; run, a small right-hand tributary to Dry Fork of Cheat River in Tucker County.
Mill; run, a small right-hand branch of Sugar Creek, a tributary to Back Fork of Elk River, in Webster and Randolph counties.
Mill; run, a small right-hand tributary to Elk River in Webster County.
Mill; run, head fork of Teter Creek, a branch of Tygarts Valley River, in Barbour County.
Millard; post village in Roane County.
Millbrook; post village in Hampshire County.
Mill Creek; mountain, a long, narrow ridge, lying parallel to the South Branch of the Potomac River, in Hardy and Hampshire counties. Altitude, 1,000 to 2,000 feet.
Mill Creek; post village in Randolph County on the West Virginia Central and Pittsburg Railway.
Miller; creek, a small right-hand branch of Meadow River, a tributary to Gauley River, in Nicholas County.
Miller; run, a left-hand branch of Miller Fork of Rock Run in Wetzel County.
Miller Knob; summit in Webster County. Altitude, 2,742 feet.
Miller Ridge; short mountainous range in Webster County, south of the Gauley River.
Millers; creek, a very small right-hand branch of Tug Fork of Big Sandy River, a tributary to Ohio River, in Logan County.
Millers; fork, a right-hand tributary to Twelvepole Creek, a tributary to Ohio River, in Wayne County.
Millers Camp; branch, a right-hand head fork of Marsh Fork of Coal River in Raleigh County.
Millers Camp Branch; post village in Raleigh County.
Millers Ridge; short spur in Greenbrier County. Altitude, 2,500 feet.
Mill Fall; run, a left-hand branch of West Fork River in Marion County.
Millhill; post village in Greenbrier County.
Mill Hill; summit in Greenbrier County.
Mill Hollow; small right-hand tributary to Kanawha River in Kanawha County.
Milligan; creek, a small right-hand tributary to Greenbrier River in Greenbrier County.
Mill Knob; summit in Nicholas County.
Millpoint; post village in Pocahontas County.

Millsboro; post village in Marshall County.

Millsite; branch, a very small right-hand tributary to Mud River, a branch of Guyandot River, in Lincoln County.

Mill Site; run, a small right-hand branch of Little Kanawha River in Gilmer County.

Mill Site; run, a small right-hand tributary to Right Fork of Buckhannon River in Upshur County.

Millstone; post village in Calhoun County.

Millstone; run, a right-hand branch of Little Kanawha River in Braxton County.

Millville; post village in Jefferson County on the Baltimore and Ohio Railroad.

Millwood; post village in Jackson County on the Baltimore and Ohio Railroad.

Milo; post village in Calhoun County.

Milroy; post village in Braxton County.

Milton; town in Cabell County on the Chesapeake and Ohio Railway. Altitude, 586 feet. Population, 582.

Mineral; county, situated in the northeastern part of the State, limited on the west and north by Potomac River. Its surface is an alternation of ridges and valleys, ranging in elevation from 800 to over 3,000 feet. Area, 332 square miles. Population, 12,883—white, 12,218; negro, 665; foreign born, 451. County seat, Keyser. The mean magnetic declination in 1900 was 2° 30'. The mean annual rainfall is 50 to 60 inches, and the mean annual temperature 45° to 50°. The county is traversed by the Baltimore and Ohio and the West Virginia Central and Pittsburg railroads.

Mineral; post village in Harrison County.

Mineralwells; post village in Wood County.

Mingo; county, situated in the southwestern part of the State, bordering on Big Sandy River, and lying on the Allegheny Plateau. It is here deeply dissected. Area, 424 square miles. Population, 11,359—white, 11,050; negro, 309; foreign born, 65. County seat, Williamson. The mean magnetic declination in 1900 was 45'. The mean annual rainfall is 50 to 60 inches, and the mean annual temperature 50° to 55°. The county is traversed by the Norfolk and Western Railway.

Mingo; post village in Randolph County.

Mingo; run, a small left-hand tributary to Valley River in Randolph County.

Mingo; run, a right-hand branch of Buffalo Creek in Brooke County.

Mingo Knob; summit in Randolph County.

Mink; post village in Kanawha County.

Minkshoal; branch, a small right-hand tributary to Elk River, a branch of Kanawha River, in Kanawha County.

Minnie; post village in Wetzel County.

Minnora; post village in Calhoun County.

Minverton; post village in Fayette County.

Mipp; post village in Wirt County.

Miracle; run, a right-hand branch of Dunkard Creek in Monongalia County.

Miracle Run; post village in Monongalia County.

Missouri; creek, a small left-hand tributary to Laurel Creek in Webster County.

Missouri; creek, a very small right-hand branch of Right Fork of Twelvepole Creek, a tributary to Ohio River, in Wayne County.

Missouri; fork, a small left-hand branch of Hewett Creek, a tributary to Little Coal River, in Boone and Logan counties.

Mitchell; branch, a very small right-hand tributary to Tug Fork of Big Sandy River in McDowell County.

Mitchell; post village in Pendleton County on the Ohio Central Lines.

Mitchell; run, a small right-hand tributary to Back Fork of Elk River in Randolph County.

Mitchell Lick; fork, a right-hand branch of Left Fork of Middle Fork of Tygarts Valley River in Randolph County.
Mitchell Ridge; mountains in Raleigh County.
Mitten Ridge; short range of mountains in Webster County. Altitude, 3,000 feet.
Mobley; post village in Wetzel County.
Moccasin; branch, a very small left-hand tributary to Guyandot River in Wyoming County.
Mod; branch, a very small left-hand tributary to Tug Fork of Big Sandy River in McDowell County.
Mod; run, a left-hand branch of Buffalo Creek in Marion County.
Modoc; post village in Greenbrier County.
Moffett Knob; summit in Pocahontas County. Altitude, 4,210 feet.
Mohr; post village in Wetzel County.
Molehill; post village in Ritchie County.
Molers; village in Jefferson County.
Moll Kelly; branch, a small left-hand tributary to Peachtree Creek, a branch of Marsh Fork of Coal River, in Raleigh County.
Molly Kincaid; branch, a very small left-hand branch of Loop Creek, a tributary to Kanawha River, in Fayette County.
Mona; post village in Monongalia County.
Monarch; post village in Kanawha County on the Ohio Central lines.
Money; run, a right-hand branch of Fishing Creek in Wetzel County.
Monitor; post village in Monroe County.
Monongah; town in Marion County on the Baltimore and Ohio Railroad. Population, 1,786.
Monongahela; river, the southernmost of the two main forks of Ohio River, the other being the Allegheny, which rises in southwestern New York. It heads in Lewis, Upshur, and Randolph counties in several large branches, West Fork, Tygart Valley, and Cheat rivers, while to the eastward heads the Youghiogheny, which flows into it near its mouth. It joins the Allegheny at Pittsburg, forming the Ohio. Length, about 190 miles; drainage area, 7,625 square miles; navigable to Morgantown.
Monongalia; county, situated in the Allegheny Plateau. It is drained by tributaries of the Monongahela. Area, 368 square miles. Population, 19,049—white, 18,747; negro, 299; foreign born, 301. County seat, Morgantown. The mean magnetic declination in 1900 was 3° 15′. The mean annual rainfall is 40 to 50 inches, and the mean annual temperature 50° to 55°. The county is traversed by the Baltimore and Ohio Railroad.
Monroe; county, situated in the southeastern part of the State. It is diversified by parallel ridges and valleys trending northeast and southwest. The western part is a plateau but little dissected and bearing numerous hills upon its surface. It is drained by tributaries of Greenbrier and New rivers. Area, 464 square miles. Population, 13,130—white, 12,300; negro, 830; foreign born, 32. County seat, Union. The mean magnetic declination in 1900 was 1° 55′. The mean annual rainfall is 50 to 60 inches, and the mean annual temperature 50° to 55°.
Monroe; post village in Randolph County.
Monroe Draft; small left-hand tributary to Howards Creek, a branch of Greenbrier River, in Greenbrier County.
Montana Mines; post village in Marion County.
Montcalm; post village in Mercer County.
Monterville; post village in Randolph County.
Montgomery; town in Fayette County on the Chesapeake and Ohio Railway and on Kanawha River. Altitude, 634 feet. Population, 1,594.

Montrose; post village in Randolph County on the West Virginia Central and Pittsburg Railway.

Moore; fork, a very small left-hand branch of Elk Creek, a tributary to Guyandot River, in Logan County.

Moore; post village in Tucker County on the West Virginia Central and Pittsburg Railway.

Moore; run, a left-hand branch of Indian Fork in Gilmer County.

Moore; run, a small left-hand tributary to Greenbrier River in Pocahontas County.

Moore Camp; branch, a small right-hand tributary to Spice Creek, a branch of Tug Fork of Big Sandy River, in McDowell County.

Moorefield; county seat of Hardy County. Population, 460.

Moorefield; river, a right-hand head branch of South Branch of the Potomac in Hardy County.

Moores; run, a left-hand branch of Rocky Fork of Ellis Creek in Gilmer County.

Mooresville; post village in Monongalia County.

Morford; post village in Roane County.

Morgan; branch, a very small right-hand tributary to Drawdy Creek, a branch of Coal River, in Boone County.

Morgan; county, situated in the northeastern part of the State, limited on the north by Potomac River. The surface consists of broad valleys alternating with narrow ridges of no great height. Area, 235 square miles. Population, 7,294—white, 7,074; negro, 220; foreign born, 68. County seat, Berkeley Springs. The mean magnetic declination in 1900 was 4°. The mean annual rainfall is 40 to 50 inches, and the mean annual temperature 45° to 50°. The county is traversed by the Baltimore and Ohio Railroad.

Morgan; run, a small left-hand tributary to Cheat River in Preston County.

Morgan Ridge; mountains in Mercer County.

Morgans Glade; post village in Preston County.

Morgansville; post village in Doddridge County on the Baltimore and Ohio Railroad.

Morgantown; county seat of Monongalia County on the Baltimore and Ohio and the Morgantown and Kingwood railroads. Population, 1,895. Altitude, 963 feet.

Morley; post village in Braxton County.

Morocco; post village in Clay County.

Morris; creek, a small left-hand tributary to Cranberry River, a branch of Gauley River, in Nicholas County.

Morris; creek, a very small left-hand tributary to Elk River in Kanawha County.

Morris; fork, a left-hand branch of Blue Creek, a tributary to Elk River, in Kanawha County.

Morris; post village in Wirt County.

Morris; run, a left-hand branch of Miller Fork of Rock Run in Wetzel County.

Morrison; fork, a very small left-hand branch of Fourmile Creek, a tributary to Guyandot River, in Lincoln County.

Morrison; fork, a left-hand branch of Little Hurricane Creek, a tributary to Kanawha River, in Putnam County.

Mosby; branch, a very small right-hand tributary to Big Cub Creek, a branch of Guyandot River, in Wyoming County.

Moscow; post village in Hancock County on the Pittsburg, Cincinnati, Chicago and St. Louis Railroad.

Moser Knob; summit in Pendleton County.

Moses; creek, a very small left-hand branch of Right Fork of Twelvepole Creek, a branch of Ohio River, in Wayne County.

Moses; run, a right-hand branch of Long Drain in Wetzel County.

Mossy; creek, a small right-hand tributary to Paint Creek, a branch of Kanawha River, in Fayette County.

GAZETTEER OF WEST VIRGINIA. 107

Mossy; post village in Fayette County.
Mound; post village in Kanawha County.
Moundsville; county seat of Marshall County on the Baltimore and Ohio Railroad. Population, 5,362. Altitude, 640 feet.
Mountain; creek, a small left-hand tributary to Bluestone River, a branch of New River, in Mercer County.
Mountain; fork, a small indirect right-hand tributary to Dry Fork, a branch of Tug Fork of Big Sandy River, in McDowell County.
Mountain; run, a right-hand branch of Sleepy Creek in Morgan County.
Mountain Cove; post village in Fayette County.
Mountain Lick; small left-hand tributary to Williams River in Pocahontas County.
Mount Carbon; post village in Fayette County on Kanawha River and on the Chesapeake and Ohio and the Powellton and Pocahontas railways. Altitude, 639 feet.
Mount Clare; post village in Harrison County on the West Virginia Central and Pittsburg Railway. Altitude, 1,001 feet.
Mount Desert; summit in Kanawha County.
Mount Harmony; village in Marion County.
Mount Hope; town in Fayette County on Dunloup Creek, a tributary to New River. Population, 351.
Mount Lookout; post village in Nicholas County. Altitude, 2,017 feet.
Mount Nebo; post village in Nicholas County.
Mount of Seneca; post village in Pendleton County.
Mount Olive; post village in Mason County.
Mount Storm; post village in Grant County.
Mount Tell; post village in Jackson County.
Mount Zion; post village in Calhoun County.
Mouse; creek, a small left-hand branch of Hominy Creek, a tributary to Gauley River, in Nicholas County.
Moyer; gap between Sandy Ridge and Jack Mountains, caused by a small right-hand branch of South Branch of the Potomac, in Pendleton County.
Moyer; run, a small left-hand tributary to South Branch of the Potomac, in Pendleton County.
Mozelle; post village in Jackson County.
Mud; fork, a small left-hand tributary to Turtle Creek, a branch of Little Coal River, in Boone County.
Mud; fork, a small left-hand tributary to Guyandot River, a branch of Ohio River, in Logan County.
Mud; post village in Lincoln County.
Muddlety; creek, a right-hand branch of Gauley River, in Nicholas County.
Muddlety; post village in Nicholas County.
Muddy; creek, a right-hand tributary to Greenbrier River, in Greenbrier County.
Muddy; run, a small left-hand tributary to Cheat River, in Preston County.
Muddy Cove; branch, a very small right-hand tributary to Big Huff Creek, a branch of Guyandot River, in Logan County.
Muddy Creek; mountain, a ridge in Greenbrier County. Altitude, 2,000 to 2,500 feet.
Mud Hole; branch, a small right-hand tributary to Clear Fork, a branch of Tug Fork of Big Sandy River, in McDowell County.
Mud Lick; a small left-hand branch of Morris Fork of Blue Creek, a tributary to Elk River, in Kanawha County.
Mud Lick; a small right-hand tributary to Little Kanawha River, in Gilmer County.
Mudlick; branch, a small right-hand tributary to Buffalo Creek, a branch of Guyandot River, in Logan County.
Mudlick; branch, a very small right-hand tributary to Gilbert Creek, a branch of Guyandot River, in Mingo County.

Mud Lick; fork, a small left-hand branch of Leatherwood Creek, a tributary to Elk River, in Kanawha County.

Mudlick; fork, a small left-hand tributary to Laural Creek, a branch of Coal River, in Boone County.

Mud Lick; fork, a small right-hand tributary to Blake Branch of Smithers Creek, a tributary to Kanawha River, in Fayette County.

Mudlick; run, a left-hand branch of Carney Fork of Rock Run, in Wetzel County.

Mudlick; run, a left-hand branch of Pritchett Creek, in Marion County.

Mud Lick; run, a small left-hand tributary to South Branch of the Potomac, in Hardy County.

Mulberry; fork, a left-hand branch of Jenkins Fork of Loop Creek, a tributary to Kanawha River, in Fayette County.

Mulberry; fork, a small right-hand tributary to Left Fork of Middle Fork of Tygart Valley River, in Randolph County.

Mullin; branch, a very small left-hand tributary to Winding Gap, a branch of Guyandot River, in Raleigh County.

Mulvane; post village in Fayette County.

Munday; post village in Wirt County.

Mundy Lick; small left-hand tributary to Greenbrier River, in Pocahontas County.

Mundy Lick Ridge; short mountainous range between Greenbrier River and Buckley Mountain, in Pocahontas County.

Munson; post village in Morgan County.

Murphytown; post village in Wood County.

Murraysville; post village in Jackson County, on the Baltimore and Ohio Railroad.

Muses Bottom; post village in Jackson County.

Musick; post village in Mingo County.

Mutton Run; post village in Hampshire County.

Muzzle; fork, a small left-hand branch of Little Huff Creek, a tributary to Guyandot River, in Wyoming County.

Myerstown; village in Jefferson County.

Myra; post village in Lincoln County.

Myrtle; post village in Mingo County.

Nancy; fork, a small right-hand tributary to Indian Creek, a branch of Guyandot River, in Wyoming County.

Napier; post village in Braxton County.

Napier Ridge; range of hills in Wayne County. Altitude, about 1,200 feet.

Narrow; branch, a very small right-hand tributary to Elk River, a branch of Kanawha River, in Kanawha County.

Nat; post village in Mason County.

Naul; creek, a right-hand branch of Little Kanawha River, in Braxton County.

Neal; branch, a small right-hand branch of Twentymile Creek, a tributary to Gauley River, in Nicholas County.

Nease; post village in Mason County.

Ned; branch, a very small left-hand tributary to Guyandot River, a branch of Ohio River, in Mingo County.

Needmore; post village in Hardy County.

Neel; village in Marion County.

Nelson; branch, a very small right-hand tributary to Little Huff Creek, a branch of Guyandot River, in Wyoming County.

Neponset; post village in Summers County.

Neptune; post village in Jackson County.

Nesselroad; post village in Jackson County.

Nestlow; post village in Wayne County.
Nestorville; post village in Barbour County.
Nettly; mountain, a short ridge west of Valley River, in Randolph County.
New; creek, a left-hand tributary to North Fork of Potomac River, in Grant County.
New; creek, a right-hand tributary to North Branch of Potomac River, in Grant and Mineral counties.
New; post village in Raleigh County.
New; river, a large branch of the Kanawha River, rising in Watauga County, N. C., and flowing in a peculiar course first north and thence westward to its junction with the Gauley River, where they form the Kanawha, in Fayette County, W. Va.
Newark; post village in Wirt County on the Little Kanawha Railroad.
Newberne; post village in Gilmer County.
Newburg; town in Preston County on the Baltimore and Ohio Railroad. Population, 751. Altitude, 755 feet.
Newcomb; creek, a very small left-hand branch of Twelvepole Creek, a tributary to Ohio River, in Wayne County.
Newcomb; creek, a small right-hand branch of East Fork of Twelvepole Creek, a tributary to Ohio River, in Wayne County.
New Creek; mountain, a broken, mountainous country in Grant and Mineral counties. Altitude, 2,000 to 2,500 feet.
Newcreek; post village in Mineral County.
New Cumberland; county seat of Hancock County on the Pittsburg, Cincinnati, Chicago and St. Louis Railroad. Population, 2,198.
Newdale; post village in Wetzel County.
New England; post village in Wood County.
Newfound; post village in Wyoming County.
Newhaven; post village in Mason County, on the Baltimore and Ohio Railroad.
New Hope; post village in Mercer County.
Newhouse; branch, a small right-hand tributary to Elk River, a branch of Kanawha River, in Kanawha County.
Newlands; run, a right-hand tributary of Short Creek, in Brooke County.
Newlandsville; post village in Pleasants County.
Newlonton; post village in Upshur County.
New Martinsville; county seat of Wetzel County. Population, 1,089.
New Milton; post village in Doddridge County.
Newport; post village in Wood County.
New Richmond; post village in Summers County, on the Chesapeake and Ohio Railway. Altitude, 1,289 feet.
Newson; branch, a small left-hand tributary to Spice Creek, a branch of Tug Fork of Big Sandy River, in McDowell County.
Newton; post village in Roane County, on the West Virginia Central and Pittsburg Railway. Altitude, 1,917 feet.
Newville; post village in Braxton County.
Next; post village in Tyler County.
Nicholas; county, situated in the central part of the State, on the Allegheny Plateau. It is drained by Gauley River and its tributaries. Area, 691 square miles. Population, 11,403—white, 11,384; negro, 19; foreign born, 245. County seat, Summersville. The mean magnetic declination in 1900 was 2°. The mean annual rainfall is 50 to 60 inches, and the mean annual temperature 50° to 55°.
Nickells Knob; summit in Greenbrier County. Altitude, 2,725 feet.
Nickells Mills; post village in Monroe County.
Nicklow; post village in Barbour County.
Nicolette; post village in Wood County on the Baltimore and Ohio Railroad.

Nigger; branch, a small right-hand tributary to Clear Fork, a branch of Tug Fork of Big Sandy River, in McDowell County.

Nigger Camp; run, a small right-hand branch of Old Lick Creek, a tributary to Holly River, in Webster County.

Nina; post village in Doddridge County.

Ninemile; creek, a small left-hand tributary to Ohio River in Cabell County.

Ninemile; creek, a small right-hand tributary to Guyandot River, a branch of Ohio River, in Lincoln County.

Ninemile; fork, a small left-hand branch of Campbell Creek, a tributary to Kanawha River, in Kanawha County.

Nixon; post village in Upshur County.

Nobe; post village in Calhoun County.

Nolan; post village in Mingo County.

Norman; run, a small left-hand tributary to Holly River in Webster County.

Normantown; post village in Gilmer County.

North; branch, a small right-hand tributary to Big Creek, a branch of Guyandot River, in Logan County.

North; river, a large left-hand branch of Great Cacapon River, rising in South Branch Mountain, in Hardy County.

North Fork; mountains in the eastern part of the State, lying between North and South forks of the Potomac, in Pendleton and Grant counties. Altitude, 2,000 to 4,000 feet.

North Fork; post village in McDowell County on the Norfolk and Western Railway and on Elkhorn Creek.

North Mill; creek, a right-hand tributary to South Branch of the Potomac, in Grant and Pendleton counties, known in its upper course as Brushy Run.

North Mountain; post village in Berkeley County on the Baltimore and Ohio Railroad. Altitude, 547 feet.

Northriver Mills; post village in Hampshire County.

Northspring; post village in Wyoming County.

Norwood; post village in McDowell County on Elkhorn Creek and on the Norfolk and Western Railway.

Noseman; branch, a very small right-hand tributary to Cooney Otter Creek, an indirect left-hand tributary to Guyandot River, in Wyoming County.

Notchlog; fork, a small left-hand tributary to Dry Branch of Cabin Creek, a tributary to Kanawha River, in Kanawha County.

Numan; post village in Doddridge County.

Nunly; mountain, a short ridge in Greenbrier County.

Nuttallburg; post village in Fayette County on New River and on the Chesapeake and Ohio Railway. Altitude, 944 feet.

Nutter; run, a small left-hand tributary to Little Kanawha River in Gilmer County.

Nutterfarm; post village in Ritchie County.

Nutterville; post village in Greenbrier County.

Nye; post village in Putnam County.

Oak; branch, a very small left-hand tributary to Long Pole Creek, a branch of Tug Fork of Big Sandy River, in McDowell County.

Oak; post village in Wood County.

Oakflat; post village in Pendleton County.

Oakgrove; post village in Mercer County.

Oakland; post village in Morgan County.

Oakvale; post village in Mercer County on the Norfolk and Western Railway. Altitude, 1,705 feet.

Oakville; post village in Roane County on the Norfolk and Western Railway.

O'Brien; creek, a small right-hand tributary to Elk River in Clay County.

O'Brien; fork, a left-hand branch of Salt Lick Fork of Little Kanawha River in Braxton County.
O'Brien; fork, a right-hand branch of Right Fork of Steer Creek in Gilmer and Braxton counties.
Oceana; county seat of Wyoming County. Population, 187.
Odaville; post village in Jackson County.
Odd; post village in Raleigh County.
Odell; post village in Kanawha County on the Clendennin and Spencer Railway.
Odessa; post village in Clay County on Porters Creek and Gauley Railway.
Ogdin; post village in Wood County.
Ohio; county, situated in the Panhandle, bordering on Ohio River. Area, 111 square miles. Population, 48,024—white, 46,765; negro, 1,251; foreign born, 6,140. County seat, Wheeling. The mean magnetic declination in 1900 was 1°. The mean annual rainfall is 40 to 50 inches, and the mean annual temperature 50° to 55°. The county is traversed by the Wheeling and Lake Erie, the Wheeling Terminal, the Baltimore and Ohio, the Cleveland, Lorain and Wheeling, the Ohio River, the Pittsburg, Cincinnati, Charleston and St. Louis, and the Wheeling and Elm Grove railroads.
Ohio; river, formed by the Allegheny and Monongahela rivers, which unite at Pittsburg, in Pennsylvania, where it is a navigable stream about 600 yards wide. It runs first northwestward to Beaver, and, after it has crossed the western boundary of Pennsylvania, flows southward to Wheeling. Below this point it forms the boundary between Ohio and West Virginia, and runs southwestward to the mouth of the Sandy River. It next forms the boundary between Kentucky and Ohio, and pursues a west-northwestward course to Cincinnati. After it strikes the eastern border of Indiana, it runs nearly southwestward with a very sinuous course and forms the boundary between Indiana and Illinois on the right and Kentucky on the left, until it enters the Mississippi at Cairo, in latitude 37° N., and about 1,200 miles from the mouth of the Great River. Drainage area, 201,720 square miles. Length, 963 miles. It is navigable throughout.
Oil; creek, a right-hand branch of Little Kanawha River in Braxton and Lewis counties.
Oilville; post village in Logan County.
Oka; post village in Calhoun County.
Okeeffe; post village in Mingo County.
Okonoko; post village in Hampshire County on the Baltimore and Ohio Railroad.
Old Camp; branch, a very small right-hand tributary to Pond Fork of Little Coal River in Boone County.
Old Field; fork, a left-hand head fork of Elk River in Pocahontas County.
Old Field; fork, a right-hand branch of Sand Fork in Lewis County.
Old Field; mountain, a short ridge in Greenbrier County. One of the peaks has an altitude of 4,244 feet.
Old Field Ridge; short spur between Black Run of North Fork of Greenbrier and North Fork of Pocahontas County.
Oldfields; post village in Hardy County. Altitude, 800 feet.
Old House; branch, a very small right-hand tributary to Pond Fork of Little Coal River in Boone County.
Old House; branch, a very small right-hand tributary to Spruce Fork of Little Coal River, in Logan County.
Old Lick; creek, a head fork of Left Fork of Holly River in Webster County.
Old Man; run, a small right-hand tributary to Cacapon River in Hampshire County.
Old Perryville; village, in McDowell County, located on Dry Fork, a tributary to Tug Fork of Big Sandy River.

Old Shop; branch, a very small right-hand tributary to Winding Gap, a branch of Guyandot River, in Raleigh County.

Old Slab; fork, a small right-hand branch of Slab Fork, a tributary to Guyandot River, in Wyoming County.

Oldtown; village in Mason County.

Old Woman; run, a very small right-hand tributary to Elk River in Braxton County.

Oley; post village in Raleigh County.

Olive; post village in Harrison County.

Olympia; post village in Wirt County.

Omps; post village in Morgan County.

Ona; post village in Cabell County on the Chesapeake and Ohio Railway. Altitude, 623 feet.

One; fork, a small indirect tributary to Buffalo Creek, a branch of Elk River, in Clay County.

Onego; post village in Pendleton County.

O'Neills Knob; summit in Greenbrier County.

Onemile; creek, a very small left-hand branch of East Fork of Twelvepole Creek, a tributary to Ohio River, in Wayne County.

Onemile; creek, a very small right-hand branch of Fourmile Creek, a tributary to Guyandot River, in Lincoln County.

Onemile; fork, a very small right-hand branch of Blue Creek, a tributary to Elk River, in Kanawha County.

Onoto; post village in Pocahontas County.

Oors; run, a right-hand tributary of Middle Wheeling Creek in Ohio County.

Oozley; branch, a small left-hand tributary to Dry Fork, a branch of Tug Fork of Big Sandy River, in McDowell County.

Opekiska; post village in Monongalia County on the Baltimore and Ohio Railroad.

Open; fork, a right-hand branch of Bell Creek, a tributary to Gauley River, in Nicholas and Clay counties.

Open; fork, a small right-hand tributary to Loop Creek, a branch of Kanawha River, in Fayette County.

Openmouth; branch, a very small left-hand branch of Right Fork of Twelvepole Creek, a tributary to Ohio River, in Logan County.

Ophelia; post village in Nicholas County.

Opossum; creek, a right-hand branch of Mill Creek, a tributary to New River, in Fayette County.

Oral; post village in Harrison County on the Baltimore and Ohio Railroad.

Orange; post village in Boone County.

Orchard; branch, a very small left-hand tributary to Tug Fork of Big Sandy River in McDowell County.

Orchard; branch, a very small left-hand branch of Laurel Creek, a tributary to New River, in Fayette County.

Orchard; branch, a small left-hand branch of Sandlick Fork of Laurel Creek, a tributary to Coal River, in Boone County.

Orchard; post village in Monroe County.

Orem; post village in Wood County.

Organcave; post village in Greenbrier County.

Orient; post village in Calhoun County.

Orleans Crossroads; post village in Morgan County on the Baltimore and Ohio Railroad.

Orlena; post village in Randolph County.

Orpha; post village in Barbour County.

Orr; post village in Preston County.

Osborne; creek, a right-hand branch of Mill Creek, a tributary to New River, in Fayette County.
Osbornes Mills; post village in Roane County.
Osceola; post village in Randolph County.
Osgood; post village in Monongalia County.
Otia; post village in Mason County.
Otter; branch, a very small left-hand branch of Blue Creek, a tributary to Elk River, in Kanawha County.
Otter; creek, a small right-hand tributary to Meadow River, in Greenbrier County.
Otter; creek, a small right-hand branch of Peters Creek, a tributary to Gauley River, in Nicholas County.
Otter; creek, a left-hand branch of Tygart Valley River in Taylor County.
Otter; fork, one of the head forks of Left Fork of Steer Creek in Braxton County.
Otter; fork, a left-hand tributary to Dry Fork of Cheat River in Tucker and Randolph counties.
Otter; fork, a very small right-hand branch of Laurel Fork, a tributary to Clear Fork of Guyandot River, in Wyoming County.
Otter; run, a right-hand branch of Pritchett Creek in Marion County.
Otto; post village in Roane County.
Overfield; post village in Barbour County.
Overhill; post village in Upshur County.
Owen; run, a small right-hand tributary to Left Fork of Steer Creek in Gilmer County.
Oxbow; post village in Ritchie County.
Oxford; post village in Doddridge County.
Pack; branch, a very small left-hand branch of Smithers Creek, a tributary to Kanawha River, in Fayette County.
Pack; branch, a small right-hand tributary to Paint Creek, a branch of Kanawha River, in Fayette County.
Pack; fork, a small left-hand branch of Rockhouse Fork of Dingus Run, a tributary to Guyandot River, in Logan County.
Packs Ferry; post village in Summers County.
Pad; fork, a small left-hand branch of Little Huff Creek, a tributary to Guyandot River, in Wyoming County.
Pad; post village in Roane County.
Padds; run, a left-hand branch of Lost Run in Taylor County.
Paddy; branch, a very small right-hand tributary to Kanawha River in Fayette County.
Paddy; branch, a right-hand branch of Trace Fork in Cabell County.
Paddy; mountain, a short ridge in Frederick and Shenandoah counties. Altitude, 2,500 to 3,000 feet.
Paddy; run, a small left-hand branch of Cedar Creek in Gilmer County.
Paddys; run, a right-hand branch of Saltlick Creek in Braxton County.
Paddy Knob; summit in Braxton County.
Padenvalley; post village in Wetzel County on the Baltimore and Ohio Railroad.
Page; post village in Putnam County.
Paint; branch, a right-hand tributary to Cabin Creek, a branch of Kanawha River, in Kanawha County.
Paint; creek, a left-hand branch of Kanawha River in Kanawha, Fayette, and Raleigh counties.
Paint; creek, a large right-hand tributary to Kanawha River in Kanawha, Fayette, and Raleigh counties.
Paint; mountain on boundary line between Fayette and Raleigh counties.

Paintcreek; post village in Kanawha County on the Chesapeake and Ohio Railway. Altitude, 622 feet.

Palace Ridge; summit in the northern part of Randolph County.

Palace Valley; post village in Upshur County.

Palmer; post village in Braxton County on the Holly River and Addison Railway.

Palser; run, a small right-hand branch of Steer Run in Gilmer County.

Pansy; post village in Grant County.

Panther; branch, a very small left-hand tributary to Clear Fork of Coal River in Raleigh County.

Panther; branch, a small right-hand branch of Blue Creek, a tributary to Elk River, in Kanawha County.

Panther; creek, a small left-hand tributary to Gauley River in Nicholas County.

Panther; creek, a small left-hand tributary to Mud River, a branch of Guyandot River, in Lincoln County.

Panther; creek, a left-hand branch of Tug Fork of Big Sandy River in McDowell County.

Panther; creek, a small right-hand tributary to Buckhannon River in Upshur County.

Panther; post village in McDowell County on the Norfolk and Western Railway.

Panther; run, a small right-hand tributary to Left Fork of Middle Fork of Tygarts Valley River in Randolph County.

Panther; run, a small right-hand tributary to Little Kanawha River in Upshur County.

Panther Camp; fork, a small left-hand branch of Spring Creek, a tributary to Greenbrier River, in Greenbrier County.

Panther Knob; summit in Summers County.

Panther Knob; summit in Wyoming County.

Panther Knob; summit in Pendleton County.

Panther Lick; run, a small left-hand tributary to Elk River in Webster County.

Panther Lick; very small right-hand tributary to Mud River, a branch of Guyandot River, in Cabell County.

Paola; post village in Doddridge County.

Paradise; post village in Putnam County.

Parchment Valley; post village in Jackson County on the Baltimore and Ohio Railroad.

Park; gap in Fork Mountains caused by Beach Lick Run, a short branch of South Fork of Cherry River, in Greenbrier County.

Parker; creek, a small left-hand branch of Kiah Fork, a tributary to Twelvepole Creek, in Wayne County.

Parkers; post village in Doddridge County.

Parkersburg; county seat of Wood County on the Baltimore and Ohio, the Baltimore and Ohio Southwestern, and the Little Kanawha railroads. Altitude, 616 feet. Population, 11,703.

Parrish; post village in Pleasants County.

Parsner; creek, a small right-hand tributary to Mud River, a branch of Guyandot River, in Lincoln County.

Parsons; county seat of Tucker County on the West Virginia Central and Pittsburg Railway.

Pasco; post village in Roane County.

Pasture; branch, a very small left-hand tributary to Beech Fork of Twelvepole Creek, a branch of Ohio River, in Wayne County.

Patrick; creek, a small left-hand branch of West Fork of Twelvepole Creek, a tributary to Ohio River, in Wayne County.

Patrick; peak, a knob of Wolf Creek Mountain in Monroe County.

GAZETTEER OF WEST VIRGINIA. 115

Patrick; post village in Kanawha County.
Patsey; post village in Roane County.
Patters; run, a left-hand branch of Big Creek in Lincoln County.
Patterson; creek, right-hand branch of North Branch of Potomac River in Grant and Mineral counties.
Patterson Creek; mountain, a narrow ridge along the boundary line of Grant and Hardy counties. Altitude, 2,000 to 2,500 feet.
Pattersons Depot; post village in Mineral County.
Patton; knob in Taylor County.
Patton; post village in Monroe County.
Paw Paw; creek, a small left-hand branch of Monongahela River in Monongalia County.
Pawpaw; town in Morgan County on the Baltimore and Ohio Railroad. Population, 693.
Payne Knob; summit in Fayette County. Altitude, 2,804 feet.
Payne Knob, summit in Webster County. Altitude, 3,126 feet.
Paynes; branch, a small left-hand tributary to Five Mile Creek, a branch of East River, in Mercer County.
Peabody; post village in Wetzel County.
Peach; creek, a small right-hand branch of Guyandot River, a tributary to Ohio River, in Logan County.
Peachtree; branch, a small right-hand tributary to Twentymile Creek, a branch of Gauley River, in Nicholas County.
Peachtree; creek, a left-hand branch of Marsh Fork of Coal River in Raleigh County.
Peachtree; post village in Raleigh County.
Peach Tree; run, a right-hand tributary to Steer Run in Gilmer County.
Peak Ridge; mountains in Wyoming County.
Pear; post village in Raleigh County.
Pearl; mountain ridge in bend of Tilhance Creek in Berkeley County.
Pearl; post village in Nicholas County.
Pearson; branch, a small right-hand branch of Muddlety Creek, a tributary to Gauley River, in Nicholas County.
Peck; post village in Logan County. Altitude, 653 feet.
Pecksrun; post village in Upshur County.
Peddler; run, a right-hand branch of Simpson Run in Taylor County.
Pedee; fork, a small left-hand tributary to Rock Creek, a branch of Little Coal River, in Boone County.
Pedlar; post village in Monongalia County.
Peeled Chestnut; gap in Big Stone Ridge on boundary between McDowell and Mercer counties.
Peel Tree; post village in Barbour County.
Peery Camp; branch, a small right-hand tributary to Clear Fork, a branch of Tug Fork of Big Sandy River, in McDowell County.
Peeryville; post village in McDowell County located on Dry Fork, a large left-hand tributary to Tug Fork of Big Sandy River.
Peet; post village in Randolph County.
Peewee; post village in Wirt County.
Pemberton; post village in Raleigh County.
Penbro; post village in Webster County.
Pence Springs; post village in Summers County on the Chesapeake and Ohio Railway.
Pendleton; county, situated in the eastern part of the State, against the boundary of Virginia. Its surface is mountainous, consisting of alternations of valleys and

ridges. It is drained northward by tributaries to the Potomac River. Area, 707 square miles. Population, 9,167—white, 9,044; negro, 123; foreign born, 6. County seat, Franklin. The mean magnetic declination in 1900 was 2°. The mean annual rainfall is 50 to 60 inches, and the mean annual temperature 45° to 50°. The county is traversed by the Ohio River Railroad.

Penfield; branch, a very small left-hand tributary to New River in Fayette County.
Peniel; post village in Roane County.
Pennsboro; town in Ritchie County on the Baltimore and Ohio Railroad. Population, 738.
Penrith; village in Hancock County.
Pentress; post village in Monongalia County.
Peora; village in Harrison County.
Pepper; post village in Barbour County.
Perkins; fork, a head fork of Cedar Creek in Braxton County.
Perry; branch, a small left-hand tributary to Buffalo Creek, a branch of Elk River, in Clay and Nicholas counties.
Perry; post village in Hardy County.
Perry Ridge; short spur north of Cranberry River in Nicholas County.
Persinger; post village in Nicholas County.
Persinger; run, a small right-hand tributary to Gauley River in Nicholas County.
Peru; post village in Hardy County.
Peter; run, a small left-hand tributary to South Branch of Potomac River in Pendleton County.
Peter Cove; creek, a small left-hand branch of East Fork of Twelvepole Creek, a tributary to Ohio River, in Wayne County.
Peter Johnson; run, a right-hand branch of Pritchet Creek in Marion County.
Peters; creek, a right-hand branch of Gauley River in Nicholas County.
Peters; creek, a right-hand branch of Little Wheeling Creek in Ohio County.
Peters; gap in Great Flat Top Mountain in Mercer County.
Peters; mountain, a long, narrow ridge in Monroe County, W. Va., and Alleghany County, Va.
Peters; mountain, a ridge in Monroe County.
Peters; mountain, a short ridge between North Fork and Moore Run, branches of Greenbrier River, in Pocahontas County.
Petersburg; post village and county seat of Grant County on South Branch of Potomac River.
Peters Cave; fork, a left-hand branch of Horse Creek, a tributary to Little Coal River, in Lincoln County.
Peters Creek; fork, a small left-hand branch of Hardway Branch of Twentymile Creek, a tributary to Gauley River, in Nicholas County.
Peterstown; town in Monroe County, situated on Rich Creek. Altitude, 1,745 feet. Population, 167.
Petes; fork, a very small right-hand branch of Falling Rock Creek, a tributary to Elk River, in Kanawha and Clay counties.
Petroleum; post village in Ritchie County on the Baltimore and Ohio Railroad. Altitude, 697 feet.
Pettit; post village in Randolph County.
Pewee; knob in Taylor County.
Peytona; post village in Boone County.
Pharoah; post village in Wayne County.
Phillip Camp; fork, a small tributary to Left Fork of Buckhannon River in Randolph County.
Philippi; county seat of Barbour County on the Baltimore and Ohio Railroad. Altitude, 1,192 feet. Population, 665.

Phillips; branch, a very small right-hand branch of Tug Fork of Chattarawha River, a tributary to Ohio River, in Logan County.
Phillips; run, a small left-hand tributary to Muddlety Creek, a branch of Gauley River, in Nicholas County.
Philoah; post village in Putnam County.
Pickaway; post village in Monroe County.
Pickens; post village in Randolph County on the Baltimore and Ohio Railroad.
Pickle; mountain, a short ridge west of the South Branch of the Potomac in Pendleton County. Altitude, 2,500 to 3,000 feet.
Pickles; fork, a small right-hand tributary to Salt Lick Fork of Little Kanawha River in Braxton County.
Piedmont; town in Mineral County on the Baltimore and Ohio and on the Cumberland and Pennsylvania railroads. Altitude, 933 feet. Population, 2,115.
Piercy; post village in Jackson County.
Pigeon; creek, a right-hand branch of Tug Fork of Big Sandy River, a tributary to Ohio River, in Logan County.
Pigeon; creek, a very small right-hand tributary to Guyandot River in Wyoming County.
Pigeon; fork, a left-hand branch of Naul Creek in Braxton County.
Pigeon; post village in Roane County.
Pigeon; run, a right-hand branch of left fork of Steer Creek in Gilmer County.
Pigeon; run, a right-hand branch of Stony Creek, tributary to Greenbrier River, in Pocahontas County.
Pigeon; station in Logan County on the Norfolk and Western Railway and at junction of Pigeon Creek with Tug Fork of Big Sandy River. Altitude, 1,299 feet.
Pigeon Knob; summit in Lincoln County. Altitude, 1,354 feet.
Pigeon Roost; a summit in Wayne County. Altitude, 1,105 feet.
Pigeon Roost; branch, a small right-hand tributary to Spruce Fork of Little Coal River in Logan County.
Pigeon Roost; creek, a left-hand branch of Big Ugly Creek, a tributary to Guyandot River in Lincoln County.
Pigeon Roost; fork, a small left-hand branch of Lower Sleith Fork in Braxton County.
Pigeon Roost; fork, a small left-hand branch of Right Fork of Stone Coal Creek in Upshur County.
Pigeon Roost; fork, a small, indirect left-hand tributary to Blue Creek, a branch of Elk River, in Kanawha County.
Pigeon Roost; fork, a right-hand branch of Lick Creek, a tributary to Little Coal River, in Boone County.
Pike; post village in Ritchie County.
Pilot; triangulation station on Great Flat Top Mountain on boundary line between Wyoming and Mercer counties.
Pinch; creek, a small left-hand tributary to Elk River in Kanawha County.
Pinch Gut; creek, a small right-hand tributary to Glade Creek, a branch of New River, in Raleigh County.
Pine; creek, a left-hand tributary to Island Creek, a branch of Guyandot River, in Logan County.
Pine; run, a right-hand branch of Indian Fork in Gilmer County.
Pine; run, a small right-hand tributary to Peter Creek, a branch of Gauley River, in Nicholas County.
Pinebluff; village in Harrison County.
Pine Glade; run, a small right-hand tributary to Gauley River in Webster County.
Pinegrove; post village in Wetzel County on the Baltimore and Ohio Railroad.

Pine Grove; run, a small right-hand tributary to Williams River in Webster County.
Pineville; post village in Wyoming County.
Piney; creek, a left-hand branch of New River in Raleigh County.
Piney; creek, a small right-hand branch of Meadow River, a tributary to Gauley River, in Greenbrier and Nicholas counties.
Piney; fork, a left-hand branch of Fishing Creek in Wetzel County.
Piney; post village in Wetzel County on the Ohio Central Lines. Altitude, 1,120 feet.
Piney; run, a right-hand branch of Pritchett Creek in Marion County.
Piney Mount; triangulation station in Cabell County. Altitude, 1,115 feet.
Piney Swamp; run, a small right-hand tributary to North Branch of Potomac River in Mineral County.
Pink; post village in Calhoun County.
Pinkerton; knob in Third Hill Mountain in Berkeley County. Elevation, 1,700 feet.
Pinnacle; creek, a left-hand branch of Guyandot River in Wyoming County.
Pinnacle; hill in Mercer County.
Pinnacle; triangulation station in Allegheny Front in Mineral County. Altitude, 3,827 feet.
Pinoak; post village in Mercer County.
Pioneer; post village in Marshall County.
Pious; mountain ridge in Morgan County. Elevation, 800 feet.
Piper; fork, a small right-hand tributary to Crooked Fork in Braxton County.
Pipestem; creek, a small left-hand tributary to New River in Summers County.
Pipestem; post village in Summers County.
Pipestem Knob; summit in Mercer County.
Pisgah; mount, a summit in Clay County. Altitude, 1,683 feet.
Pisgah; post village in Preston County.
Pisgah; run, a very small left-hand tributary to Elk River, a branch of Kanawha River, in Clay County.
Pittman; post village in Fayette County.
Plankcabin; creek, a small left-hand branch of Second Creek, a tributary to Greenbrier River, in Monroe County.
Plant; post village in Lewis County.
Plantation; fork, a left-hand tributary to O'Brien Fork in Braxton County.
Plantation; fork, a head fork of Right Fork of Steer Creek in Braxton County.
Pleasant; creek, a left-hand branch of Tygart Valley River in Taylor County.
Pleasant; run, a small left-hand tributary to Left Fork of Middle Fork of Tygart Valley River in Randolph County.
Pleasant; run, a small left-hand tributary to Shavers Fork of Cheat River in Randolph County.
Pleasantdale; post village in Hampshire County.
Pleasanthill; post village in Preston County.
Pleasant Retreat; post village in Clay County.
Pleasantrun; post village in Tucker County.
Pleasants; county, situated in the northwestern part of the State, bordering on the Ohio River. Area, 142 square miles. Population, 9,341—white, 9,335; negro, 6; foreign born, 83. County seat, Saint Marys. The mean magnetic declination in 1900 was 2°. The mean annual rainfall is 40 to 50 inches, and the mean annual temperature 50° to 55°. The county is traversed by the Ohio River Railroad.
Pleasants; post village in Pleasants County.
Pleasant Valley; town and post village in Marshall County. Population, 180.
Pleasantview; post village in Jackson County on the Baltimore and Ohio Railroad.

GAZETTEER OF WEST VIRGINIA. 119

Pliny; post village in Putnam County.
Plum; fork, a right-hand branch of Grove Creek in Clay County.
Plum; post village in Tyler County.
Plum; run, a left-hand branch of Buffalo Creek in Marion County.
Plum; run, a right-hand branch of Tygart Valley River in Taylor County.
Plum Orchard; creek, a small right-hand branch of Paint Creek, a tributary to Kanawha River, in Fayette County.
Plummer; knob in Taylor County. Elevation, 1,500 feet.
Plummer; run, a right-hand branch of Booths Creek in Taylor County.
Pluto; post village in Raleigh County.
Plymah; branch, a right-hand branch of Twelvepole Creek in Wayne County.
Plymouth; post village in Putnam County on the Ohio Central Lines.
Poca; post village in Putnam County on the Ohio Central Lines. Altitude, 573 feet.
Poca; river, a small left-hand tributary to Ohio River rising in Roane County.
Pocahontas; county, situated in the eastern part of the State. Its surface is mountainous, consisting of a broken plateau, deeply dissected. It is drained by Greenbrier River. Area, 858 square miles. Population, 8,572—white, 7,947; negro, 625; foreign born, 345. County seat, Marlington. The mean magnetic declination in 1900 was 2° 5'. The mean annual rainfall is 50 to 60 inches, and the mean annual temperature 45° to 50°.
Pocotaligo; post village in Kanawha County.
Pocotaligo; river, a right-hand branch of Kanawha River in Putnam, Kanawha, and Roane counties.
Pocosin; fork, a small right-hand branch of Rich Creek, a tributary to Bluestone River.
Poindexter; branch, a small left-hand tributary to Hurricane Creek, a branch of Kanawha River, in Putnam County.
Point; mountain, a short ridge in Greenbrier County. Altitude, 3,500 feet.
Point; mountain, a broken, mountainous range in Webster and Randolph counties.
Point; mountain, a short ridge in Greenbrier and Pocahontas counties.
Point; mountain, a short ridge between Back Fork of Elk River and Elk River in Webster County.
Point; run, a left-hand branch of Little Wheeling Creek in Ohio County.
Point Lick; fork, a left-hand branch of Campbell Creek, a tributary to Kanawha River, in Kanawha County.
Point Mountain; run, a small left-hand tributary to Back Fork of Elk River in Webster County.
Point Pleasant; county seat of Mason County on the Baltimore and Ohio and the Ohio Central railroads. Altitude, 563 feet. Population, 1,934.
Points; post village in Hampshire County.
Pointy Knob; summit in Tucker County. Altitude, 4,286 feet.
Polandale; post village in Wood County.
Polard; post village in Tyler County.
Polemic; run, a small left-hand tributary to Little Birch River in Braxton County.
Poley Ridge; short spur west of Greenbrier River in Greenbrier County. Altitude, 2,500 feet.
Pollock; mountain, a summit in Greenbrier County. Altitude, 3,900 feet.
Pompeys Knob; summit in Webster County north of Gauley River.
Pond; fork, a small left-hand branch of Middle Fork of Blue Creek, a tributary to Elk River, in Kanawha County.
Pond; fork, a right-hand head fork of Little Coal River, a branch of Coal River, in Boone County.
Pond Gap; height in Kanawha County.
Pondgap; post village in Kanawha County.

Pond Lick; creek, a small left-hand tributary to Howards Creek, a branch of Greenbrier River, in Greenbrier County.

Pondlick; post village in Mason County on the West Virginia Central and Pittsburg Railway.

Pond Mill; run, a small left-hand tributary to North Fork of Potomac River in Pendleton County.

Pond Range; short ridge in the central part of Pendleton County. Altitude, 2,500 to 3,000 feet.

Pond Trace; branch, a very small left-hand branch of Right Fork of Twelvepole Creek, a tributary to Ohio River, in Logan County.

Pool; post village in Nicholas County.

Poplar; creek, a small left-hand tributary to Birch River, a branch of Elk River, in Nicholas County.

Poplar; fork, a small left-hand tributary to Kanawha River in Putnam County.

Poplar; post village in Webster County on the Baltimore and Ohio Railroad.

Poplar Lick; small left-hand tributary to Left Fork of Steer Creek in Gilmer County.

Poppa; post village in Wayne County.

Porter; post village in Clay County on the Charleston, Clendennin and Sutton and the Porters Creek and Gauley railroads.

Porter Knob; summit in Cabell County. Altitude, 1,252 feet.

Porter Knob; summit in Wayne County. Altitude, 1,407 feet.

Porters; branch, a very small left-hand tributary to Kanawha River in Kanawha County.

Porters; creek, a left-hand tributary to Elk River in Clay County.

Porters Falls; post village in Wetzel County on the Baltimore and Ohio Railroad.

Portersville; post village in Lincoln County.

Porterwood; post village in Tucker County on the West Virginia Central and Pittsburg Railway.

Posey; run, a small right-hand branch of Oil Creek in Braxton County.

Pot; branch, a small left-hand tributary to Trace Fork of Davis Creek, a branch of Kanawha River, in Kanawha County.

Potato; branch, a very small right-hand tributary to Laurel Creek, a branch of Coal River, in Boone County.

Potato; hill, a summit on boundary line between Raleigh and Fayette counties. Altitude, 3,256 feet.

Potato; hill, a summit in Webster County.

Potato Hill; run, a small left-hand tributary to Back Fork of Elk River in Webster County.

Potato Hole Knob; summit in Webster County.

Potomac; river, heading in the northeastern part of the State, in two branches, North and South. North Branch heads near Fairfax Stone and flows northeast, forming a part of the north boundary of the State. After its junction with South Branch, some miles below Cumberland, it continues along the north boundary to Harpers Ferry, the easternmost point of the State.

Potomac; village in Ohio County.

Pound; fork, a very small right-hand branch of Fourmile Creek, a tributary to Guyandot River, in Lincoln County.

Pound Mill; branch, a very small right-hand tributary to Big Huff Creek, a branch of Guyandot River, in Logan County.

Pound Mill; run, a small left-hand tributary to Valley River in Randolph County.

Powell; branch, a small left-hand tributary to Spruce Fork of Little Coal River, a branch of Coal River, in Boone County.

Powell; creek, a small left-hand tributary to Birch River, a branch of Elk River, in Nicholas County.
Powell; fork, a small left-hand tributary to Leatherwood Fork of Elk River in Webster County.
Powell; mountains, a short ridge in Nicholas County. Its highest peak is 2,316 feet.
Powell Knob; summit in Gilmer County. Altitude, 1,460 feet.
Powells; post village in Marion County on the Baltimore and Ohio Railroad.
Powellton; fork, a right-hand branch of Armstrong Creek, a tributary to Kanawha River, in Fayette County.
Powellton; town in Fayette County on the Powellton and Pocahontas Railway and on Powellton Fork of Kanawha River. Population, 503. Altitude, 904 feet.
Powers; post village in Wood County.
Powhatan; post village in McDowell County on the Norfolk and Western Railway and on South Fork of Elkhorn Creek.
Powley; creek, a small right-hand tributary to Greenbrier River in Summers County.
Pratt; post village in Kanawha County, on the Chesapeake and Ohio Railway.
Press Kincaid; branch, a very small right-hand branch of Loop Creek, a tributary to Kanawha River, in Fayette County.
Preston; county, situated in the northern part of the State on the Allegheny Plateau, here not greatly dissected, and having an average elevation of about 3,000 feet. Area, 671 square miles. Population, 22,727—white, 22,565; negro, 162; foreign born, 482. County seat, Kingwood. The mean magnetic declination in 1900 was 3° 30′. The mean annual rainfall is 40 to 50 inches, and the mean annual temperature 45° to 50°. The county is traversed by the West Virginia Northern and the Baltimore and Ohio railroads.
Preston; post village in Wayne County.
Prestonia; post village in Webster County.
Pretty Ridge; mountains in Wyoming County.
Pretty Ridge; short spur of North Fork Mountain in Pendleton County. Elevation, 2,000 feet.
Price; branch, a very small right-hand tributary to Little Coal River, a branch of Coal River, in Boone County.
Price; branch, a very small right-hand tributary to Beech Fork of Twelvepole Creek, a branch of Ohio River, in Wayne County.
Price; fork, a small left-hand tributary to Hominy Creek, a branch of Gauley River, in Nicholas and Greenbrier counties.
Pride; post village in Mercer County.
Priestly; post village in Lincoln County.
Prince; post village in Fayette County on the Chesapeake and Ohio Railway and on New River. Altitude, 1,188 feet.
Princeton; county seat of Mercer County. Altitude, 2,450 feet.
Pringle; fork, a small left-hand tributary to Right Fork of Stone Coal Creek in Upshur County.
Pringle; run, a small left-hand tributary to Cheat River in Preston County.
Pritchard; post village in Ritchie County.
Procious; post village in Clay County.
Proctor; post village in Wetzel County on the Baltimore and Ohio Railroad.
Proctors; creek, a small left-hand branch of Ohio River in Wetzel County.
Progress; post village in Braxton County.
Props; gap in Long Ridge, caused by a small right-hand branch of the South Branch of Potomac River, in Pendleton County.
Prospect Valley; village in Harrison County.

Prosperity; post village in Raleigh County.
Providence; post village in Jackson County.
Pruett; branch, a very small right-hand tributary to Dry Fork, a branch of Tug Fork of Big Sandy River, in McDowell County.
Pruntytown; village in Taylor County.
Pugh; post village in Webster County.
Pullman; post village in Ritchie County.
Puncheon Camp; branch, a very small right-hand branch of Blue Creek, a tributary to Elk River, in Kanawha County.
Purgitsville; post village in Hampshire County.
Pursley; post village in Tyler County.
Push; post village in Doddridge County.
Putnam; county situated in the western part of the State on the lower slopes of the Allegheny Plateau; it is traversed by Kanawha River, which drains it. Area, 353 square miles. Population, 17,330—white, 16,951; negro, 379; foreign born, 107. County seat near Winfield. The mean magnetic declination in 1900 was 1° 15′. The mean annual rainfall is 40 to 50 inches, and the mean annual temperature 50° to 55°. The county is traversed by the Kanawha and Michigan and the Chesapeake and Ohio railways.
Pyle; mountain, a short ridge west of Greenbrier River in Pocahontas County. Altitude, 2,500 to 3,275 feet, the latter being the height of one peak.
Pyles; fork, a small left-hand branch of Monongahela River in Monongalia County.
Quaker Knob; summit in Webster County. Altitude, 2,722 feet.
Queens; post village in Upshur County.
Queens Camp; fork, a small left-hand branch of Milam Creek, a tributary to East Fork of Twelvepole Creek, in Wayne County.
Queen Shoal; creek, a small left-hand tributary to Elk River in Clay County.
Queens Ridge; post village in Wayne County.
Queer; branch, a small left-hand tributary to Cranberry River in Webster County.
Quiet Dell; post village in Harrison County.
Quincy; post village in Kanawha County.
Quinnimont; post village in Fayette County on the Chesapeake and Ohio Railway and on New River. Altitude, 1,195 feet.
Racine; post village in Boone County. Altitude, 665 feet.
Racoon; creek, a small right-hand tributary to Teter Creek, a branch of Tygarts Valley River, in Barbour County.
Racoon; creek, a right-hand tributary to Valley River in Preston County.
Raccoon; creek, a small right-hand branch of Beech Fork of Twelvepole Creek, a tributary to Ohio River, in Wayne County.
Racy; post village in Ritchie County.
Radnor; post village in Wayne County on the Norfolk and Western Railway.
Rafe; run, a very small left-hand tributary to Valley River in Randolph County.
Ragland; post village in Mingo County.
Raider; fork, a small left-hand tributary to Twenty Mile Creek in Nicholas County.
Raines; fork, a very small left-hand branch of Sycamore Creek, a tributary to Clear Fork of Coal River, in Raleigh County.
Raleigh; county, situated in the southern part of the State, on the Allegheny Plateau, here having an average elevation of 2,500 feet, and is not greatly dissected. It is drained by tributaries of the Kanawha and New rivers. Area, 560 square miles. Population, 12,436—white, 12,076; negro, 360; foreign born, 33. County seat, Beckley. The mean magnetic declination in 1900 was 1° 15′. The mean annual rainfall is 50 to 60 inches, and the mean annual temperature 50° to 55°.
Raleigh; post village of Raleigh County on the Chesapeake and Ohio Railway. Altitude, 2,440 feet.

Raleman; mountain, a short ridge in Pendleton County. Altitude, 3,000 feet.
Ralph; branch, a very small right-hand tributary to Clear Fork, a branch of Guyandot River, in Wyoming County.
Ralston; run, a small left-hand tributary to Valley River in Randolph County.
Ramsey; post village in Fayette County.
Rams Horn; spur of Allegheny Front in Pocahontas County.
Randall; post village in Monongalia County on the Baltimore and Ohio Railroad.
Randolph; county, situated in the eastern part of the State. The surface is entirely mountainous, the western part lying on the Allegheny Plateau, and the eastern part consisting of heavy parallel ridges, trending northeast and southwest, separated by limestone valleys. It is drained by tributaries to the North Branch of the Potomac and to the Monongahela River. Area, 1,086 square miles. Population, 17,670—white, 17,149; negro, 519; foreign born, 698. County seat, Elkins. The mean magnetic declination in 1900 was 2° 30'. The mean annual rainfall is 50 to 60 inches, and the mean annual temperature 45° to 50°. The county is traversed by the West Virginia Central and Pittsburg Railway.
Ranger; post village in Lincoln County.
Ranger; run, a left-hand branch of West Virginia Fork of Dunkard Creek in Monongalia County.
Ratcliff; run, a small left-hand tributary to Buckhannon River in Upshur County.
Rattlesnake Draft; very small right-hand tributary to Paint Creek, a branch of Kanawha River, in Fayette County.
Ravenrock; post village in Pleasants County on the Baltimore and Ohio Railroad.
Ravens Eye; post village in Fayette County.
Ravenswood; town in Jackson County. Population, 1,074. Altitude, 544 feet.
Raymond; run, a right-hand tributary of North Fork of Fishing Creek in Wetzel County.
Raymond City; post village in Putnam County on the Ohio Central Lines.
Read; fork, a left-hand tributary to Grass Run in Gilmer County.
Reader; creek, a right-hand branch of Fishing Creek in Wetzel County.
Reader; post village in Wetzel County on the Baltimore and Ohio Railroad.
Real Gap; height in Little Mountain in Grant County.
Red; creek, a right-hand tributary to Dry Fork of Cheat River in Tucker and Randolph counties.
Redbird; post village in Raleigh County.
Red Bridge; run, a small left-hand tributary to Shavers Fork of Cheat River in Randolph County.
Redcreek; post village in Tucker County.
Redhill; post village in Wood County.
Redhouse Shoals; post village in Putnam County on the Ohio Central Lines.
Redknob; post village in Roane County.
Red Lick; mountain, a short ridge in Pocahontas County. The altitude of one peak is 4,671 feet.
Red Lick; small left-hand tributary to Oil Creek in Lewis County.
Redmud; post village in Mason County.
Red Oak; creek, a small right-hand tributary to North Branch of Potomac River in Grant County.
Red Oak Knob; summit in Webster County. Altitude, 3,750 feet.
Red Oak Ridge; mountains in Mercer County.
Red River; fork, a small left-hand branch of Fourmile Creek, a tributary to Guyandot River, in Lincoln County.
Redstar; station in Fayette County on the Chesapeake and Ohio Railway and on Dunloup Creek, a tributary to New River.
Red Sulpher Springs; post village in Monroe County.

Reed; creek, a left-hand tributary to South Branch of Potomac River in Pendleton County.

Reeds; creek, a small left-hand tributary to North Fork of Potomac River in Pendleton County.

Reedsville; post village in Preston County.

Reedy; branch, a very small right-hand tributary to Guyandot River in Wyoming County.

Reedy; branch, a small right-hand tributary to Clear Fork, a branch of Guyandot River, in Wyoming County.

Reedy; town in Roane County on the Baltimore and Ohio Railroad. Population, 300.

Reedyripple; post village in Wirt County.

Reedyville; post village in Roane County.

Reeses Mill; post village in Mineral County.

Reid; post village in Cabell County.

Removal; post village in Webster County.

Rena; post village in Putnam County.

Rend; post village in Fayette County.

Renicks Valley; post village in Greenbrier County, on the Chesapeake and Ohio Railway.

Renius; post village in Wood County.

Replete; post village in Webster County.

Reuben; right-hand branch of Pritchett Creek in Marion County.

Revel; post village in Gilmer County.

Revere; post village in Gilmer County.

Rex; post village in Putnam County.

Rezrode; post village in Pendleton County.

Reynolds; branch, a very small right-hand tributary to Kanawha River in Kanawha County.

Reynoldsville; post village in Harrison County.

Rhine; fork, a head tributary to Youghiogheny River in Preston County.

Rice; post village in Wayne County.

Rices; run, a left-hand branch of Garrison Run in Ohio County.

Rich; branch, a small left-hand tributary to Pond Fork of Little Coal River in Boone County.

Rich; creek, a very small left-hand tributary to Guyandot River in Wyoming County.

Rich; creek, a small left-hand tributary to Guyandot River, a branch of Ohio River, in Logan County.

Rich; creek, a left-hand tributary to Bluestone River in Mercer County.

Rich; creek, a small left-hand branch of East Fork of Twelvepole Creek, a tributary to Ohio River, in Wayne County.

Rich; creek, a small right-hand tributary to New River in Monroe County.

Rich; knob in Cabell County. Altitude, 1,047 feet.

Rich; mountain, a ridge lying west of Valley River in the northwestern part of Randolph County.

Rich; mountain, a ridge lying east of Laurel Fork of Cheat River in the eastern part of Randolph County.

Rich; post village in Logan County.

Richardson; post village in Calhoun County.

Rich Knob; summit in Greenbrier County. Altitude, 3,848 feet.

Richlands; post village in Greenbrier County.

Rich Mountain; post village in Randolph County.

Rich Patch; creek, a small left-hand tributary to Howards Creek, a branch of Greenbrier River, in Greenbrier County.

Richwood; post village in Nicholas County, on the Baltimore and Ohio Railroad.
Richwood; run, a right-hand branch of South Fork of Fishing Creek in Wetzel County.
Riddle; branch, a very small right-hand tributary to Big Huff Creek, a branch of Guyandot River, in Logan County.
Riddleboch; run, a small right-hand tributary to South Fork of Potomac River in Hardy County.
Ridersville; post village in Morgan County.
Ridge; post village in Morgan County.
Ridgedale; post village in Monongalia County on the Baltimore and Ohio Railroad.
Ridgeley; post village in Mineral County on the West Virginia Central and Pittsburg Railway.
Ridgeville; post village in Mineral County.
Ridgeway; village in Berkeley County on the Cumberland Valley Railroad.
Riffle; branch, an indirect right-hand tributary to Tommy Creek, a head fork of Guyandot River, in Raleigh County.
Riffle; run, a small right-hand tributary to Little Kanawha River in Braxton County.
Riffles; creek, a small right-hand tributary to Valley River in Randolph County.
Riggs; branch, a very small right-hand tributary to Kanawha River in Fayette County.
Rilla; post village in Calhoun County.
Rinehart; post village in Harrison County.
Riney; mountain in Cabell County. Altitude, 1,107 feet.
Ring; branch, a small right-hand tributary to Dry Fork, a branch of Tug Fork of Big Sandy River, in McDowell County.
Rio; post village in Hampshire County.
Ripley; county seat of Jackson County on the Baltimore and Ohio Railroad. Population, 579.
Rippon; post village in Jefferson County on the Norfolk and Western Railway. Altitude, 516 feet.
Rising Sun; branch, a small left-hand tributary to Little Bluestone Creek, a branch of Bluestone River, in Summers County.
Ritchie; county, situated in the western part of the State, near the foot of the Allegheny Plateau. Area, 457 square miles. Population, 18,901—white, 18,875; negro, 26; foreign born, 120; county seat, Harrisville. The mean magnetic declination in 1900 was 2°. The mean annual rainfall is 40 to 50 inches, and the mean annual temperature 50° to 55°. The county is traversed by the Baltimore and Ohio Railroad.
Bitter; post village in McDowell County at junction of upper Shannon Branch with Tug Fork of Big Sandy River.
River; fork, a left-hand tributary to Coal River in Boone County.
River; run, a left-hand branch of Tygart Valley River in Marion County.
River Laurel; branch, a very small left-hand tributary to Tug Fork of Big Sandy River in McDowell County.
River Road; run, a very small right-hand tributary to Greenbrier River in Summers County.
Riverside; post village in Kanawha County.
Riverton; post village in Pendleton County.
Rivesville; town in Marion County. Population, 164.
Roach; branch, a small left-hand tributary to West Fork, a branch of Pond Fork of Little Coal Creek, in Boone County.
Roach; post village in Cabell County.
Road; branch, a very small left-hand tributary to Big Ugly Creek, a branch of Guyandot River, in Lincoln County.

Road; branch, a small right-hand tributary to Cranberry River in Webster County.

Road; branch, a very small right-hand tributary to Little Huff Creek, a branch of Guyandot River, in Wyoming County.

Road; fork, a small left-hand tributary to Twentymile Creek, a branch of Gauley River, in Nicholas County.

Road; fork, a small left-hand branch of Peters Cave Fork of Horse Creek, a tributary to Little Coal River, in Lincoln County.

Road; fork, a left-hand tributary to Trace Fork of Mud River, a branch of Guyandot River, in Lincoln County.

Road; fork, a small left-hand branch of Big Huff Creek, a tributary to Guyandot River, in Wyoming County.

Road; fork, a small left-hand tributary to Tug Fork of Big Sandy River in McDowell County.

Road; fork, a small left-hand tributary to Buffalo Creek, a branch of Elk River, in Clay and Nicholas counties.

Road; fork, a small right-hand branch of Seng Camp Creek, a tributary to Spruce Fork of Little Coal River, in Logan County.

Road; fork, a small right-hand branch of Fuqua Creek, a tributary to Coal River, in Lincoln County.

Road; fork, a small right-hand branch of Rock Camp Fork of Twentymile Creek, a tributary to Gauley River, in Nicholas and Clay counties.

Road; fork, a small right-hand branch of Left Fork of Witchers Creek, a tributary to Kanawha River, in Kanawha County.

Road; fork, a right-hand branch of Grove Creek in Clay County.

Road; run, a small left-hand branch of Oil Creek in Braxton County.

Road; run, a small right-hand tributary to Little Birch River in Braxton County.

Roane; county, situated in the western part of the State near the foot of the Allegheny Plateau. Area, 547 square miles. Population, 19,852—white, 19,820; negro, 32; foreign born, 52. County seat, Spencer. The mean magnetic declination in 1900 was 1° 30′. The mean annual rainfall is 40 to 50 inches, and the mean annual temperature 50° to 55°. The county is traversed by the Ohio River Railroad.

Roanoke; post village in Lewis County on the Baltimore and Ohio Railroad. Altitude, 1,053 feet.

Roaring; creek, a small left-hand tributary to Seneca Creek, a branch of North Fork of Potomac River, in Pendleton County.

Roaring; creek, a small right-hand branch of Valley River in Randolph County.

Roaring; plains, summit near the Allegheny Front, lying on the boundary line between Randolph and Pendleton counties.

Robbins; fork, a small left-hand branch of Spring Creek, a tributary to Greenbrier River, in Greenbrier County.

Roberts; post village in Doddridge County.

Roberts; run, a left-hand branch of Long Drain in Wetzel County.

Robertsburg; post village in Putnam County on the Ohio Central Lines.

Robertson; right-hand branch of Tygarts Valley River in Marion County.

Robinette; branch, a very small left-hand tributary to Guyandot River in Wyoming County.

Robinette; branch, a very small left-hand tributary to Buffalo Creek, a branch of Guyandot River, in Logan County.

Robinson; branch, a very small left-hand branch of Loop Creek, a tributary to Kanawha River, in Fayette County.

Robinson; creek, a small right-hand tributary to Pond Fork of Little Coal River, a branch of Coal River, in Boone County.

GAZETTEER OF WEST VIRGINIA.

Robinson; fork, a left-hand tributary to Buffalo Creek, a branch of Elk River, in Nicholas and Clay counties.
Robinson; fork, a small left-hand tributary to Twentymile Creek, a branch of Gauley River, in Nicholas County.
Robinson; run, a left-hand branch of Monongahela River in Monongalia County.
Robinson; run, a small left-hand branch of the Right Fork of Holly River in Braxton County.
Robinson; run, a right-hand branch of Lunice Creek, a tributary to South Branch of Potomac River, in Grant County.
Robinson Gap; height in Grant County.
Robinsons Mill; post village in Wetzel County.
Robson; post village in Fayette County.
Rock; branch, a very small left-hand tributary to Piney Creek, a branch of New River, in Raleigh County.
Rock; branch, a small left-hand tributary to Beaver Creek, a branch of Piney Creek, in Raleigh County.
Rock; creek, a small right-hand tributary to Marsh Fork of Coal River in Raleigh County.
Rock; creek, a right-hand tributary to Little Coal River, a branch of Coal River, in Boone County.
Rock; post village in Mercer County.
Rock; run, a small left-hand tributary to Greenbrier River in Pocahontas County.
Rock; run, a right-hand branch of Sand Fork in Lewis County.
Rock Camp; branch, a small left-hand branch of Peter Creek, a tributary to Gauley River, in Nicholas County.
Rock Camp; creek, a small, indirect left-hand tributary to Indian Creek in Monroe County.
Rock Camp; fork, a right-hand branch of Twentymile Creek, a tributary to Gauley River, in Nicholas and Clay counties.
Rock Camp; fork, a right-hand branch of Bell Creek, a tributary to Gauley River, in Clay County.
Rock Camp; fork, a small right-hand branch of Blue Creek, a tributary to Elk River, in Kanawha County.
Rock Camp; mountain, a short ridge in Greenbrier County.
Rockcamp; post village in Monroe County.
Rock Camp; run, a small left-hand branch of Spring Creek, a tributary to Greenbrier River, in Greenbrier County.
Rock Camp; run, a small right-hand tributary to Elk River in Braxton County.
Rock Camp; run, a very small right-hand tributary to Gauley River in Nicholas County.
Rock Camp; run, a left-hand branch of Tanner Creek in Gilmer County.
Rock Camp Knob; summit in Greenbrier County.
Rock Castle; creek, a small right-hand branch of Guyandot River in Wyoming County.
Rockcastle; post village in Jackson County.
Rockcave; post village in Upshur County.
Rockford; post village in Harrison County.
Rockgap; post village in Morgan County.
Rock House; branch, a very small left-hand tributary to Gauley River in Webster County.
Rockhouse; branch, a small left-hand tributary to Tug River in McDowell County.
Rockhouse; branch, a very small left-hand tributary to Guyandot River in Wyoming County.

Rockhouse; branch, a small left-hand branch of Road Fork, a tributary to Trace Fork of Mud River, in Lincoln County.

Rockhouse; branch, a small left-hand tributary to Guyandot River, a branch of Ohio River, in Logan County.

Rockhouse; branch, a small right-hand tributary to Elkhorn Creek in McDowell County.

Rockhouse; branch, a very small right-hand tributary to Island Creek, a branch of Guyandot River, in Logan County.

Rockhouse; creek, a small left-hand branch of Mud Fork of Guyandot River, a tributary to Ohio River, in Logan County.

Rockhouse; creek, a very small left-hand tributary to Spruce Fork of Little Coal River in Logan County.

Rockhouse; creek, a small right-hand branch of Clear Fork, a tributary to Coal River, in Raleigh County.

Rockhouse; fork, a small left-hand branch of Big Hart Creek, a tributary to Guyandot River, in Logan County.

Rockhouse; fork, a small left-hand tributary to Clear Fork of Guyandot River in Wyoming County.

Rockhouse; fork, a small left-hand tributary to Marsh Fork of Coal River in Raleigh County.

Rockhouse; fork, a right-hand tributary to Pigeon Creek, a branch of Tug Fork of Big Sandy River, in Logan County.

Rockhouse; fork, a head fork of Dingus Run, a tributary to Guyandot River, in Logan County.

Rockland; post village in Hardy County on the Chesapeake and Ohio Railway.

Rocklick; branch, a very small right-hand tributary to Pond Fork of Little Coal River in Boone County.

Rock Lick; a small left-hand branch of Arbuckle Creek, a tributary to New River, in Fayette County.

Rock Lick; a small right-hand tributary to Williams River in Webster County.

Rocklick; fork; a small left-hand tributary to Leatherwood Creek, a small branch of Elk River, in Clay County.

Rocklick; post village in Marshall County.

Rocklick; run, a right-hand branch of Buffalo Creek in Marion County.

Rock Narrow; branch, a very small left-hand tributary to Tug Fork of Big Sandy River in McDowell County.

Rockoak; post village in Hardy County.

Rockport; post village in Wood County.

Rockruffle; run, a right-hand tributary of Little Kanawha River in Gilmer County.

Rocksdale; post village in Calhoun County.

Rockview; post village in Wyoming County.

Rockville; post village in Preston County.

Rocky; fork, a left-hand branch of Pocotaligo River, a tributary to Kanawha River, in Kanawha County.

Rocky; fork, a left-hand tributary to Indian Fork in Gilmer and Lewis counties.

Rocky; run, a very small left-hand branch of Big Laurel Creek, a tributary to Cherry River, in Greenbrier County.

Rocky; run, a small left-hand tributary to Buckhannon River in Upshur County.

Rocky; run, a small right-hand tributary to Williams River in Webster County.

Rocky; run, a small right-hand branch of Thorn Run, a tributary to South Branch of Potomac River, in Pendleton County.

Rockyfork; post village in Kanawha County.

Rocky Knob; summit in Putnam County. Altitude, 1,170 feet.

Rodamers; post village in Preston County.

Roderfield; post village in McDowell County on the Norfork and Western Railway and on Tug Fork of Big Sandy River.
Rodgers; mountain, a summit in Pocahontas County. Altitude, 3,176 feet.
Roe; post village in Kanawha County.
Rohr; post village in Preston County.
Roller; fork, a small right-hand branch of Kiah Fork, a tributary to Twelvepole Creek, in Wayne County.
Rollins; post village in Mason County.
Rome; post village in Kanawha County.
Romines Mills; post village in Harrison County.
Romney; county seat of Hampshire County on the Baltimore and Ohio Railroad. Population, 580.
Romont; post village in Fayette County.
Ronceverte; town in Greenbrier County on Greenbrier River and on the Chesapeake and Ohio Railway. Population, 968. Altitude, 1,663 feet.
Ronda; post village in Kanawha County.
Roneyspoint; post village in Ohio County on the Baltimore and Ohio Railroad. Altitude, 829 feet.
Roneyspoint; run, a right-hand branch of Little Wheeling Creek in Ohio County.
Rook; branch, a very small right-hand tributary to Left Fork of Mud River in Lincoln County.
Roose; creek, a very small left-hand tributary to Mud River, a branch of Guyandot River, in Cabell County.
Rorebagh; run, a small right-hand tributary to South Fork of Potomac River in Hardy County.
Rosbysrock; post village in Marshall County. Altitude, 787 feet.
Rose; branch, a very small right-hand tributary to Little Huff Creek, a branch of Guyandot River, in Wyoming County.
Rosedale; post village in Braxton County.
Rosen; creek, a small left-hand tributary to North Fork of Greenbrier River in Pocahontas County.
Roseville; post village in Fayette County.
Rosina; post village in Kanawha County.
Ross; post village in Wetzel County.
Ross; run, a small right-hand tributary to Salt Lick Fork of Little Kanawha River in Braxton County.
Rough; run, a small right-hand tributary to Cranberry River in Webster County.
Rough; run, a small right-hand tributary to South Fork of Potomac River in Pendleton County.
Rough; run, a small right-hand tributary to Left Fork of Middle Fork of Valley River in Randolph County.
Rough Gap; run, a very small right-hand tributary to Elk River in Randolph County.
Round Bottom; branch, a very small right-hand tributary to Coal River, a branch of Kanawha River, in Boone County.
Roundbottom; post village in Wayne County on the Baltimore and Ohio Railroad.
Roundknob; post village in Putnam County.
Round Knob; summit in Pocahontas County.
Round Knob; summit in Raleigh County.
Round Knob; summit in Randolph County.
Rover; post village in Wirt County.
Rowlesburg; town in Preston County on the Baltimore and Ohio Railroad. Altitude, 1,402 feet. Population, 652.

Roxalana; post village in Roane County.
Roy; post village in Roane County.
Rubens; branch, a left-hand branch of Buck Fork of Twelvepole Creek in Wayne County.
Rucker; branch, a very small right-hand tributary to Little Coal River, a branch of Coal River, in Boone County.
Ruckman; post village in Hampshire County.
Ruddle; post village in Pendleton County.
Ruffner; branch, a small left-hand tributary to Little Sandy Creek, a small branch of Elk River, in Kanawha County.
Ruffner; branch, a very small right-hand tributary to Kanawha River in Kanawha County.
Rugger; run, a small left-hand tributary to Right Fork of Buckhannon River in Upshur County.
Rum; creek, a small right-hand tributary to Guyandot River in Logan County.
Rupert; post village in Greenbrier County.
Ruraldale; post village in Upshur County.
Rush; creek, a very small left-hand tributary to Kanawha River in Kanawha County.
Rush; fork, a small right-hand tributary to Elk River in Braxton County.
Rush; run, a small left-hand tributary to Monongahela River in Lewis County.
Rush; run, a very small left-hand tributary to New River in Fayette County.
Rush Knob; summit in Lewis County. Altitude, 1,642 feet.
Rushrun; post village in Fayette County on the Chesapeake and Ohio Railway and on New River.
Rushville; post village in Roane County.
Rusk; post village in Ritchie County.
Russell; creek, a very small left-hand tributary to Guyandot River, a branch of Ohio River, in Cabell County.
Russellville; post village in Fayette County. Altitude, 1,092 feet.
Russet; post village in Calhoun County.
Ruth; post village in Kanawha County.
Rutherford; post village in Ritchie County on the Cairo and Kanawha Valley Railroad.
Ryan; post village in Roane County.
Rye; post village in Wood County.
Rymer; village in Marion County.
Sago; post village in Upshur County on the Baltimore and Ohio Railroad. Altitude, 1,425 feet.
Saint Albans; town in Kanawha County on the Chesapeake and Ohio Railroad. Population, 816. Altitude, 593 feet.
Saint Clara; post village in Doddridge County.
Saint Cloud; post village in Monongalia County.
Saint George; town in Tucker County. Population, 152.
Saint Joseph; post village in Marshall County.
Saint Leo; post village in Monongalia County.
Saint Marys; county seat of Pleasants County on the Baltimore and Ohio Railroad. Population, 825.
Salama; post village in Pleasants County on the Baltimore and Ohio Railroad.
Salem; town in Harrison County on the Baltimore and Ohio Railroad. Population, 746.
Sally; run, a small right-hand tributary to Gauley River in Webster County.
Salt Block; run, a small right-hand tributary to Left Fork of Right Fork of Buckhannon River in Randolph County.

Salt Lick; branch, a very small left-hand tributary to New River in Fayette County.
Salt Lick; fork, a left-hand branch of Little Kanawha River in Braxton County.
Salt Lick; run, a small left-hand tributary to Leading Creek in Randolph County.
Saltlick Bridge; post village in Braxton County.
Salt Rock; post village in Cabell County on the Chesapeake and Ohio Railway.
Salt Sulphur; branch, a very small left-hand tributary to Guyandot River, a branch of Ohio River, in Lincoln County.
Salt Sulphur Springs; post village in Monroe County.
Saltwell; village in Harrison County.
Sam; branch, a very small right-hand tributary to Guyandot River in Wyoming County.
Sam; branch, a small right-hand branch of Big Clear Creek, a tributary to Meadow River, in Greenbrier County.
Samaria; post village in Marion County.
Sammy; run, a left-hand branch of Sand Fork in Lewis County.
Samp; post village in Webster County.
Sam Ridge; short spur between Big Clear Creek and its branch, Sam Creek, in Greenbrier County.
Sancho; post village in Tyler County.
Sand; branch, a very small left-hand tributary to Big Huff Creek, a branch of Guyandot River, in Logan County.
Sand; creek, a very small right-hand tributary to Guyandot River, a branch of Ohio River, in Lincoln County.
Sand; fork, a small left-hand tributary to Middle Fork of Mud River, a branch of Guyandot River, in Lincoln County.
Sand; fork, a small right-hand branch of Paint Creek, a tributary to Kanawha River, in Raleigh County.
Sand; fork, a right-hand branch of West Fork of Monongahela River in Lewis County.
Sand; fork, a small right-hand branch of Buffalo Creek, a tributary to Elk River, in Clay County.
Sand; fork, a right-hand branch of Little Kanawha River in Lewis and Gilmer counties. It rises in Lewis County and flows southwestward to its junction with Sand Fork in Gilmer County.
Sand; river, a small right-hand tributary to Gauley River in Webster County.
Sand; run, a very small right-hand tributary to Elk River, a large branch of Kanawha River, in Kanawha County.
Sand; run, a small right-hand tributary to French Creek in Upshur County.
Sand; run, a right-hand head fork of Laurel Fork of French Creek in Upshur County.
Sanders; post village in Wyoming County.
Sandfork; post village in Gilmer County situated on Little Kanawha River.
Sandhill; post village in Marshall County.
Sand Lick; branch, a small left-hand tributary to Big Huff Creek, a branch of Guyandot River, in Logan County.
Sandlick; branch, a very small left-hand tributary to Guyandot River, a branch of Ohio River, in Logan County.
Sand Lick; branch, a very small right-hand branch of Blue Creek, a tributary to Elk River, in Kanawha County.
Sand Lick; branch, a very small right-hand tributary to Bluestone River in Mercer County.
Sand Lick; creek, a right-hand branch of Marsh Fork of Coal River in Raleigh County.

Sand Lick; creek, a small left-hand tributary to Tug Fork of Big Sandy River in McDowell County.

Sandlick; fork, a left-hand branch of Laurel Creek, a tributary to Coal River, in Boone County.

Sandlick; run, a right-hand branch of Right Fork of Simpson Creek in Taylor County.

Sand Ridge; hill west of the South Branch of Potomac River in Pendleton County.

Sandrun; post village in Upshur County.

Sandusky; post village in Tyler County.

Sandy; creek, a small left-hand branch of Ohio River in Jackson County.

Sandy; creek, a right-hand branch of Valley River formed by two forks, Little and Big Sandy creeks, forming boundary line between Taylor and Barbour and between Barbour and Preston counties.

Sandy; post village in Monongalia County on the Baltimore and Ohio Railroad.

Sandy Huff; branch, a small right-hand tributary to Tug Fork of Big Sandy River in McDowell County.

Sandy Huff; post village in McDowell County.

Sandy Ridge; short ridge in Pendleton County. Altitude, 2,500 to 3,000 feet.

Sandy Ridge; mountains in Hampshire County.

Sandy Ridge; short range east of Greenbrier River in Pocahontas County.

Sandyville; post village in Jackson County on the Baltimore and Ohio Railroad.

Sang; run, a left-hand head fork of Laurel Fork of French Creek in Upshur County.

Sangamore; fork, a small right-hand branch of Open Fork of Bell Creek, a tributary to Gauley River, in Clay County.

Sanoma; post village in Wirt County.

Santifee; post village in Summers County.

Sapp; run, a right-hand branch of Booths Creek in Marion County.

Sarah; post village in Cabell County.

Sardis; post village in Harrison County.

Sassafras; post village in Mason County.

Sattes; post village in Kanawha County on the Ohio Central Lines.

Saulsbury; post village in Wood County.

Saulsbury; run, a small left-hand branch of Deer Creek, a tributary to North Fork of Greenbrier River, in Pocahontas County.

Saulsville; post village in Wyoming County.

Saunders; creek, a very small left-hand tributary to Mud River, a branch of Guyandot River, in Cabell County.

Savage; post village in Mineral County.

Savanah; post village in Greenbrier County.

Saw Mill; run, a small left-hand tributary to Buckhannon River in Upshur County.

Sawyer; run, a small left-hand tributary to Back Fork of Elk River in Webster County.

Saxon; post village in Raleigh County.

Scab; run, a right-hand branch of Tygarts Valley River in Taylor County.

Scary; creek, a very small left-hand tributary to Middle Fork of Mud River in Lincoln County.

Scary; creek, a small left-hand tributary to Kanawha River in Putnam County.

Scary; post village in Putnam County on the Chesapeake and Ohio Railway. Altitude, 591 feet.

Scheidler; run, a right-hand branch of Little Fishing Creek in Wetzel County.

Scherr; post village in Grant County.

Schilling; post village in Roane County.

Schoolcraft; run, a small left-hand tributary to Left Fork of Middle Fork of Tygarts Valley River, in Randolph County.

GAZETTEER OF WEST VIRGINIA.

Schoolhouse; branch, a very small right-hand tributary to Pocotaligo River, a branch of Kanawha River, in Kanawha County.
Schoolhouse; branch, a small right-hand tributary to Twomile Creek, a branch of Guyandot River, in Lincoln County.
Schoolhouse; branch, a very small left-hand tributary to Clear Fork, a branch of Guyandot River, in Wyoming County.
Schoolhouse; fork, a small, indirect left-hand tributary to Blue Creek, a branch of Elk River, in Kanawha County.
Schoolhouse; post village in Jackson County on the Baltimore and Ohio Railroad.
Schoolhouse; run, a left-hand tributary to Indian Fork in Gilmer County.
Schoonover Knob; summit in Clay County. Altitude, 1,595 feet.
Schultz; post village in Pleasants County.
Scidmore; run, a very small left-hand tributary to Elk River in Braxton County.
Scott; branch, a very small left-hand tributary to Fields Creek, a branch of Kanawha River, in Kanawha County.
Scott; branch, a very small left-hand tributary to Glade Creek, a branch of New River, in Raleigh County.
Scott; fork, a left-hand fork of Westfall Fork of Cedar Creek in Braxton County.
Scott; post village in Wood County on the Chesapeake and Ohio Railway. Altitude, 694 feet.
Scott; run, a left-hand branch of Buffalo Creek in Brooke County.
Scottdale; post village in Marion County.
Scott Depot; post village in Putnam County.
Scotts; branch, a small left-hand tributary to Rich Creek, a branch of New River, in Monroe County.
Scotts; run, a left-hand branch of Miracle Run in Monongalia County.
Scrabble; creek, a small right-hand tributary to Gauley River in Fayette County.
Scrafford; post village in Monongalia County.
Scratchers; run, a left-hand branch of Prickett Run in Marion County.
Seaman; post village in Roane County on the Baltimore and Ohio Railroad.
Second; branch, a left-hand branch of Hurricane Creek in Putnam County.
Second; creek, a left-hand branch of Greenbrier River in Monroe and Greenbrier counties.
Second Big; run, a small right-hand tributary to Oil Creek in Lewis County.
Secondcreek; post village in Monroe County.
Sedalia; post village in Doddridge County.
Sedan; post village in Hampshire County.
See All; summit in Pocahontas County.
Seebert; post village in Pocahontas County, on the Chesapeake and Ohio Railway.
See Camp; gap in hills caused by Schoolcraft Run, a small tributary to Monongahela River, in Randolph County.
Seemly; post village in Grant County.
Selbyville; post village in Upshur County.
Sell; post village in Preston County.
Senate; branch, a right-hand branch of Lilly Fork of Buffalo Creek, a tributary to Elk River, in Clay County.
Seneca; creek, a left-hand tributary to North Fork of Potomac River in Pendleton County.
Seneca; creek, a right-hand branch of North Fork of Potomac River in Pendleton County.
Seneca; town in Monongalia County. Population, 723.
Seng; branch, a very small left-hand tributary to Mulberry Fork of Loop Creek, a branch of Kanawha River, in Fayette County.
Seng; creek, a very small right-hand tributary to Coal River in Boone County.

Seng; fork, a small right-hand tributary to Hopkins Fork of Laurel Creek, a branch of Coal River, in Boone County.

Seng; post village in Logan County.

Seng Camp; creek, a small right-hand tributary to Spruce Fork of Little Coal River in Logan County.

Serena; post village in Clay County.

Servia; post village in Braxton County.

Seth; post village in Boone County.

Settle; post village in Mason County.

Sevenmile; creek, a small left-hand tributary to Ohio River in Cabell County.

Sevenpines; village in Marion County.

Sewell; creek, a small left-hand tributary to Meadow River in Greenbrier County.

Sewell; post village in Fayette County on New River and on the Chesapeake and Ohio Railway. Altitude, 1,003 feet.

Seymourville; post village in Grant County.

Shabby Room; branch, a very small right-hand tributary to Spice Creek, a branch of Tug Fork of Big Sandy River, in McDowell County.

Shad; post village in Roane County.

Shadrick; fork, a right-hand branch of Hughes Creek, a tributary to Kanawha River, in Kanawha County.

Shadyspring; post village in Raleigh County.

Shafter; post village in Pendleton County.

Shamblings Mills; post village in Roane County.

Shanghai; post village in Berkeley County.

Shanks; post village in Hampshire County.

Shannon; post village in Ohio County.

Shannon Mill; creek, a very small right-hand tributary to Guyandot River in Wyoming County.

Sharp Knob; summit in Pocahontas County. Altitude, 4,545 feet.

Shaver; fork, a right fork of Westfall Fork of Cedar Creek in Braxton County.

Shavers; mountain, a ridge east of Shavers Fork of Cheat River in Randolph County.

Shavers; run, a small right-hand tributary to Valley River in Randolph County.

Shaw; post village in Mineral County on the West Virginia Central and Pittsburg Railway. Altitude, 1,290 feet.

Shawnee; post village in Pleasants County.

Sheep; run, a left-hand branch of North Fork of Fishing Creek in Wetzel County.

Shelby; run, a left-hand branch of Berkeley Run in Taylor County.

Shell Camp Ridge; narrow, broken mountains between Big Clear Creek and Smokehouse Branch, a fork of Big Clear Creek, in Greenbrier County. Altitude, 4,000 feet.

Shelley; post village in Clay County.

Shelton; post village in Clay County on the Charleston, Clendennin and Sutton Railroad.

Shenandoah; mountain, a broken range of mountains originating in Bath County, Virginia, and extending northeasterly through Hardy and Hampshire counties, West Virginia. Altitude, 1,500 to 3,000 feet.

Shenandoah Junction; post village in Jefferson County on the Baltimore and Ohio and Norfolk and Western railroads. Altitude, 512 feet.

Shenango; creek, a right-hand branch of Fishing Creek in Wetzel County.

Shepherd Spring; branch, a small right-hand tributary to Dunloup Creek, a branch of New River, in Raleigh County.

Shepherdstown; town in Jefferson County on the Norfolk and Western Railway. Population, 1,184.

Sheppard; post village in Mingo County.

Sheridan; post village in Lincoln County on the Chesapeake and Ohio Railway.
Sherman; post village in Jackson County on the Baltimore and Ohio Railroad.
Sherrard; post village in Marshall County.
Shiloh; post village in Tyler County.
Shinnston; town in Harrison County. Population, 535.
Shirkey; branch, a small right-hand branch of Blue Creek, a tributary to Elk River, in Kanawha County.
Shirley; post village in Tyler County.
Shoal; branch, a very small right-hand tributary to Twelvepole Creek, a branch of Ohio River, in Wayne County.
Shoals; post village in Wayne County, on the Norfolk and Western Railway.
Shock; post village in Braxton County.
Shock; run, a small left-hand branch of Suttleton Creek, a tributary to Greenbrier River, in Pocahontas County.
Shockley; branch, a small left-hand tributary to Millers Camp Branch of Marsh Fork of Coal River in Raleigh County.
Shock Mill; fork, a small left-hand tributary to Right Fork of Steer Creek in Braxton County.
Shooks; run, a small right-hand tributary to Moorefield River in Hardy County.
Shoomaker Knob; summit in Greenbrier County.
Shop; branch, a very small right-hand tributary to Indian Creek, a branch of Guyandot River, in Wyoming County.
Shops; post village in Putnam County.
Short; branch, a small right-hand tributary to Fifteenmile Fork of Cabin Creek, a branch of Kanawha River, in Kanawha County.
Short; branch, a small left-hand tributary to Davis Creek, a branch of Kanawha River, in Kanawha County.
Short; branch, a very small left-hand tributary to Tug Fork of Big Sandy River in McDowell County.
Short; creek, a left-hand branch of Ohio River in Ohio County.
Short; creek, a very small right-hand branch of Wolf Creek, a tributary to New River, in Fayette County.
Short; creek, a very small right-hand tributary to Coal River, a branch of Kanawha River, in Boone County.
Short; mountain, a summit in Greenbrier County.
Short; mountain in Morgan County. Elevation, 1,388 feet.
Short; run, a small right-hand tributary to Middle Fork of Tygarts Valley River in Randolph County.
Short; run, a very small right-hand tributary to Left Fork of Buckhannon River in Randolph County.
Short Bend; creek, a small right-hand branch of Little Hart Creek, a tributary to Guyandot River, in Lincoln County.
Short Bend; fork, a small right-hand branch of Fourteenmile Creek, a tributary to Guyandot River, in Lincoln County.
Shortcreek; post village in Brooke County on the Pittsburg, Cincinnati, Chicago and St. Louis Railway.
Short Pole; branch, a very small right-hand tributary to Tug Fork of Big Sandy River in McDowell County.
Shreeve; run, a very small left-hand tributary to Little Kanawha River in Braxton County.
Shrewsbury; post village in Kanawha County.
Shriner; run, a left-hand branch of West Virginia Fork of Dunkard Creek in Monongalia County.
Shryock; post village in Greenbrier County.

Shumate; branch, a small left-hand tributary to Marsh Fork of Coal River in Raleigh County.

Siberia; post village in Mercer County.

Sidney; post village in Wayne County.

Sigman; post village in Putnam County.

Siloam; post village in Mason County.

Silverhill; post village in Wetzel County.

Silverton; post village in Jackson County, on the Baltimore and Ohio Railroad.

Simmon; creek, a small left-hand tributary to Bluestone River in Mercer County.

Simmon; run, a small left-hand tributary to Right Fork of Buckhannon River in Upshur County.

Simmons; branch, a very small left-hand tributary to Clear Fork, a branch of Guyandot River, in Wyoming County.

Simmons; creek, a small right-hand tributary to Kanawha River in Kanawha County.

Simmons; creek, a small right-hand tributary to Kanawha River in Kanawha County.

Simmons; mountain, a short ridge between Dry Run and Hammer Run, left-hand branches of South Branch of the Potomac, in Pendleton County.

Simoda; post village in Pendleton County.

Simon; branch, a very small right-hand tributary to Middle Fork of Mud River in Lincoln County.

Simons; post village in Barbour County.

Simpson; post village in Taylor County, on the Baltimore and Ohio Railroad.

Simpson; run, a small right-hand branch of Little Sandy Creek in Preston County.

Sims; branch, a very small right-hand tributary to Paint Creek, a branch of Kanawha River, in Raleigh County.

Sincerity; post village in Wetzel County.

Sinclair; post village in Preston County.

Sinking; creek, a right-hand branch of Little Kanawha River in Gilmer County.

Sinking; creek, a small stream in Greenbrier County, rising in Big Clear Mountain. It flows southward a short distance and sinks.

Sinks Grove; post village in Monroe County.

Sioto; post village in Lincoln County.

Sir Johns; run, a right-hand branch of Potomac River in Morgan County.

Sir Johns Run; post village in Morgan County, on the Baltimore and Ohio Railroad.

Sissonville; post village in Kanawha County.

Sistersville; city in Tyler County. Population, 2,979.

Sixmile; creek, a small left-hand branch of Lens Creek, a tributary to Kanawha River, in Kanawha County.

Sixmile; creek, a small left-hand tributary to Spruce Fork of Little Coal River in Boone County.

Sixmile; creek, a small right-hand tributary to Guyandot River, a branch of Ohio River, in Lincoln County.

Sixmile; post village in Boone County.

Skelt; post village in Webster County.

Skidmore; post village in Jackson County.

Skidmore; run, a small right-hand branch of Little Kanawha River in Gilmer County.

Skillet; creek, a very small right-hand tributary to Gilbert Creek, a branch of Guyandot River, in Mingo County.

Skin; creek, a right-hand tributary to West Fork of Monongahela River in Lewis County.

GAZETTEER OF WEST VIRGINIA.

Skin; fork, a small left-hand tributary to Pond Fork of Little Coal River in Boone County.
Skin; fork, a very small right-hand tributary to Guyandot River in Wyoming County.
Skinner; fork, a small left-hand tributary to Surveyor Fork, a branch of Marsh Fork of Coal River, in Raleigh County.
Skin Poplar; branch, a small right-hand tributary to Laurel Fork, a branch of Spruce Fork of Little Coal River, in Boone County.
Skin Poplar; gap, a height in Guyandot Mountain in Raleigh County. Altitude, 2,360 feet.
Skitter; creek, a very small left-hand tributary to Paint Creek, a branch of Kanawha River, in Fayette County.
Skull Run; post village in Jackson County.
Skyle; creek, a small right-hand tributary to Birch River in Webster County.
Skyles; post village in Webster County.
Slab; creek, a very small left-hand tributary to Mud River, a branch of Guyandot River, in Lincoln County.
Slab; fork, a right-hand tributary to Guyandot River in Raleigh and Wyoming counties.
Slab Camp; creek, a small left-hand tributary to Greenbrier River in Greenbrier County.
Slab Camp; fork, a left-hand branch of French Creek, a tributary to Buckhannon River, in Upshur County.
Slab Camp; mountain, a short ridge in Greenbrier County. Altitude, 3,000 to 3,050 feet.
Slab Camp; run, a small right-hand tributary to Williams River in Webster County.
Slab Creek; run, a small right-hand branch of Cedar Creek in Braxton County.
Slack; branch, a small left-hand tributary to Blue Creek, a branch of Elk River, in Kanawha County.
Slanesville; post village in Hampshire County.
Slap Camp; run, a right-hand tributary of Right Fork of Skin Creek in Gilmer County.
Slash Lick; creek, a small left-hand tributary to Howards Creek, a branch of Greenbrier River, in Greenbrier County.
Slate; post village in Wood County.
Slate Lick; small right-hand branch of Campbell Creek, a tributary to Kanawha River, in Kanawha County.
Slate Lick Knob; summit in Pocahontas County.
Slater; branch, a very small right-hand tributary to Kanawha River in Kanawha County.
Slater; creek, a very small right-hand tributary to New River in Fayette County.
Slater; station in Fayette County on the Chesapeake and Ohio Railway and at junction of Slater Creek and New River. Altitude, 1,108 feet.
Slaty; fork, a small right-hand branch of Old Field Fork of Elk River in Pocahontas County.
Slatyfork; post village in Pocahontas County.
Slaty Ridge; broken mountainous country in Pocahontas County.
Slaughter; creek, a small left-hand tributary to Kanawha River in Kanawha County.
Slaunch; fork, a left-hand head fork of Panther Creek, a branch of Tug Fork of Big Sandy River, in McDowell County.
Sleepy; creek, a small left-hand tributary to Hurricane Creek, a branch of Kanawha River, in Putnam County.
Sleepy; creek, a right-hand branch of Potomac River in Morgan County.
Sleepy Creek; mountain in Berkeley and Morgan counties. Elevation, 1,800 feet.

Sleith; post village in Braxton County.

Sleps; branch, a very small right-hand tributary to Elk River in Webster County.

Slick Rock; branch, a very small left-hand tributary to Big Huff Creek, a branch of Guyandot River, in Wyoming County.

Slick Rock; branch, a small right-hand tributary to Tug Fork of Big Sandy River in McDowell County.

Sliding Hill; run, a small right-hand branch of Little Kanawha River in Gilmer County.

Slipcamp; run, a right-hand branch of Indian Fork Run in Gilmer County.

Slippery Gut; branch, a small left-hand tributary to Little Coal River, a branch of Coal River and indirect tributary to Kanawha River, in Boone County.

Sloan; post village in Wood County.

Slowers; branch, a very small left-hand tributary to Beech Fork of Twelvepole Creek, a branch of Ohio River, in Wayne County.

Smith; branch, a small right-hand branch of Bell Creek, a tributary to Gauley River, in Fayette County.

Smith; branch, a very small left-hand branch of Dunloup Creek, a tributary to New River, in Fayette County.

Smith; branch, a very small left-hand tributary to Pinnacle Creek, a branch of Guyandot River, in Wyoming County.

Smith; branch, a very small left-hand tributary to New River in Mercer County.

Smith; creek, a small right-hand tributary to Coal River, a branch of Kanawha River, in Kanawha County.

Smith; creek, a left-hand tributary to South Branch of Potomac River in Pendleton County.

Smith; creek, a small left-hand tributary to Guyandot River, a branch of Ohio River, in Cabell County.

Smithers; creek, a small right-hand tributary to Kanawha River in Kanawha and Fayette counties.

Smithfield; post village in Wetzel County on the Baltimore and Ohio Railroad.

Smithton; post village in Doddridge County on the Baltimore and Ohio Railroad. Altitude, 795 feet.

Smithville; post village in Ritchie County.

Smoke Camp Knob; summit in Pocahontas County.

Smoke Hole Settlement; neighborhood at the base of the South Fork of the Potomac at the east base of North Fork Mountains, in Pendleton and Grant counties.

Smokehouse; branch, a small right-hand branch of South Fork of Big Clear Creek, a tributary to Meadow River, in Greenbrier County.

Smokehouse; fork, a small right-hand branch of Big Heart Creek, a tributary to Guyandot River, in Logan County.

Smoot; post village in Greenbrier County on the Baltimore and Ohio Railroad.

Snake; fork, a small right-hand tributary to Elk River in Clay County.

Snake; run, a small right-hand tributary to Muddy Creek, a branch of Greenbrier River, in Greenbrier County.

Snake Root; branch, a small right-hand tributary to Clear Fork, a branch of Tug Fork of Big Sandy River, in McDowell County.

Snap; branch, a small left-hand tributary to Guyandot River, a branch of Ohio River, in Logan County.

Snow; mount in Pendleton County. Altitude, 4,500 feet.

Snowden; post village in Lincoln County.

Snowhill; post village in Nicholas County on the Ohio Central Lines.

Snowy; creek, a left-hand tributary to Youghiogheny River in Preston County.

Snyder Knob; summit in Randolph County.

Snyders Mills; village in Jefferson County.

Soab; branch, a very small right-hand branch of Tug Fork of Big Sandy River, a tributary to Ohio River, in Logan County.
Soak; creek, a small left-hand tributary to Piney Creek, a branch of New River, in Raleigh County.
Soak; post village in Raleigh County.
South; fork, a small head tributary to Left Fork of Buckhannon River in Randolph County.
South; fork, a right-hand head tributary to Snowy Creek, a branch of Youghiogheny River, in Preston County.
South Branch; mountain, a narrow ridge in Hardy and Hampshire counties. Altitude, 1,500 to 3,000 feet.
Southbranch Depot; post village in Hampshire County.
South Elkins; town in Randolph County. Population, 206.
South Fork; mountain, broken range in the eastern part of the State. Altitude, 1,500 to 3,000 feet.
South Mill; creek, a right-hand tributary to South Branch of Potomac River in Grant and Pendleton counties.
South Millcreek; post village in Pendleton County.
South Morgantown; town in Monongalia County. Population, 405.
Southside; post village in Mason County.
Souttell; run, a left-hand branch of Short Creek in Ohio County.
Sow; branch, a very small right-hand tributary to Laurel Branch, a tributary to Clear Fork of Guyandot River, in Wyoming County.
Spangler; branch, a very small left-hand tributary to Winding Gulf, a branch of Guyandot River, in Raleigh County.
Spangler; fork, a small left-hand branch of Middle Fork of Blue Creek, a tributary to Elk River, in Kanawha County.
Spangler; post village in Kanawha County.
Spanishburg; post village in Mercer County, located on Bluestone River. Altitude, 2,074 feet.
Spanker; branch, a very small right-hand tributary to Marsh Fork of Coal River in Raleigh County.
Sparrow; creek, a small left-hand tributary to Spruce Fork of Little Coal River, a branch of Coal River, in Boone County.
Sparrow; run, a small left-hand tributary to Holly River in Braxton County.
Spaulding; post village in Mingo County.
Speed; branch, a very small left-hand tributary to Sycamore Creek, a branch of Clear Fork of Coal River, in Raleigh County.
Speed; post village in Roane County.
Spencer; branch, a small right-hand tributary to Boyer Fork of Piney Creek, a branch of New River, in Raleigh County.
Spencer; county seat of Roane County on the Baltimore and Ohio Railroad. Population, 737.
Spice; creek, a very small right-hand tributary to Guyandot River in Mingo County.
Spice; creek, a small left-hand tributary to Tug Fork of Big Sandy River in McDowell County.
Spice; creek, a small left-hand tributary to South Forth of Tug River in McDowell County.
Spice; run, a small left-hand tributary to Greenbrier River on boundary line between Pocahontas and Greenbrier counties.
Spice; run, a small right-hand tributary to Williams River in Webster County.
Spice; run, a very small right-hand tributary to Gauley River in Nicholas County.
Spice Laurel; branch, a small left-hand tributary to Spice Creek, a branch of Tug Fork of Big Sandy River, in McDowell County.

Spicelick; fork, a head fork of Joe Creek, a tributary to Coal River, in Boone County.

Spider; creek, a right-hand branch of Pinnacle Creek, a tributary to Guyandot River, in Wyoming County.

Spider Ridge; mountains in Wyoming County.

Spilman; post village in Mason County on the Baltimore and Ohio Railroad.

Spottswood; post village in Logan County.

Spread Bend; mountain, a short ridge north of Elk River in Clay County. Altitude, 1,000 feet.

Spring; branch, a very small right-hand tributary to Twelvepole Creek, a branch of Ohio River, in Wayne County.

Spring; branch, a small right-hand branch of Rock Camp Fork of Twentymile Creek, a tributary to Gauley River, in Nicholas County.

Spring; creek, a small right-hand tributary to Greenbrier River in Greenbrier County.

Spring; creek, a right-hand branch of Grass Run in Gilmer County.

Spring; creek, a small left-hand tributary to Ohio River, rising in Roane County.

Spring; fork, a left-hand branch of Ben Creek, a tributary to Tug Fork of Big Sandy River, in Mingo County.

Spring; fork, a small left-hand branch of Campbell Creek, a tributary to Kanawha River, in Kanawha County.

Spring Creek; post village in Greenbrier County on the Chesapeake and Ohio Railway.

Springdale; post village in Fayette County.

Springfield; town in Hampshire County on the Baltimore and Ohio Railroad. Population, 143.

Springgap; post village in Hampshire County.

Springgarden; post village in Roane County.

Springhill; post village in Kanawha County on the Chesapeake and Ohio, the Kanawha and Coal River, and the Ohio Central Lines railroads. Altitude, 597 feet.

Sprive; run, a small right-hand tributary to Left Fork of Steer Creek in Braxton County.

Spruce; branch, a very small left-hand branch of Right Fork of Twelvepole Creek, a tributary to Ohio River, in Wayne County.

Spruce; fork, a stream in Logan and Boone counties, uniting with Pond Fork to form Little Coal River.

Spruce; fork, a small left-hand tributary to Right Fork of Middle Fork of Little Kanawha River in Webster County.

Spruce; fork, a small left-hand tributary to Horse Creek, a branch of Little Coal River, in Boone County.

Spruce; fork, a left-hand head fork of Little Coal River, a branch of Coal River, in Boone and Logan counties.

Spruce; fork, a small right-hand tributary to Right Fork of Stone Coal Creek in Upshur County.

Spruce; fork, a small right-hand branch of Brier Creek, a tributary to Coal River, in Kanawha Count.

Spruce; fork, a small right-hand branch of Blue Creek, a tributary to Elk River, in Kanawha County.

Spruce; fork, a small right-hand tributary to Birch River, a branch of Elk River, in Webster County.

Spruce; fork, a very small right-hand tributary to Clear Fork of Coal River in Raleigh County.

Spruce; fork, a right-hand tributary to Wolf Creek in Braxton County.

Spruce; run, a small right-hand tributary to Cedar Creek in Gilmer County.

Spruce; run, a right-hand tributary to Cheat River in Preston County.
Spruce; run, a small right-hand branch of Brushy Fork of Muddlety Creek, a tributary to Gauley River, in Nicholas County.
Spruce; run, a small right-hand branch of Dry Creek, a tributary to Howards Creek, in Greenbrier County.
Spruce; mountain, a short ridge lying west of the North Fork of the Potomac, parallel to the Timber Ridge, in Pendleton County.
Spruce Knob; summit in Pocahontas County. Altitude, 4,730 feet.
Spruce Knob; summit of Spruce Mountain in Pendleton County. Altitude, 4,860 feet.
Spruce Low; gap caused by Spruce Fork of Blue Creek.
Spruce Pine Hollow; small right-hand tributary to Kanawha River in Kanawha County.
Spurlock; branch, a very small left-hand tributary to Beech Fork of Twelvepole Creek, a branch of Ohio River, in Wayne County.
Spurlockville; post village in Lincoln County.
Squealer Knob; summit in Raleigh County.
Squirejim; post village in McDowell County.
Stafford; branch, a very small right-hand tributary to Guayandot River in Mingo County.
Stafford; post village in Mingo County.
Stags; run, a small left-hand branch of Patterson Creek, a tributary to North Branch of Potomac River, in Mineral County.
Stalnaker; post village in Lewis County.
Stamping; creek, a small right-hand tributary to Greenbrier River in Pocahontas County.
Stanaford; branch, a small left-hand tributary to Piney Creek, a branch of New River, in Raleigh County.
Stanley; fork, a very small right-hand tributary to Mud River, a branch of Guyandot River, in Boone County.
Stanley; post village in Ritchie County.
Starkey; run, a left-hand tributary of Buffalo Creek in Marion County.
State; fork, a right-hand branch of Pyles Fork of Buffalo Creek in Marion County.
Staten; post village in Calhoun County.
Staten; run, a very small right-hand tributary to Kanawha River in Kanawha County.
State Road; run, a left-hand branch of Paw Paw Creek in Marion County.
Statler Run; post village in Monongalia County.
Statts Mills; post village in Jackson County.
Steel; post village in Wood County.
Steel; run, a right-hand branch of Little Fishing Run in Wetzel County.
Steel Trap; branch, a very small left-hand tributary to Tug Fork of Big Sandy River in McDowell County.
Steener; fork, a left-hand tributary of Lynn Camp Run in Wetzel County.
Steep; run, a small right-hand tributary to Wolf Creek in Braxton County.
Steep Gut; branch, a very small right-hand branch of Tug Fork of Big Sandy River, a tributary to Ohio River, in Logan County.
Steer; creek, a small left-hand tributary to Ohio River in Calhoun County.
Steer; run, a right-hand branch of Left Fork of Steer Creek in Gilmer County.
Stevens; branch, a small right-hand tributary to Marsh Fork of Coal River in Raleigh County.
Stevens; post village in Mason County on the Baltimore and Ohio Railroad.
Stewart; creek, a small left-hand tributary to Little Bluestone Creek in Summers County.

Stewart; creek, a right-hand branch of Little Kanawha River in Gilmer County.
Stewart; run, a small right-hand tributary to Valley River in Randolph County.
Stewartstown; post village in Monongalia County.
Still; run, a small right-hand tributary to Guyandot River in Wyoming County.
Stillhouse; branch, a small right-hand tributary to Twentymile Creek, a branch of Gauley River, in Nicholas County.
Stillhouse; branch, a very small right-hand tributary to Peters Creek, a branch of Gauley River, in Nicholas County.
Still House; branch, a small left-hand tributary to Leatherwood Fork of Elk River in Webster County.
Stillhouse; run, a small left-hand tributary to Birch River, a branch of Elk River, in Nicholas County.
Stillman; post village in Upshur County.
Stillwell; post village in Wood County.
Stinking Lick; creek, a very small right-hand tributary to New River in Summers and Monroe counties.
Stinson; branch, a small left-hand tributary to Left Fork of Mud River, a branch of Guyandot River, in Lincoln County.
Stinson; post village in Calhoun County.
Stitt; branch, a very small right-hand tributary to Davis Creek, a branch of Kanawha River, in Kanawha County.
Stockerts; post village in Upshur County.
Stockton; post village in Mason County.
Stockton; station in Fayette County on the Kanawha and Michigan Railway and on Kanawha River. Altitude, 618 feet.
Stockton Knob; summit in Fayette County. Altitude, 3,252 feet.
Stolling; fork, a small left-hand tributary to Laurel Creek, a branch of Coal River, in Boone County.
Stone; fork, a very small left-hand tributary to Beech Fork of Twelvepole Creek, a branch of Ohio River, in Wayne County.
Stone; run, a small right-hand tributary to Valley River in Barbour County.
Stonecliff; post village in Fayette County on New River and on the Chesapeake and Ohio Railway. Altitude, 1,076 feet.
Stone Coal; branch, a very small right-hand tributary to Clear Fork of Coal River in Raleigh County.
Stonecoal; branch, a very small right-hand tributary to Mud River, a branch of Guyandot River, in Lincoln County.
Stone Coal; branch, a small right-hand tributary to Spice Creek, a branch of Tug Fork of Big Sandy River, in McDowell County.
Stone Coal; creek, a right-hand branch of Tommy Creek, a head fork of Guyandot River, in Raleigh County.
Stonecoal; post village in Wayne County.
Stone Coal; run, a small right-hand tributary to Left Fork of Middle Fork of Tygarts Valley River in Randolph County.
Stonewall; post village in Raleigh County on the Chesapeake and Ohio Railway.
Stony; creek, a small left-hand tributary to Elk River in Braxton County.
Stony; creek, a small left-hand tributary to Greenbrier River in Summers County.
Stony; creek, a small right-hand tributary to Greenbrier River in Pocahontas County.
Stony; post village in Hampshire County.
Stony; river, a large right-hand tributary to North Branch of Potomac River in Grant County.
Stony; run, a small left-hand tributary to Elk Water in Randolph County.
Stony; run, a small left-hand branch of Suttleton Creek, a tributary to Greenbrier River, in Pocahontas County.

Stony; run, a small right-hand tributary to South Fork of Potomac River in Pendleton County.

Stony Creek; mountain, a short ridge north of Greenbrier River, in Pocahontas County. Altitude, 2,500 to 3,500 feet.

Stony Ridge; mountains in Mercer County.

Stotlers Crossroads; post village in Morgan County.

Stout; creek; a very small left-hand tributary to Guyandot River, a branch of Ohio River, in Lincoln County.

Stouts Mills; post village in Gilmer County situated on Little Kanawha River.

Stover; branch, a very small right-hand tributary to Coal River, a branch of Kanawha River, in Boone County.

Stover; fork, a small left-hand tributary to Clear Fork of Coal River in Raleigh County.

Stover; fork, a small left-hand tributary to Piney Creek, a branch of New River, in Raleigh County.

Stover; fork, a very small right-hand tributary to Sycamore Creek, a branch of Clear Fork of Coal River, in Raleigh County.

Stover; post village in Tucker County on the Dry Fork Railroad.

Straight; creek, a small left-hand tributary to Gauley River in Webster County.

Straight; fork, a head fork of Little Skin Creek in Lewis County.

Straight; fork; a small left-hand tributary to West Fork of Monongahela River in Lewis County.

Straight; fork, a very small left-hand tributary to Huff Creek, a branch of Guyandot River, in Wyoming County.

Straight; fork, a left-hand tributary to Middle Fork of Mud River, a branch of Guyandot River, in Lincoln County.

Straight Creek; mountain, a short ridge north of Williams River in Webster County.

Strange; creek, a small left-hand tributary to Elk River in Nicholas and Braxton countries.

Strangecreek; post village in Braxton County.

Streeter; post village in Summers County.

Stroud; creek, a small right-hand tributary to Gauley River, in Nicholas and Webster counties.

Stroud Knobs; summit in Nicholas County.

Strouds; post village in Webster County.

Stump; run, a small right-hand tributary to South Fork of Potomac River in Hardy County.

Stumptown; post village in Gilmer County.

Stumpy; creek, a very small left-hand tributary to Mud River, a branch of Guyandot River, in Lincoln County.

Sturms Mill; village in Marion County.

Styles; run, a left-hand branch of Long Drain in Wetzel County.

Suck; creek, a small right-hand branch of Little Bluestone Creek, a tributary to Bluestone River, in Summers County.

Sue; post village in Greenbrier County.

Sugar; branch, a very small left-hand tributary to Hominy Creek, a branch of Gauley River, in Nicholas County.

Sugar; creek, a right fork of Laurel Creek, a tributary to Valley River, in Barbour County.

Sugar; creek, a right-hand branch of Back Fork of Elk River in Webster and Randolph counties.

Sugar; creek, a very small right-hand tributary to Big Huff Creek, a branch of Guyandot River, in Logan and Wyoming counties.

Sugar; creek, a small left-hand branch of Twomile Creek, a tributary to Kanawha River, in Kanawha County.

Sugar; creek, a very small left-hand branch of Dunloup Creek, a tributary to New River, in Fayette County.

Sugar; creek, a small left-hand tributary to Williams River in Pocahontas County.

Sugar; run, a left-hand branch of Fish Creek in Wetzel County.

Sugar; run, a very small right-hand tributary to Guyandot River in Wyoming County.

Sugar; run, a left-hand branch of Paw Paw Creek in Marion County.

Sugar; run, a small right-hand tributary to Left Fork of Middle Fork of Tygarts Valley River in Randolph County.

Sugar; ran, a left-hand branch of West Virginia Fork of Dunkard Creek in Monongalia County.

Sugar Camp; branch, a very small left-hand tributary to Mulberry Fork of Loop Creek, a branch of Kanawha River, in Fayette County.

Sugar Camp; branch, a small left-hand branch of Twentymile Creek, a tributary to Gauley River, in Nicholas County.

Sugar Camp; branch, a small right-hand tributary to Paint Creek, a branch of Kanawha River, in Kanawha County.

Sugar Camp; branch, a very small right-hand branch of Hughes Creek, a tributary to Kanawha River, in Kanawha County.

Sugar Camp; branch, a very small right-hand branch of Kelly Creek, a tributary to Kanawha River, in Kanawha County.

Sugarcamp; branch, a very small right-hand tributary to Davis Creek, a branch of Kanawha River, in Kanawha County.

Sugar Camp; branch, a very small right-hand tributary to Guyandot River in Wyoming County.

Sugarcamp; creek, a very small right-hand branch of Davis Creek, a tributary to Kanawha River, in Kanawha County.

Sugarcamp; post village in Doddridge County.

Sugar Camp; run, a small right-hand tributary to Elk River in Braxton County.

Sugar Camp; run, a left-hand tributary of Booths Creek in Harrison County.

Sugar Camp; run, a small left-hand tributary to Knapp Creek, a branch of Greenbrier River, in Pocahontas County.

Sugar Camp Knob; summit in Greenbrier County.

Sugarcamp Knob; summit in Lincoln County.

Sugar Creek; mountain, a short ridge between Williams River and Williams River Mountain in Pocahontas County.

Sugargrove; post village in Pendleton County.

Sugar Grove Knob; summit in Nicholas County. Altitude, 3,028 feet.

Sugar Knob; summit in Braxton County. Altitude, 1,630 feet.

Sugar Knob; summit in Greenbrier County.

Sugar Run; branch, a small left-hand tributary to Rich Creek, a branch of New River, in Monroe County.

Sugartree; branch, a very small right-hand tributary to Mud River, a branch of Guyandot River, in Boone County.

Sugar Tree; branch, a very small right-hand branch of Tug Fork of Big Sandy River, a tributary to Ohio River, in Logan County.

Sugar Tree; branch, a small left-hand tributary to Tug Fork of Big Sandy River in McDowell County.

Sugartree; fork, a left-hand tributary to Middle Fork of Mud River, a branch of Guyandot River, in Lincoln County.

Sugar Tree Bench; mountains, a short spur of Yew Mountains in Greenbrier and Pocahontas counties.

Sugar Valley; post village in Pleasants County.
Suke; creek, a small left-hand branch of Little Huff Creek, a tributary to Guyandot River, in Wyoming County.
Sulphur; post village in Mineral County.
Sulphur; run, a small right-hand branch of Hughes Fork, in Braxton County.
Sulphur Spring; fork, a small right-hand branch of Fourteenmile Creek, a tributary to Guyandot River, in Lincoln County.
Sulphur Spring; fork, a small left-hand branch of Fourmile Creek, a tributary to Guyandot River, in Lincoln County.
Sulphur Spring; fork, a small left-hand branch of Peters Cave Fork of Horse Creek, a tributary to Little Coal River, in Lincoln County.
Summers; county, situated in the southern part of the State on the summit of the Allegheny Plateau, which here presents the broken, mountainous surface with numerous high points, the highest 3,945 feet, Keeney Knob. Area, 368 square miles. Population, 16,265—white, 15,149; negro, 1,115; foreign born, 64. County seat, Hinton. The mean magnetic declination in 1900 was 1° 30′. The mean annual rainfall is 50 to 60 inches, and the mean annual temperature 50° to 55°. The county is traversed by the Chesapeake and Ohio Railway.
Summers; post village in Doddridge County.
Summersville; county seat of Nicholas County. Population, 223.
Summersville; mountain in Nicholas County. Altitude, 2,584 feet.
Summit Point; post village in Jefferson County on the Baltimore and Ohio Railroad. Altitude, 623 feet.
Sunhill; post village in Wyoming County.
Sunlight; post village in Greenbrier County.
Sunnyside; post village in Fayette County on the Chesapeake and Ohio Railway and on New River. Altitude, 842 feet.
Sunrise; branch, a small right-hand branch of Trace Creek, a tributary to Middle Fork of Mud River, in Lincoln County.
Sunset; branch, a small left-hand tributary to Trace Creek, a branch of Middle Fork of Mud River, in Lincoln County.
Sunset; post village in Pocahontas County.
Surveyor; fork, a left-hand head fork of Marsh Fork of Coal River, in Raleigh County.
Sutherland; post village in Kanawha County.
Sutphin; branch, a very small left-hand tributary to Piney Creek, a branch of New River, in Raleigh County.
Suttleton; creek, a small left-hand tributary to Greenbrier River in Pocahontas County.
Sutton; county seat of Braxton County on the Baltimore and Ohio Railroad. Population, 864. Altitude, 823 feet.
Sutton; run, a small left-hand tributary to North Fork of Greenbrier River in Pocahontas County.
Sutton; run, a small right-hand tributary to Birch River in Nicholas County.
Swago; creek, a small right-hand tributary to Greenbrier River in Pocahontas County.
Swago; mountain, a short ridge in central part of Pocahontas County. Altitude, 3,500 to 4,000 feet.
Swamp; branch, a very small left-hand tributary to Guyandot River, a branch of Ohio River, in Cabell County.
Swamp; run, a small right-hand tributary to Valley River in Barbour County.
Swamprun; post village in Upshur County.
Swann; post village in Cabell County.

Sweedlin Hill; short ridge lying east of South Fork of the Potomac in Pendleton County.
Sweep; run, a left-hand branch of Booths Creek in Harrison and Morgan counties.
Sweetland; post village in Lincoln County.
Sweetsprings; post village in Monroe County.
Sweet Water; branch, a very small right-hand branch of Right Fork of Twelvepole Creek, a tributary to Ohio River, in Wayne County.
Swell Knob; summit in Fayette County.
Swift; run, a small right-hand tributary to Greenbrier River, in Summers County.
Swoopes Knobs; group of summits in Monroe County.
Sycamore; branch, a small right-hand tributary to Big Huff Creek, a branch of Guyandot River, in Wyoming County.
Sycamore; branch, a small right-hand tributary to Big Cub Creek, a branch of Guyandot River, in Wyoming County.
Sycamore; branch, a very small right-hand tributary to West Fork of Twelvepole Creek, a branch of Ohio River, in Wayne County.
Sycamore; branch, a small right-hand tributary to Paint Creek, a branch of Kanawha River, in Kanawha and Fayette counties.
Sycamore; creek, a very small right-hand branch of Tug Fork of Big Sandy River, a tributary to Ohio River, in Logan County.
Sycamore; creek, a small right-hand branch of Little Kanawha River in Gilmer County.
Sycamore; creek, a small left-hand branch of Clear Fork of Coal River in Raleigh County.
Sycamore; creek, a right-hand branch of Trace Fork in Putnam County.
Sycamore; fork, a small right-hand tributary to Laurel Fork, a branch of Spruce Fork of Little Coal River, in Boone County.
Sycamore; fork, a small right-hand tributary to Left Fork of Mud River, a branch of Guyandot River, in Lincoln County.
Sycamore; fork, a left-hand tributary to Middle Fork of Mud River, a branch of Guyandot River, in Lincoln County.
Sycamore; post village in Calhoun County.
Sycamore Dale; village in Harrison County.
Sylvia; branch, a very small left-hand tributary to Guyandot River, a branch of Ohio River, in Mingo County.
Tabler; post village in Berkeley County on the Cumberland Valley Railroad.
Tablerock; post village in Raleigh County.
Table Rock; summit in Kanawha County. Altitude, 1,756 feet.
Tackett; creek, a small left-hand branch of Coal River, a tributary to Kanawha River, in Kanawha County.
Tackey; fork, a small left-hand tributary to North Fork of Greenbrier River in Pocahontas County.
Tacy; post village in Barbour County.
Tague; fork, a small right-hand tributary to Right Fork of Steer Creek in Braxton County.
Takein; creek, a very small right-hand tributary to Piney Creek, a branch of New River, in Raleigh County.
Talcott; post village in Summers County on the Chesapeake and Ohio Railway. Altitude, 1,512 feet.
Tallmansville; post village in Upshur County.
Tallow Knob; summit in Pocahontas County.
Tallyho; post village in Wood County.
Tank; branch, a very small right-hand tributary to Piney Creek, a branch of New River, in Raleigh County.

GAZETTEER OF WEST VIRGINIA.

Tanner; fork, a right-hand branch of Little Kanawha River in Gilmer County.
Tanner; fork, a small left-hand tributary to Right Fork of Steer Creek in Gilmer County.
Tanner; post village in Gilmer County.
Tantrough; branch, a very small right-hand tributary to Guyandot River, a branch of Ohio River, in Lincoln County.
Tantrough; run, a right-hand branch of Fish Creek in Wetzel County.
Tappan; post village in Taylor County.
Tarcoat; creek, a left-hand tributary to North River in Hampshire County.
Tariff; post village in Roane County.
Tate; creek, a small right-hand branch of Elk River in Braxton County.
Tate; post village in Braxton County.
Tate; run, a small right-hand branch of Peters Creek, a tributary to Gauley River, in Nicholas County.
Tater Knob; run, a small right-hand tributary to Back Fork of Holly River in Webster County.
Taylor; branch, a small left-hand tributary to Gauley River in Nicholas County.
Taylor; county, situated on the Allegheny Plateau. Drained by tributaries to the Monongahela River. Area, 132 square miles. Population, 14,978—white, 14,553; negro, 423; foreign born, 384. County seat, Grafton. The mean magnetic declination in 1900 was 4° 5'. The mean annual rainfall is 40 to 50 inches, and the mean annual temperature 45 to 50°. The county is traversed by the Baltimore and Ohio Railroad.
Taylor; fork, a left-hand tributary to Buffalo Creek, a branch of Elk River, in Nicholas and Clay counties.
Taylor; fork, a left-hand branch of Jenkins Fork of Loop Creek, a tributary to Kanawha River, in Fayette County.
Taylor; run, a very small right-hand tributary to Elk River in Braxton County.
Tea; branch, a small right-hand tributary to South Fork of Tug River in McDowell County.
Tea; creek, a small right-hand tributary to Williams River in Pocahontas County.
Tea Creek; mountain, a short ridge at foot of Gauley Mountain in Pocahontas County. Altitude, 3,500 to 4,000 feet.
Tearcoat Hill; town between North Fork of Lunice Creek and Brushy Run in Grant County.
Teays; post village in Putnam County.
Teddy; post village in Clay County.
Teeny Knob; summit in Braxton County.
Ten Mile; creek, a small right-hand tributary to Buckhannon River in Upshur County.
Tenmile; creek, a small left-hand branch of Guyandot River, a tributary to Ohio River, in Lincoln County.
Tenmile; fork, a small left-hand branch of Campbell Creek, a tributary to Kanawha River, in Kanawha County.
Tenmile; fork, a left-hand branch of Cabin Creek, a tributary to Kanawha River, in Kanawha County.
Tenmile; fork, a left-hand tributary to Paint Creek, a branch of Kanawha River, in Kanawha County.
Tenmile; post village in Upshur County on the Baltimore and Ohio Railroad. Altitude, 1,608 feet.
Terra Alta; town in Preston County on the Baltimore and Ohio Railroad. Population, 616.
Tesla; post village in Braxton County.
Teter; creek, a right-hand tributary to Valley River in Barbour County.

Texas; post village in Tucker County on the Baltimore and Ohio Railroad. Altitude, 883 feet.

Texel; post village in Randolph County.

Thacker; creek, a small right-hand branch of Tug Fork of Big Sandy River, a tributary to Ohio River, in Logan County.

Thacker; post village in Mingo County on the Norfolk and Western Railway.

Thayer; post village in Fayette County.

The; creek, a small left-hand tributary to Back Fork of Elk River in Randolph County.

The Big Bend; a portion of Greenbrier River, forming a big bend, in Summers County.

The Loop; a bend in Meadow River, a branch of Gauley River.

The Pond; summit in Raleigh County.

The Roughs; hills in Mingo County.

The Sinks; valley at the head of Gandy Creek in Randolph County.

Third; run, a small right-hand branch of Little Kanawha River in Gilmer County.

Thoburn; village in Marion County.

Thomas; creek, a small left-hand tributary to Greenbrier River in Pocahontas County.

Thomas; mountain, a short ridge between Laurel and Moore runs, branches of Greenbrier River, in Pocahontas County.

Thomas; town in Tucker County, on the West Virginia Central and Pittsburg Railway. Population, 2,126.

Thompson; post village in Marshall County on the Baltimore and Ohio Railroad.

Thompson; run, a small right-hand tributary to Valley River in Randolph County.

Thorn; post village in Pendleton County.

Thorn; run, a small left-hand tributary to Patterson Creek, a branch of North Branch of Potomac River, in Grant County.

Thorn; run, a right-hand tributary to South Branch of Potomac River in Pendleton County.

Thornton; post village in Taylor County on the Baltimore and Ohio Railroad. Altitude, 1,038 feet.

Thorny; creek, a small left-hand tributary to Greenbrier River in Pocahontas County.

Thorny Bottom; right-hand tributary to Cacapon River in Hardy County.

Thorny Creek; mountain, a short ridge between Thorny Creek and Greenbrier River in Pocahontas County. Altitude, 3,000 feet.

Thorny Flat; summit of Back Alleghany Mountains in Pocahontas County.

Thoroughfare; branch, a small right-hand tributary to Paint Creek, a branch of Kanawha River, in Kanawha County.

Three Churches; post village in Hampshire County.

Three Fork; creek, a right-hand tributary to Valley River in Taylor County.

Three Forks; run, a small left-hand tributary to Left Fork of Middle Fork of Tygarts Valley River in Randolph County.

Three Forks; very small left-hand tributary to Buffalo Creek, a branch of Guyandot River, in Logan County.

Three Lick; small right-hand branch of Oil Creek in Lewis County.

Three Lick; small right-hand branch of Little Skin Creek in Lewis County.

Three Lick; run, a right-hand branch of Oil Creek in Gilmer County.

Threemile; creek, a left-hand branch of Ohio River in Cabell County.

Threemile; fork, a small right-hand tributary to Whiteoak Creek, a branch of Coal River, in Boone County.

Threemile; fork, a very small left-hand branch of Smithers Creek, a tributary to Kanawha River, in Fayette County.

Three Springs; branch, a small left-hand tributary to Big Huff Creek, a branch of Guyandot River, in Logan County.
Third Heel; mountain in Berkeley County. Elevation, 1,777 feet.
Thurmond; post village in Fayette County on New River and on the Chesapeake and Ohio Railway. Altitude, 1,056 feet.
Tichenal; post village in Harrison county.
Tigarts Valley; river, a right-hand branch of the Monongahela, joining it at Fairmont.
Tilhance; creek, a right-hand tributary of Potomac River in Berkeley County.
Timber Ridge; mountains lying parallel with Spruce Mountains, west of the North Fork of the Potomac, in Pendleton County. Altitude, 2,000 to 4,000 feet.
Timothy; run, a small right-hand branch of Clover Lick Fork in Lewis County.
Tincture; fork, a left-hand tributary of Middle Fork of Mud River in Lincoln County.
Tiney; creek, a small left-hand tributary to Little Coal River, a branch of Coal River, in Lincoln County.
Tipton; post village in Nicholas county.
Tobacco; run, a small left-hand tributary to Little Kanawha River in Lewis County.
Todd; run, a right-hand branch of Middle Wheeling Run in Ohio County.
Tollgate; post village in Ritchie County on the Baltimore and Ohio Railroad.
Tom; branch, a small right-hand tributary to Paint Creek, a branch of Kanawha River, in Kanawha and Fayette counties.
Tom; branch, a very small right-hand tributary to Coal River in Raleigh County.
Tom; branch, a very small right-hand tributary to North Fork of Elkhorn Creek in McDowell County.
Tom; creek, a very small right-hand tributary to Guyandot River, a branch of Ohio River, in Cabell County.
Tom; creek, a very small left-hand branch of Twelvepole Creek, a tributary to Ohio River, in Wayne County.
Tom; creek, a small right-hand tributary to Meadow River, a branch of Gauley River, in Greenbrier County.
Tom; fork, a small left-hand tributary to Coal River, a branch of Kanawha River, in Lincoln County.
Tom; run, a small left-hand branch of Cedar Creek in Braxton County.
Tom; run, a very small left-hand tributary to New River in Summers County.
Tom; run, a small right-hand tributary to Sand Fork in Lewis County.
Tomahawk; village in Berkeley County.
Tomahawk; run, a left-hand branch of Indian Fork in Lewis County.
Tom Bailey; branch, a small right-hand tributary to Glen Fork, a branch of Laurel Branch of Clear Fork of Guyandot River, in Wyoming County.
Tommy; creek, a left-hand head fork of Guyandot River in Raleigh County.
Tommy Ridge; mountains in Raleigh County.
Toney; creek, a very small right-hand tributary to Coal River, a branch of Kanawha River, in Boone County.
Toney; fork, a small right-hand tributary to Clear Fork of Coal River in Raleigh County.
Toney; fork, a right-hand branch of Clear Fork of Guyandot River in Wyoming County.
Toney; fork, a small right-hand branch of Buffalo Creek, a tributary to Guyandot River, in Logan County.
Toney; fork, a small right-hand branch of Big Huff Creek, a tributary to Guyandot River, in Wyoming County.
Tony; branch, a small left-hand tributary to Right Fork of Lower Creek, a branch of Mud River, in Cabell County.

Tony; branch, a very small left-hand tributary to Big Ugly Creek, a branch of Guyandot River, in Lincoln County.
Tooley; post village in Wayne County.
Tophet; post village in Summers County.
Topins Grove; post village in Jackson County.
Top of Alleghany; post village in Pocahontas County.
Tornado; post village in Kanawha County. Altitude, 608 feet.
Town; branch, a very small right-hand tributary to Guyandot River, a branch of Ohio River, in Logan County.
Town; creek, a very small left-hand tributary to Paint Creek, a branch of Kanawha River, in Fayette County.
Town; mountain, a summit in Pendleton County near Franklin.
Town Creek Knob; summit of Paint Mountain on boundary line between Raleigh and Fayette counties. Altitude, 3,088 feet.
Trace; branch, a very small left-hand tributary to Horse Creek, a branch of Little Coal River, in Lincoln County.
Trace; branch, a left-hand head fork of Elk Creek, a tributary to Guyandot River, in Logan County.
Trace; branch, a small right-hand tributary of Slab Fork, a branch of Guyandot River, in Wyoming County.
Trace; branch, a very small right-hand tributary to South Fork of Elkhorn Creek in McDowell County.
Trace; creek, a small left-hand tributary to Mud River, a branch of Guyandot River, in Cabell County.
Trace; creek, a small left-hand tributary to Middle Fork of Mud River in Lincoln County.
Trace; creek, a very small right-hand tributary to Guyandot River, a branch of Ohio River, in Cabell County.
Trace; fork, a head fork of Strange Creek in Nicholas County.
Trace; fork, a small left-hand branch of Big Hart Creek, a tributary to Guyandot River, in Logan County.
Trace; fork, a small left-hand tributary to Panther Creek, a branch of Tug Fork of Big Sandy River, in McDowell County.
Trace; fork, a small left-hand branch of Hurricane Creek, a tributary to Kanawha River, in Putnam County.
Trace; fork, a small left-hand branch of Fourmile Creek, a tributary to Guyandot River, in Lincoln County.
Trace; fork, a small left-hand branch of Huff Creek, a tributary to Guyandot River, in Wyoming County.
Trace; fork, an indirect left-hand tributary to Indian Creek, a branch of Guyandot River, in Wyoming County.
Trace; fork, a left-hand branch of Davis Creek, a tributary to Kanawha River, in Kanawha County.
Trace; fork, a right-hand branch of Pigeon Creek, a tributary to Tug Fork of Big Sandy River, in Logan County.
Trace; fork, a right-hand branch of Tanner Fork, and tributary to Little Kanawha River, in Gilmer County.
Trace; fork, a small right-hand branch of Joe Creek, a tributary to Coal River, in Boone County.
Trace; fork, a large right-hand branch of Mud River in Lincoln and Putnam counties.
Trace; run, a small left-hand tributary to Little Kanawha River in Lewis and Upshur counties.
Trace; run, a small left-hand branch of Cedar Creek in Braxton County.

Trace Fork; branch, a small left-hand branch of Sandlick Fork of Laurel Creek, a tributary to Coal River, in Boone County.
Tract Hill; short ridge in the central part of Pendleton County. Altitude, 2,000 to 2,500 feet.
Trail; fork, a right-hand branch of Long Drain River in Wetzel County.
Travellers Repose; post village in Pocahontas County.
Tressel; post village in Pendleton County.
Triadelphia; town in Ohio County on the Baltimore and Ohio Railroad. Altitude, 735 feet. Population, 287.
Tribble; post village in Mason County.
Trilby; post village in Ritchie County.
Triplets; run, a right-hand branch of Little Kanawha River in Braxton County.
Triplett; fork, a right-hand branch of O'Brien Fork in Braxton County.
Triplett; post village in Roane County.
Tristan; post village in Roane County.
Triune; post village in Monongalia County.
Trough; creek, a right-hand branch of Kiah Fork of Twelvepole Creek in Wayne County.
Trough; fork, a small right-hand branch of Laurel Fork, a tributary to Clear Fork of Guyandot River, in Wyoming County.
Trough; fork, a small left-hand tributary to Laurel Fork, a branch of Spruce Fork of Little Coal River, in Boone County.
Trout; post village in Greenbrier County.
Trout; run, a small left-hand tributary to Left Fork of Right Fork of Buckhannon River in Randolph County.
Trout; run, a small right-hand tributary to South Branch of Potomac River in Pendleton and Hampshire counties.
Trout; run, a right-hand tributary to Cacapon River in Hardy County.
Trout; run, a small right-hand tributary to Left Fork of Right Fork of Buckhannon River in Randolph County.
Troy; town in Gilmer County. Population, 148.
Trubie; run, a small right-hand tributary to Buckhannon River in Upshur County.
True; post village in Summers County.
Truebada; post village in Gilmer County, situated on Little Kanawha River.
Tuckahoe; post village in Greenbrier County on the Chesapeake and Ohio Railway and on Dry Creek. Altitude, 2,035 feet.
Tucker; county, situated in the northern part of the State on the Allegheny Plateau. The average elevation is not far from 3,000 feet. Area, 440 square miles. Population, 13,433—white, 13,077; negro, 353; foreign born, 1,508. County seat, Parsons. The mean magnetic declination in 1900 was 3°. The mean annual rainfall is 50 inches, and the mean annual temperature 45° to 50°. The county is traversed by the West Virginia Central and Pittsburg Railway.
Tucker; post village in Wirt County.
Tucker; run, a right-hand branch of Lost Creek in Taylor County.
Tuckers; run, a small right-hand tributary to South Branch of Potomac River in Hardy County.
Tudell; post village in Wayne County.
Tug; fork, a small left-hand tributary to Birch River, a branch of Elk River, in Nicholas County.
Tug Fork of Big Sandy; fork, large branch of Big Sandy River, heading in McDowell County; it flows northwest, forming a portion of the western boundary of the State and joining Levisa Fork at Louisa.
Tugg; creek, a very small right-hand tributary to New River in Summers County.

Tug River; post village in McDowell County, located on Tug Fork of Big Sandy River.

Tunnelton; town in Preston County on the Baltimore and Ohio and the West Virginia Northern railroads. Altitude, 1,820 feet. Population, 479.

Turkey; branch, a very small left-hand branch of Right Fork of Twelvepole Creek, a tributary to Ohio River, in Wayne County.

Turkey; branch, a very small left-hand tributary to Piney Creek, a branch of New River, in Raleigh County.

Turkey; creek, a very small right-hand tributary to Guyandot River in Wyoming County.

Turkey; creek, a very small right-hand branch of Tug Fork of Big Sandy River in Mingo County.

Turkey; creek, a very small right-hand tributary to New River in Fayette County.

Turkey; creek, a small left-hand tributary to Trace Fork of Mud River, a branch of Guyandot River, in Putnam and Lincoln counties.

Turkey; creek, a small left-hand branch of Indian Creek, a tributary to New River, in Monroe County.

Turkey; creek, a small left-hand tributary to Gauley River in Webster County.

Turkey; fork, a left-hand tributary to Buffalo Creek, a branch of Elk River, in Nicholas County.

Turkey; mountain, a short ridge north of Williams River in Webster County. Altitude, 3,500 to 3,887 feet, the latter being the height of one of its peaks.

Turkey; post village in Mingo County.

Turkey; run, a small right-hand tributary to Right Fork of Middle Fork of Little Kanawha River in Upshur County.

Turkey; run, a right-hand branch of Plummer Run in Taylor County.

Turkey Bone; mountain, a short ridge in the western part of Randolph County. Altitude, 3,000 to 3,500 feet.

Turkey Camp Knob; summit in Wayne County.

Turkey Gap; branch, a very small right-hand tributary to South Fork of Elkhorn Creek in McDowell County.

Turkey Knob; branch, a very small right-hand tributary to Dunloup Creek, a branch of New River, in Fayette County.

Turkeylick; run, a right-hand branch of Tanner Creek in Gilmer County.

Turkey Ridge; mountains in Wyoming County.

Turkey Ridge; short spur between Taylor Ridge and Turkey Creek in Nicholas County.

Turkey Wallow; branch, a very small left-hand tributary to Indian Creek, a branch of Guyandot River, in Wyoming County.

Turley; branch, a small right-hand tributary to Dunloup Creek, a branch of New River, in Fayette County.

Turnhole; branch, a very small right-hand tributary to Tug Fork of Big Sandy River in McDowell County.

Turnrow; branch, a very small right-hand tributary to Indian Creek, a branch of Guyandot River, in Wyoming County.

Turtle; creek, a left-hand tributary to Little Coal River, a branch of Coal River, in Boone County.

Turtlecreek; post village in Boone County.

Twelve Mile; creek, a small left-hand tributary to East River, a branch of New River, in Mercer County.

Twelvepole; creek, a left-hand branch of Ohio River, formed by two forks, east and west, which rise in Wayne County.

Twelvepole; creek, a left-hand tributary to Ohio River in Wayne County.

Twentymile; creek, a right-hand tributary to Gauley River, a large branch of Kanawha River, in Nicholas County.
Twiggs; post village in Pleasants County.
Twilight; village in Ohio County.
Twin; branch, a small right-hand tributary to Tug Fork of Big Sandy River in McDowell County.
Twin; branches, small right-hand tributaries to Cranberry River, in Webster County.
Twin Sugars; summit in Greenbrier County.
Twisted Gun Gap; height in Mingo County. Altitude, 1,422 feet.
Twistville; post village in Braxton County.
Two; run, a small right-hand tributary to Crooked Fork of Steer Creek in Gilmer County.
Two and Three Quarters Mile; creek, a small left-hand tributary to Kanawha River in Kanawha County.
Two Lick; small right-hand tributary to Oil Creek in Lewis County.
Two Lick; run, a right-hand tributary to Little Birch River in Braxton County.
Twomile; branch, a small left-hand branch of Twentymile Creek, a tributary to Gauley River, in Nicholas County.
Twomile; branch, a very small left-hand branch of Dunloup Creek, a tributary to New River, in Fayette County.
Twomile; branch, a very small right-hand tributary to Glade Creek, a branch of New River, in Raleigh County.
Twomile; creek, a small right-hand tributary to Guyandot River, a branch of Ohio River, in Lincoln County.
Twomile; creek, a small right-hand tributary to Kanawha River in Kanawha County.
Twomile; creek, a very small left-hand branch of East Fork of Twelvepole Creek, a tributary to Ohio River, in Wayne County.
Twomile; fork, a small left-hand branch of Whiteoak Creek, a tributary to Coal River, in Boone County.
Tygart; creek, a small left-hand tributary to Ohio River in Wood County.
Tygart; post village in Randolph County on the Baltimore and Ohio Railroad.
Tygarts Valley; large branch of Monongahela River, heading in Randolph County. Its course is generally north through Barbour and Taylor counties to its mouth at Fairmont in Marion County.
Tyler; county, situated in the northwestern part of the State, bordering on Ohio River; situated at the foot of the slope of the Allegheny Plateau. Area, 269 square miles. Population, 18,252—white, 18,153; negro, 94; foreign born, 295. County seat, Middlebourne. The mean magnetic declination in 1900 was 2° 30′. The mean annual rainfall is 40 to 50 inches, and the mean annual temperature 50° to 55°. The county is traversed by the Ohio River Railroad.
Tyler; creek, a very small right-hand tributary to Guyandot River, a branch of Ohio River, in Cabell County.
Tyler; creek, a small right-hand tributary to Kanawha River in Kanawha County.
Tyner; post village in Wood County.
Tyrconnell Mines; post village in Taylor County.
Tyrone; post village in Monongalia County.
Uffington; post village in Monongalia County on the Baltimore and Ohio Railroad.
Ugly; branch, a small right-hand tributary to Marsh Fork of Coal River in Raleigh County.
Uler; post village in Roane County.
Ungers Store, post village in Morgan County.
Union; county seat of Monroe County. Population, 256.

Union Mills; post village in Pleasants County.
Unionridge; post village in Cabell County.
Uniontown; post village in Wetzel County.
Unknown; branch, a very small right-hand tributary to Paint Creek, a branch of Kanawha River, in Fayette County.
Uno; post village in Wyoming County.
Unus; post village in Greenbrier County.
Upland; post village in Mason County.
Upper; gap, height of Huff Mountain in Wyoming County.
Upper; creek, a very small right-hand tributary to Elk River, a large branch of Kanawha River, in Clay County.
Upper; mountain; a summit between two forks of Moore Run, a left-hand branch of Greenbrier River, in Pocahontas County.
Upper; run, a right-hand branch of South Fork of Fishing Creek in Wetzel County.
Upper Bee Tree; run, a small left-hand tributary to Back Fork of Elk River in Randolph County.
Upper Belcher; branch, a small left-hand tributary to Elkhorn Creek, a branch of Tug Fork of Big Sandy River, in McDowell County.
Upper Birch; run, a very small left-hand tributary to Elk River in Clay County.
Upper Cove; headwaters of Lost River in Hardy County.
Upperglade; post village in Webster County.
Upper Hensley; creek, a small right-hand tributary to Tug Fork of Big Sandy River in McDowell River.
Upper Level; run, a left-hand branch of Cedar Creek in Gilmer County.
Upper Lick; small left-hand tributary to Laurel Fork, a branch of Spruce Fork of Little Coal River, in Boone County.
Upper Mill; creek, a small left-hand tributary to Elk River in Braxton County.
Upper Pond Lick; small left-hand tributary to Shavers Fork of Cheat River in Randolph County.
Upper Road; branch, a small right-hand tributary to Clear Fork, a branch of Guyandot River, in Wyoming County.
Upper Shannon; branch, a small right-hand tributary to Tug Fork of Big Sandy River in McDowell County.
Upper Shant; run, a small right-hand tributary to Back Fork of Elk River in Randolph County.
Upper Shaver; run, a small left-hand tributary to Left Fork of Steer Creek in Braxton County.
Upper Sleith; fork, a small left-hand tributary to Right Fork of Steer Creek in Braxton County.
Upper Sturgeon; branch, a head fork of Big Cub Creek, a tributary to Guyandot River, in Wyoming County.
Upper Threemile; fork, a small right-hand branch of Blue Creek, a tributary to Elk River, in Kanawha County.
Upper Tony Camp; run, a small right-hand tributary to Dry Fork of Cheat River in Randolph County.
Uppertract; post village in Pendleton County.
Upper Two; run, a small left-hand tributary to Left Fork of Steer Creek in Gilmer County.
Upshur; county situated in the central part of the State. It is drained northward by Buckhannon River. Area, 326 square miles. Population, 14,696—white, 14,473; negro, 221; foreign born, 106. County seat, Buckhannon. The mean magnetic declination in 1900 was 2° 30′. The mean annual rainfall is 50 inches, and the mean annual temperature 45° to 50°. The county is traversed by the Baltimore and Ohio Railroad.

Upton; branch, a very small left-hand tributary to Mud River, a branch of Guyandot River, in Lincoln County.
Upton; creek, a very small left-hand tributary to Kanawha River in Kanawha County.
Upton; village in Marion County.
Utica; post village in Jackson County.
Uvilla; post village in Jefferson County.
Vadis; post village in Lewis County.
Vall; creek, a small left-hand tributary to Dry Fork, a branch of Tug Fork of Big Sandy Creek, in McDowell County.
Valley; fork, a left-hand branch of Middle Fork of Mud River, a tributary to Guyandot River, in Lincoln County.
Valley; fork, a right-hand branch of Elk River in Randolph County.
Valley; mount, a summit in Pocahontas County. Altitude, 3,500 feet.
Valley; river, a tributary to Monongahela River.
Valleybend; post village in Randolph County on the West Virginia Central and Pittsburg Railway.
Valleydale; post village in Greenbrier County.
Valleyfalls; post village in Marion County, on the Baltimore and Ohio Railroad. Altitude, 969 feet.
Valleyfork; post village in Clay County.
Valley Furnace; post village in Barbour County.
Valley Grove; branch, a small right-hand branch of Elk Twomile Creek, a tributary to Elk River, in Kanawha County.
Valleygrove; post village in Ohio County on the Baltimore and Ohio Railroad.
Valleyhead; post village in Randolph County.
Valley Mills; post village in Wood County.
Valleypoint; post village in Preston County.
Van; post village in Boone County.
Vancamp; post village in Wetzel County.
Van Clevesville; post village in Berkeley County on the Baltimore and Ohio Railroad. Altitude, 500 feet.
Vandalia; post village in Lewis County.
Vandegrift; post village in Randolph County.
Vanetta; creek, a very small right-hand tributary to Guyandot River, a branch of Ohio River, in Lincoln County.
Vannoys Mill; post village in Barbour County.
Vanvoorhis; post village in Monongalia County on the Baltimore and Ohio Railroad.
Varney; post village in Mingo County.
Vaughan; post village in Nicholas County on the Chesapeake and Ohio Railway.
Vegan; post village in Upshur County.
Venable; branch, a very small left-hand tributary to Kanawha River in Kanawha County.
Venison; fork, a right-hand branch of Perkins Fork in Braxton County.
Venus; post village in Gilmer County.
Veranda; post village in Mason County.
Victor; post village in Fayette County.
Victoria; post village in Preston County.
Vienna; post village in Wood County on the Baltimore and Ohio Railroad.
View; village in Greenbrier County.
Vilas; post village in Ritchie County.
Villa; post village in Kanawha County.
Vincen; post village in Wetzel County.

Viney; mountain, a ridge in Pocahontas County.
Vinton; post village in Nicholas County.
Viola; post village in Marshall County.
Virgie; post village in Clay County.
Viropa; post village in Harrison County on the Baltimore and Ohio Railroad.
Vista; post village in Raleigh County.
Vivian; post village in McDowell County on the Norfolk and Western Railway and on Elkhorn Creek. Altitude, 1,502 feet.
Volcano; post village in Wood County on the Baltimore and Ohio Railroad.
Volga; post village in Barbour County on the Baltimore and Ohio Railroad.
Waddles; run, a right-hand branch of Short Creek in Ohio County.
Wade; fork, a left-hand branch of Little Sycamore Creek, a tributary to Elk River, in Clay County.
Wade; post village in Wetzel County.
Wadestown; post village in Monongalia County.
Wagner Knob; summit in Pendleton County.
Wainville; post village in Webster County.
Waites; run, a small right-hand tributary to Cacapon River in Hardy County.
Waiteville; post village in Monroe County.
Waldo; post village in Putnam County.
Walker; fork, a right-hand branch of Conyer Fork, a tributary to Cedar Creek, in Braxton County.
Walker; post village in Wood County on the Baltimore and Ohio Railroad.
Walker Ridge; short spur in Grant County.
Walkers; creek, a small left-hand branch of Ohio River in western Virginia.
Walkersville; post village in Lewis County.
Wall; branch, a very small right-hand tributary to Clear Fork, a branch of Guyandot River, in Wyoming County.
Wallace; branch, a very small left-hand tributary to Guyandot River, in Wyoming County.
Wallace; post village in Harrison County on the Baltimore and Ohio Railroad.
Wallow Hole; fork, a small left-hand tributary to Buffalo Creek, a branch of Elk River, in Clay County.
Wallow Hole; mountain, a short spur east of Greenbrier River in Greenbrier County. Altitude, 2,000 to 2,500 feet.
Wallow Hole Knob; summit in Clay County.
Walnut; creek, a very small left-hand tributary to Elk River in Kanawha County.
Walnut; fork, a small right-hand tributary to Elk River in Braxton County.
Walnut; gap, a height in Wyoming County. Altitude, 2,716 feet.
Walnut; post village in Calhoun County.
Walnut; run, a small right-hand tributary to Left Fork of Steer Creek in Braxton County.
Walnutgrove; post village in Roane County on the Charleston, Clendennin and Sutton Railroad.
Walnut Knob; summit in Clay County.
Walton; post village in Roane County on the Chesapeake and Ohio Railway.
Wanless; post village in Pocahontas County on the Cairo and Kanawha Valley Railroad.
Wappocomo; post village in Hampshire County.
War; branch, a very small right-hand tributary to Tug Fork of Big Sandy River in McDowell County.
War; creek, a small left-hand tributary to Dry Fork, a branch of Tug Fork of Big Sandy River, in McDowell County.
Warden; post village in Raleigh County.

Warden; run, a right-hand tributary of Little Wheeling Creek in Ohio County.
Wardensville; town and post village in Hardy County. Population, 152.
Ward Knob; summit in Randolph County.
Wards; run, a small right-hand tributary to Valley River in Randolph County.
Warfield; post village in Clay County on the Porters Creek and Gauley Railroad.
Warford; post village in Summers County.
Warm Hollow; branch, a very small right-hand branch of Tug Fork of Big Sandy River, a tributary to Ohio River, in Logan County.
Warren; post village in Jackson County on the Baltimore and Ohio Railroad.
Warrior; fork, a left-hand branch of Buffalo Creek in Marion County.
Washburn; post village in Ritchie County.
Wash Hill; fork, a left-hand tributary to Horse Creek, a branch of Little Coal River, in Boone County.
Washington; post village in Wood County on the Baltimore and Ohio Railroad.
Wasp; post village in Pleasants County.
Watering Pond; small left-hand tributary to North Fork of Greenbrier River in Pocahontas County.
Watering Pond Knob; summit in Pocahontas County.
Waterloo; post village in Mason County.
Watkins; post village in Tyler County.
Watson; branch, a very small right-hand tributary to Kanawha River in Kanawha County.
Watson; island in Kanawha River in Kanawha County.
Watson (Capon Springs); town in Marion County. Population, 18.
Watts; branch, a very small left-hand tributary to West Fork of Twelvepole Creek, a branch of Ohio River, in Wayne County.
Wattsville; post village in Clay County.
Waverly; post village in Wood County on the Baltimore and Ohio Railroad.
Way; run, a left-hand branch of South Fork of Fishing Creek in Wetzel County.
Wayne; county, situated in the southwestern part of the State on the lower slopes of the Allegheny Plateau. It is drained mainly by Twelvepole Creek. Area, 545 square miles. Population, 23,619—white, 23,298; negro, 321; foreign born, 51. County seat, Wayne. The mean magnetic declination in 1900 was 30′. The mean annual rainfall is 40 to 50 inches, and the mean annual temperature 50° to 55°. The county is traversed by the Norfolk and Western and the Chesapeake and Ohio railways.
Wayne; county seat of Wayne county on the Norfolk and Western Railway.
Wayside; post village in Monroe County.
Weaver; post village in Randolph County on the Belington and Beaver Creek Railroad.
Weavers Knob; summit in Greenbrier County. Altitude, 2,931 feet.
Webster; county, situated in the central part of the State, on the Allegheny Plateau, and drained by tributaries to Little Kanawha River. Area, 590 square miles. Population, 8,862—white, 8,850; negro, 12; foreign born, 74. County seat, Addison. The mean magnetic declination in 1900 was 2° 10′. The mean annual rainfall is 50 to 60 inches, and the mean annual temperature 45° to 50°. The county is traversed by the Baltimore and Ohio Railroad.
Webster; post village in Taylor County on the Baltimore and Ohio Railroad. Altitude, 1,022 feet.
Webster Springs; county seat of Webster County. Population, 297.
Weiss Knob; summit of Canaan Mountain in Tucker County. Altitude, 4,490 feet.
Welch; county seat of McDowell County at junction of Elkhorn Creek with Tug Fork of Big Sandy River and on the Norfolk and Western Railway. Altitude, 1,297 feet. Population, 442.

Welcome; post village in Marshall County.
Wellford; post village in Kanawha County.
Wellington; post village in Roane County.
Wells; post village in Marshall County on the Baltimore and Ohio Railroad.
Wells; run, a right-hand branch of Buffalo Creek in Brooke County.
Wellsburg; county seat of Brooke County on the Pittsburg, Cincinnati, Chicago and St. Louis Railroad. Population, 2,588. Altitude, 635 feet.
Welsh Glade; summit in Webster County on the Pittsburg, Cincinnati, Chicago and St. Louis Railway. Altitude, 2,222 feet.
Wesley; post village in Wood County.
West; fork, a large right-hand branch of Pond Fork of Little Coal River in Boone County.
West; post village in Wetzel County.
West; run, a right-hand branch of Monongahela River in Monongalia County.
West Columbia; village in Mason County on the Baltimore and Ohio Railroad. Population, 205.
West End; post village in Preston County on the Baltimore and Ohio Railroad. Altitude, 945 feet.
Westfall; fork, a small right-hand branch of Cedar Creek in Braxton County.
West Liberty; post village in Ohio County.
West Milford; town in Harrison County. Population, 187.
Weston; county seat of Lewis County on the Baltimore and Ohio Railroad. Altitude, 824 feet.
West Union; county seat of Doddridge County on the Baltimore and Ohio Railroad. Population, 623. Altitude, 800 feet.
Wet; branch, a left-hand tributary to Cabin Creek, a branch of Kanawha River, in Kanawha County.
Wetzel; county, situated in the northwestern part of the State, bordering on Ohio River and lying at the foot of the slope of the Allegheny Plateau. Area, 365 square miles. Population, 22,880—white, 22,440; negro, 439; foreign born, 393. County seat, New Martinsville. The mean magnetic declination in 1900 was 2° 30′. The mean annual rainfall is 40 to 50 inches, and the mean annual temperature 50° to 55°. The county is traversed by the Ohio River and the Baltimore and Ohio railroads.
Wharncliffe; post village in Mingo County on the Norfolk and Western Railway. Altitude, 822 feet.
Wheatland; post village in Jefferson County on the Norfolk and Western Railway.
Wheeler; fork, a small right-hand tributary to Skin Creek in Lewis County.
Wheeler; small islands in Kanawha River in Fayette County.
Wheeling; creek, a small left-hand branch of Ohio River, rising in Pennsylvania and flowing west into Ohio River.
Wheeling; county seat of Ohio County on the Baltimore and Ohio, the Pittsburg, Cincinnati, Chicago and St. Louis, and the Wheeling and Lake Erie railroads. Altitude, 645 feet.
Whetstone; creek, a left-hand branch of Fish Creek in Wetzel County.
Whetstone; post village in Clay County.
Whetstone; run, a small left-hand tributary to South Branch of Potomac River in Pendleton County.
Whetstone; run, a right-hand branch of Buffalo Creek in Marion County.
Whisler; run, a left-hand branch of Dunkard Creek in Monongalia County.
Whitcomb; post village in Greenbrier County on the Chesapeake and Ohio Railway.
White; post village in Preston County.
White; run, a right-hand tributary of Potomac River in Berkeley County.
Whiteday; post village in Monongalia County.

Whiteman; branch, a small right-hand branch of Aaron Fork of Little Sandy Creek, a tributary to Elk River, in Kanawha County.

Whiteoak; branch, a very small right-hand tributary to East Fork of Twelvepole Creek, a branch of Ohio River, in Wayne County.

Whiteoak; branch, a very small right-hand branch of Laurel Fork, a tributary to Clear Fork of Guyandot River, in Wyoming County.

Whiteoak; branch, a small right-hand tributary to Laurel Fork, a branch of Spruce Fork of Little Coal River, in Boone County.

Whiteoak; branch, a very small right-hand tributary to Indian Creek, a branch of Guyandot River, in Wyoming County.

Whiteoak; branch, a small left-hand tributary to Panther Creek, a branch of Tug Fork of Big Sandy River, in McDowell County.

Whiteoak; branch, a very small left-hand tributary to Coal River, a branch of Kanawha River, in Boone County.

Whiteoak; creek, a left-hand branch of Dunloup Creek, a tributary to New River, in Fayette County.

Whiteoak; creek, a very small left-hand tributary to Guyandot River, a branch of Ohio River, in Mingo County.

Whiteoak; creek, a small right-hand tributary to Clear Fork of Coal River in Raleigh County.

Whiteoak; creek, a small right-hand tributary to Coal River, a branch of Kanawha River, in Boone County.

White Oak; fork, a small indirect left-hand tributary to Blue Creek, a branch of Elk River, in Kanawha County.

White Oak; fork, a small right-hand tributary to Williams River in Webster County.

Whiteoak; fork, a small right-hand branch of Loop Creek, a tributary to Kanawha River, in Fayette County.

White Oak; mountain, a short ridge north of Williams River, in Webster County. Altitude, 3,500 feet.

White Oak; mountain, a broken mountainous range, forming the boundary between Raleigh and Summers counties. Altitude, 3,418 feet.

Whiteoak; post village in Ritchie County.

White Oak; run, a small right-hand tributary to Left Fork of Steer Creek in Gilmer County.

Whitepine; post village in Calhoun County.

White Rock; mountain, a short ridge east of Greenbrier River in Greenbrier County. Altitude, 2,500 to 3,212 feet, the latter the height of one peak.

Whites; branch, a small right-hand tributary to West Fork, a branch of Pond Fork of Little Coal River, in Boone County.

Whites; run, a left-hand branch of Cheat River in Monongalia County.

Whites Creek; post village in Wayne County.

Whites Draft; small left-hand tributary to Anthony Creek, a branch of Greenbrier River, in Greenbrier County.

Whites Trace; very small left-hand tributary to Spruce Fork of Little Coal River in Logan County.

White Sulphur Springs; post village in Greenbrier County on Howards Creek and on the Chesapeake and Ohio Railway. Altitude, 2,000 feet.

Whitewater; small left-hand branch of Peter Creek, a tributary to Gauley River, in Nicholas County.

Whitfield; post village in Ohio County.

Whitman; run, a small left-hand tributary to Valley River in Randolph County.

Whitman Flats; summit in Randolph County.

Whitman Knob; summit in Randolph County.

Whitmans; run, a small left-hand tributary to Anthony Creek, a branch of Greenbrier River, in Greenbrier County.
Wick; post village in Tyler County.
Wickwire; run, a right-hand branch of Tygarts Valley River in Taylor County.
Wide Mouth; creek, a left-hand tributary to Bluestone River in Mercer County.
Wiggins; post village in Summers County on the Chesapeake and Ohio Railway.
Wikel; post village in Monroe County.
Wilbur; post village in Tyler County.
Wildcat; post village in Lewis County.
Wild Cat; run, a small left-hand tributary to Skin Creek in Lewis County.
Wild Cat Knob; summit in Nicholas County. Altitude, 2,837 feet.
Wilderness; fork, a middle fork of Fork Creek, a tributary to Coal River, in Boone County.
Wilding; post village in Jackson County.
Wiley; fork, a right-hand branch of North Fork of Fishing Creek in Wetzel County.
Wiley Spring; branch, a small left-hand tributary to Devils Fork, a branch of Guyandot River, in Raleigh County.
Wileyville; post village in Wetzel County.
Wilkerson; branch, a very small left-hand tributary to Pocotaligo River, a branch of Kanawha River, in Kanawha County.
Willey; fork, a right-hand branch of North Fork of Fishing Creek in Wetzel County.
Willey; post village in Monongalia County.
William; post village in Tucker County on the West Virginia Central and Pittsburg Railway.
William Camp; run, a small right-hand tributary to Gauley River in Webster County.
Williams; fork, a left-hand tributary to Trace Fork of Mud River, a branch of Guyandot River, in Lincoln County.
Williams; river, a large left-hand branch of Gauley River, rising in Pocahontas County, and flowing northwesterly through Webster County to its mouth.
Williamsburg; post village in Greenbrier County.
Williamson; branch, a very small right-hand branch of Tug Fork of Big Sandy River, a tributary to Ohio River, in Logan County.
Williamson; branch, a very small right-hand tributary to Guyandot River in Wyoming County.
Williamson; county seat of Mingo County on the Norfolk and Western Railway.
Williamson; station in Logan County on the Norfolk and Western Railway and on Tug Fork of Big Sandy River.
Williamsport; post village in Grant County, situated on Patterson Creek. Altitude, 988 feet.
Williams River; mountain, a ridge extending from Webster County into Pocahontas. Altitude, 3,000 to 4,000 feet.
Williamstown; post village in Wood County.
Willis; branch, a very small left-hand tributary to Paint Creek, a branch of Kanawha River, in Fayette County.
Willow; post village in Pleasants County.
Willowbend; post village in Monroe County.
Willowdale; post village in Jackson County.
Willowgrove; post village in Jackson County, on the Baltimore and Ohio Railroad.
Willowton; post village in Mercer County.
Willowtree; post village in Jackson County.
Wills; creek, a left-hand branch of Little Sandy Creek, a tributary to Elk River, in Kanawha County.

Wilmore; station in McDowell County on the Norfolk and Western Railway and on Tug Fork of Big Sandy River.
Wilmoth; run, a small right-hand tributary to Valley River in Randolph County.
Wilson; branch, a small left-hand branch of Laurel Creek, a tributary to New River, in Fayette County.
Wilson; branch, a very small right-hand tributary to Kanawha River in Kanawha County.
Wilson; creek, a small right-hand branch of Twelvepole Creek, a tributary to Ohio River, in Wayne County.
Wilson; fork, a small left-hand branch of Laurel Patch Run in Braxton County.
Wilson; post village in Grant County on North Fork of Potomac River and on the West Virginia Central and Pittsburg Railway. Altitude, 2,512 feet.
Wilson; run, a small right-hand tributary to South Fork of Potomac River in Hardy and Pendleton counties.
Wilson; run, a right-hand branch of South Fork of Fishing Creek in Wetzel County.
Wilsonburg; post village in Harrison County, on the Baltimore and Ohio Railroad.
Wilsondale; post village in Wayne County on the Chesapeake and Ohio Railway and on the Right Fork of Twelvepole Creek.
Wilsonia; post village and railway station in Grant county, situated on North Branch of Potomac River, also on West Virginia Central and Pittsburgh Railway. Altitude, 2,747 feet.
Wilson Knob; summit in Upshur County.
Winding Gulf; right-hand head fork of Guyandot River in Raleigh County.
Wind Mill; gap, in Great Flat Top Mountain in Mercer County.
Windmill Gap; branch, a right-hand tributary to North Fork of Elkhorn Creek in McDowell County.
Windom; post village in Wyoming County on the West Virginia Central and Pittsburg Railway.
Windy; post village in Wirt County.
Windy; run, a small right-hand tributary to Little Birch River in Braxton County.
Windy; run, a small right-hand tributary to Valley River in Randolph County.
Winfield; county seat of Putnam County. Population, 338.
Wingrove; branch, a small right-hand tributary to Sand Lick Creek, a branch of Marsh Fork of Coal River, in Raleigh County.
Winifrede; post village in Kanawha County on the Chesapeake and Ohio Railway and the Winifrede Railroad.
Winnie; village in Wirt County.
Winona; post village in Fayette County.
Winters; run, a right-hand tributary of Wheeling Creek in Marshall County.
Wirt; county, situated in the western part of the State on the lower slope of the Alleghany Plateau. Area, 254 square miles. Population, 10,284—white, 10,220; negro, 64; foreign born, 19. County seat, Elizabeth. The mean magnetic declination in 1900 was 3°. The mean annual rainfall is 40 to 50 inches, and the mean annual temperature 50° to 55°. The county is traversed by the Little Kanawha Railroad.
Wise; post village in Monongalia County.
Wise; run, a left-hand branch of West Virginia Fork of Dunkard Creek in Monongalia County.
Wiseburg; post village in Jackson County.
Witchers; creek, a left-hand tributary to Kanawha River in Kanawha County.
Wolf; creek, a small left-hand tributary to Greenbrier River in Summers County, joining it at The Big Bend.

Wolf; creek, a small left-hand tributary to Greenbrier River in Monroe County.
Wolf; creek, a small left-hand tributary to Bluestone River in Mercer County.
Wolf; a left-hand tributary to New River in Fayette County.
Wolf; creek, a left-hand branch of Skin Creek, a tributary to West Fork of Monongahela River, in Lewis County.
Wolf; creek, a left-hand tributary to Elk River in Braxton County.
Wolf; creek, a small right-hand tributary to Cheat River in Preston County.
Wolf; gap in Pretty Ridge in Wyoming County.
Wolf; hill in Morgan County. Elevation, 900 feet.
Wolf; run, a small right-hand tributary to Skin Creek in Lewis County.
Wolf; run, a right-hand branch of Fish Creek in Wetzel County.
Wolf Creek; mountain, a short ridge in Monroe County. Altitude, 2,500 to 2,810 feet, the highest point the height of one peak.
Wolf Creek; mountain, a short, curved ridge in Summers County. Altitude, 2,000 to 2,500 feet.
Wolfcreek; post village in Monroe County on the Chesapeake and Ohio Railway.
Wolf Fork; mountain, a short ridge in Lewis County.
Wolfpen; branch, a very small right-hand branch of Big Sycamore Creek, a tributary to Elk River, in Clay County.
Wolf Pen; branch, a small right-hand tributary to Clear Fork, a branch of Tug Fork of Big Sandy River, in McDowell County.
Wolfpen; branch, a very small right-hand tributary to Beech Fork of Twelvepole Creek, a branch of Ohio River, in Wayne County.
Wolfpen; branch, a small right-hand tributary to Indian Creek, a branch of Guyandot River, in Wyoming County.
Wolfpen; branch, a small right-hand branch of Little Sandy Creek, a tributary to Elk River, in Kanawha County.
Wolfpen; branch, a very small left-hand tributary to Guyandot River in Wyoming County.
Wolfpen; branch, a very small left-hand tributary to Clear Fork of Guyandot River in Wyoming County.
Wolf Pen; run, a small left-hand tributary to Birch River in Braxton County.
Wolf Pen; run, a small left-hand tributary to West Fork of Monongahela River in Lewis County.
Wolf Pen; run, a right-hand branch of Sand Fork in Lewis County.
Wolf Pen; run, a small right-hand branch of Stewart Creek in Gilmer County.
Wolf Pen; run, a small right-hand tributary to Right Fork of Steer Creek in Braxton County.
Wolf Pen Ridge; short range in the central part of Pocahontas County.
Wolfpit; fork, a small left-hand tributary to Little Coal River, a branch of Coal River, in Lincoln County.
Wolfrun; post village in Marshall County.
Wolf Summit; post village in Harrison County on the Baltimore and Ohio Railroad.
Womelsdorf; post village in Randolph County.
Wood; county, situated in the western part of the State on the Ohio River and lying at the foot of the Allegheny Plateau. Area, 357 square miles. Population, 34,452—white, 33,528; negro, 922; foreign born, 925. County seat, Parkersburg. The mean magnetic declination in 1900 was 1° 10′. The mean annual rainfall is 40 to 50 inches, and the temperature 50° to 55°. The county is traversed by the Baltimore and Ohio, the Baltimore and Ohio Southwestern, the Little Kanawha, and Ohio River railroads.
Woodbine; post village in Nicholas County.

Woodlands; post village in Marshall County.
Woodrow; post village in Morgan County on the West Virginia Central and Pittsburg Railway.
Woodruff; post village in Marshall County on the Baltimore and Ohio Railroad.
Woodrum; branch, a very small right-hand branch of Powellton Fork of Armstrong Creek, a tributary to Kanawha River, in Fayette County.
Woods; run, a small right-hand tributary to Greenbrier River in Pocahontas County.
Woods; run, a right-hand branch of Wheeling Creek in Ohio County.
Woodward; branch, a small right-hand branch of Twomile Creek, a tributary to Kanawha River, in Kanawha County.
Woodyard; post village in Roane County.
Woodzell; post village in Webster County.
Woosley; post village in Wyoming County.
Workman; branch, a small right-hand tributary to Pond Fork of Little Coal River, a branch of Coal River, in Boone County.
Workman; branch, a very small right-hand tributary to Pinnacle Creek, a branch of Guyandot River, in Wyoming County.
Workman; creek, a small left-hand tributary to Clear Fork of Coal River in Raleigh County.
Workman Knob; summit in Boone County.
Worley; post village in Monongalia County on the Chesapeake and Ohio Railway.
Worth; post village in McDowell County.
Worthington; post village in Marion County on the Baltimore and Ohio Railroad.
Wrack Timber; run, a small right-hand tributary to Holly River in Webster County.
Wright; post village in Raleigh County on the Chesapeake and Ohio Railway.
Wyant; fork, a right-hand branch of Grass Run in Gilmer County.
Wyatt; post village in Harrison County.
Wyatt; run, a left-hand branch of Left Fork of Steep Creek in Braxton County.
Wylies; falls in New River on boundary between Mercer and Summers counties.
Wyoma; post village in Mason County.
Wyoming; county, situated in the southern part of the State and drained by Guyandot River. The Allegheny Plateau is here deeply dissected. Area, 526 square miles. Population, 8,380—white, 8,286; negro, 94; foreign born, 5. County seat, Oceana. The mean magnetic declination in 1900 was 1°. The mean annual rainfall is 50 to 60 inches, and the mean annual temperature 50° to 55°.
Yankeedam; post village in Clay County on the Charleston, Clendennin and Sutton Railroad.
Yeager; post village in Mason County.
Yeager; run, a left-hand branch of West Virginia Fork of Dunkard Creek in Monongalia County.
Yelk; post village in Pocahontas County.
Yellow; creek, a small right-hand tributary to Blackwater River in Tucker County.
Yellowspring; post village in Hampshire County.
Yellow Spring; run, a left-hand branch of Sleepy Creek in Morgan County.
Yew; mountains, a broken mountainous range extending into Greenbrier and Webster counties. Altitude, 3,000 to 4,000 feet.
Yokum; post village in Upshur County.
Yokums Knob; summit in the Allegheny Mountains in Randolph County. Altitude, 4,330 feet.
Yorkville; post village in Wayne County.
Youngs; mountain, a summit in Day Mountain in Pocahontas County.

Youngs Knob; summit in Kanawha County.
Zackville; post village in Wirt County.
Zar; post village in Preston County.
Zebs; creek, a small left-hand tributary to Valley River in Barbour and Randolph counties.
Zela; post village in Nicholas County.
Zenith; post village in Monroe County.
Zinnia; post village in Doddridge County.
Zona; post village in Roane County.
Zypho; post village in Harrison County.

O

www.ingramcontent.com/pod-product-compliance
Lightning Source LLC
Chambersburg PA
CBHW020357170426
43200CB00005B/199